INSIDE, LOOKING OUT

HARPER'S
MAGAZINE
PRESS

INSIDE,

LOOKING OUT

A Personal Memoir

By Harding Lemay

A HARPER'S MAGAZINE PRESS BOOK

Published in Association with

Harper & Row   •   New York

For Dorothy

Beyond the various people mentioned in these pages, some under fictitious names, I would like to acknowledge my gratitude to William Maxwell of The New Yorker, my editor, Herman Gollob, and my agents, John A. S. Cushman and Phoebe Larmore, without whose encouragement and assistance these memories would still be in my head.

PART ONE

...on the farm... 1922–1939

A few years ago, my oldest sister and her husband stopped by our New York apartment on their way to visit his relatives. During the course of catching up with the news of our other brothers and sisters living in various parts of the country, my sister, whom I shall call Evangeline, inadvertently gave me the answer to a riddle that has baffled me for twenty years or more—why I have scarcely any memories of my life before I was ten. We were talking of our youngest brother, Floyd, who is now past thirty and still talks baby talk, which I find almost impossible to understand, although my wife, with more patience, and less irritation, manages to make some sense out of his conversations with us, which are usually by telephone. With her customary bluntness, Evangeline said, "We never worried about Floyd's speech when he was little because you and Lionel talked the same way until you were about ten. We thought he'd outgrow it as you did."

I didn't believe her. The scramble for attention in a large family often means that the only person one ever really listens to is oneself. Very likely the reason she believed that I (never mind about Lionel) didn't talk clearly was that she didn't listen closely. But then she went on to recite, to the amusement of my own children, a little jingle of incomprehensible vowels and consonants that Lionel and I chanted as we brushed our teeth:

> Ut and don an al aron
> We bus or tee al day.
> Ut and don an al aron
> To tate de pec away.

I could no longer deny it. And the explanation of why I have so few early memories was suddenly clear to me. It may or may not be true for others, but I am certain that my own memories began when I learned to speak clearly. Such early recollections as I do have are of books I read and movies I saw, for my attention was not on what was happening around me, but fixed unwaveringly on the printed page and the silver screen.

I was born in 1922, wedged into the fifth place of thirteen children, and was named after the President. Evangeline, of course, was named after the heroine of Longfellow's poem. Most of the other children were given names equally unusual in the predominantly French-Canadian community where we lived. Since Catholic children at that time and in that place (and perhaps still and in all places) were obliged to be christened with at least one saint's name, we all bore those as middle names, but were called by the first names my mother chose for us. The three oldest boys were Rudolph, Ambrose, and Lionel. After me in my early childhood came Annabelle and Clarence. There were six more. The thirteenth child, Cyril, was born just before I ran away from home, in 1939. He was my godson, and he lived for a little over a year. Lionel (whom we called Frenchie) was killed in Korea a year or so before my mother's death in 1953. So there are eleven of us now. We do not see each other often, and when we do come together we tend to talk about our childhoods. For each of us'

4

there is a different childhood, with quite different and sometimes contradictory memories.

Big families were not uncommon where we lived. Ours was by no means the largest in the community. Every hand nature provided was needed for chores and in the fields. The more hands at work outdoors, the more hands were needed in the kitchen, so girls as well as boys were welcome. Since children were, in most cases, less expensive to come by than horses and cows, they were often treated with an indifference no sensible farmer would display toward his livestock. My father, however, was not a sensible farmer. I doubt whether he was, by inclination, a farmer at all. He had managed creameries in various towns in the immediate vicinity, and in the early twenties he bought his own, situated by a crossroads some way out of town, and made a fairly successful business of it. Rumor, within the family and outside of it, says that he added to his income by occasional bootlegging; a delivery of freshly churned butter to farms and towns in Quebec became a delivery of unlabeled bottles of whiskey on the way back. Whether or not this is true, one of my few very early memories is of automobiles roaring down a dirt road behind the creamery, and of the clanging of the gate in the arcade of sorts that connected the creamery with the house we lived in. Bootlegging was far from unknown to most border families; my mother's younger brother, Charlie, was shot and killed near Montreal, by a border patrol, while running whiskey illegally to the States.

My mother had been brought up on a farm that was part of an Indian reservation (my great-great-grandmother or great-great-grandfather was half Indian, so far as I can make out; Evangeline says it was a generation earlier, which makes the fraction of Indian blood fairly minute), and she persuaded my father to sell the creamery and buy a hundred-and-fifty-acre farm, where the boys could grow up under the benign influences of country life. My older brothers were already showing a tendency to get into trouble. They had drowned several of her prize Plymouth Rocks

5

in the stream behind the creamery. (They wanted to see if hens could swim.) When they were tired of having Evangeline tag along behind them, they left her soaking headfirst in the rain barrel and went off fishing. They also locked me, at the age of four, in the automatic electric churn in the deserted creamery and turned on the switch. Even when all the evidence proved her wrong, my mother still wouldn't admit that her boys were anything worse than prankish. "They're not bad boys," she told a schoolteacher who had been tripped up from behind while going down a flight of stairs. "They're just mischievous." She thought, I suppose, that a farm was a safer place for mischievous boys in that they could at least be put to use.

So, in the fall of 1929, when I was seven, the family, with six boys and two girls, moved to the big farmhouse where I spent all but one of the years I remember before I left home. In the pastures there were cows, horses, and goats, and in the barnyards there were pigs, chickens, ducks, dogs, and cats. As for all farm children, there was a never-ending round of chores, of course, and when I could escape from them I did. There was a swimming hole, down past the cornfields, with beaver-made dams and boy-made rafts, and, best of all, there were three ponies, to be shared among the six oldest children.

It was not really an unpleasant life, but a gradual sense of deprivation is inevitable, I think, in a large family. There are, in effect, no parents, since parental attentiveness and concern can be stretched only so far and no farther. When I recall my childhood now, I realize that very early I was searching elsewhere for (and very often finding) the attention I craved at home. A serious little boy with good manners fills a considerable void in the lives of aging spinster schoolteachers and childless country wives. And to a child accustomed to women drudging in the kitchen and the barn, the very sight of a woman in a flowered dress and high heels is inexplicably touching—the unfamiliar kind of beauty that only town women have. I remember a teacher in the one-room schoolhouse we all attended until the sixth grade who wore a different dress every day. I don't know whether the women who teach in country schools now are what they were in my childhood: plain, strong, capable farm girls who stood up against bullies sometimes bigger and stronger than they were, and with good humor and a fierce determination conveyed the rudiments of reading, arithmetic, geography, and spelling. I particularly remember two sisters, Florence and Beatrice Baxter, who, one after the other, taught the eighteen to twenty children (five of whom seemed always to be various Lemays) in the school. One Miss Baxter was dark-haired and the other was red-haired, but which was which, and which one held me on her lap and told me stories, I long ago forgot. When I was in Europe as a soldier during the Second World War, a friend in New York sent me the *Iliad* and several of the Greek tragedies, and, although reading them for the first time, I had the feeling that I recognized the characters and situations. Finally, I came to the conclusion that Miss Baxter had told me stories from Greek mythology (holding the little boy who couldn't speak properly on her lap), and that those bigger-than-life-size people had been tucked away in my mind ever since, waiting to be rediscovered.

Unlike my brothers, I spent as little time as possible in the barn and in the fields, and I did not have the country boy's interest in hunting and fishing. I was the quiet one in a family of noisy boys, and it must have been that inability to speak properly that clamped me early and permanently into the safety of books and movies.

Listening to Rudolph and Ambrose recite, haltingly and inaccurately, sections of *Il Penseroso* and *The Ancient Mariner*, I knew that if those two were able to do it at all, I could do it better, and I did. Perhaps it was at this point that I began to speak clearly. Stretched out on a plank at the top of the silo, I read Sir Walter Scott and Grace Livingston Hill and Gene Stratton Porter and whatever other books I could borrow from my teachers or from the neighbors. When I wanted to go to the movies, I told my mother that I was going to play with a farm boy up the road, and sneaked out through the pastures to the highway that led to the Schine movie palace in Crescent, ten miles away. I watched Norma Shearer, in a white wedding gown and a blond wig, gently slide into Leslie Howard's arms in *Smilin' Through* after Fredric March, crazed with jealousy, had shot her at the altar. I saw the red stain spreading through the white satin, even though it was some years before technicolor; they provided the stain, I provided the color.

In the darkened movie theatre, with synthetic stars twinkling in the deep blue of the artificial sky above me, or in the dove-surrounded solitude of the silo, I absorbed a distinct and cherished model of behavior and attitudes that made me an alien whenever I moved among actual people. I was little more than twelve when, walking along the deserted highway after seeing Ann Harding and Robert Montgomery in *Biography of a Bachelor Girl*, I realized that I, too, could live as they did, wearing a suit and tie every day, and eating dinner with lighted candles and a tablecloth beneath the plates. At that moment, I decided to run away from the overalls and the oilcloth. For the next five years, I hugged my secret to myself as I watched Kay Francis and Ruth Chatterton enduring their personal troubles with graceful, mute-voiced dignity, and as my own mother drifted, unnoticed, into insanity.

During the long dark winter evenings, when the rest of the house was chilly, the family gathered in the kitchen. My father read the Crescent evening newspaper. My mother sat at the table, surrounded by unwashed pots and pans. My sisters ironed their dresses or did their homework, and the boys sat sullenly staring out the window, hoping to see an automobile flash its headlights from a country road, or a distant barn afire against the snow. I lay on the floor behind the wood-burning cookstove, reading. I read about white boys who were kidnaped and raised by the Indians, society ladies adrift on a sea of immorality, orphans who turned out to be heirs to a lavish English county estate. I read anything that fell into my hands, much of it trash, and, reading, I forgot the constant humiliation of being the only frail boy in the family, whose eyes, gradually failing (no doubt partly because of reading in the dim light behind the stove), excluded him from playing ball games in the fields during the warm months, and from doing acrobatic stunts on the swings and trapezes my father devised in the hayloft for winter afternoons. After a while, I no longer envied my brothers their games. And, once having learned to speak clearly, I found my weapon in a quick and bitter tongue, which I used often and indiscriminately, secure in the protective shield my mother threw around me: "Leave him alone, Rudolph, he's sickly. . . ." Sometimes, on the road coming home from school, or in the pastures on my own solitary excursions, Rudolph or one of the others found me and, if I didn't run away quickly enough, taught me how little protection an absent shield provides.

At a family reunion several years ago, my brother Clarence and I for the first time were able to talk candidly about the way we felt about each other as children. "What I remember about you," I told him, "is that if you caught me on the road coming home from school, you'd jump out from under a culvert or behind a tree and rub my nose in cow manure."

"And all I remember about you," he replied, "is that you always held your nose so high in the air I wanted to rub it in the filthiest thing I could find."

The boy with the book is the enemy in such a family: an enemy to the boys with the guns and the fishing rods; an enemy to the girls who believe that books belong to girls, not to boys; and eventually an enemy to the father and mother, for from his books he learns about a life which denies and then defies theirs.

As approval from my teachers increased, the approval of my brothers and of my father at home decreased. I could ignore the opinions of my brothers, but no boy wants to be disliked by his father. Mine was a mystery to me then, as he still is today. I remember him as a slight, wiry man with small hands and feet, and I also remember that he was always working—cutting down the trees in the woods, sharpening scythes against the grindstone, mending fences in the pastures—and that he punished me almost daily because I didn't do my chores around the house and barn, but that he let Ambrose, Rudolph, and Frenchie off with shouted warnings of future punishment. He had his favorites, and Evangeline was the favorite of them all. If Rudolph and Ambrose asked him for money to spend, he would give a quarter to Rudolph and a dime to Ambrose, and turn away, stony-faced, from the latter's protests. As his sons grew older, he encouraged them openly to take up the vices of men—I remember seeing Rudolph standing in the barn with four or five of my father's friends sharing a bottle of whiskey, passed from hand to hand, when he was no more than thirteen. Quick-witted and opinionated, my father ridiculed my mother's family for their pretensions (all the girls had gone to secretarial or normal school) and spoke maliciously of their Indian blood before all us children. My mother, easily inflamed, usually threw something at him in reply. On the dining-room wallpaper there was a large brown splotch where she had once hurled a cup of coffee at him, but I don't remember that he ever struck her. He reserved such treatment for his sons. Once, as a very small boy, I picked myself up from the farther end of the woodshed where he had kicked me after I had innocently repeated a word I had heard one of my brothers use. I began to avoid him by the time I was twelve. At meals or in the barn, if I saw his face—with its long nose, thin lips, and dark inscrutable eyes behind his glasses—turned in my direction, my heart stopped still until he looked away.

Long after he was dead, I learned from one of his sisters that he had run away from home when he was thirteen and worked from daylight to dark on farms and in factories, until he married my mother, who was a teacher in a one-room schoolhouse. The years passed, the children came, and he was the man I knew, or refused to know, or the man who refused to let his children know him. Long before we moved from the creamery, I remember coming around the corner and seeing my young mother standing beside a rain barrel, dipping a comb in the water and running it through her long black hair. The sun struck her features and, before my love-filled gaze, I saw her turn, face aglow, toward my father coming from the creamery door. He put his arms around her and they kissed with a tender intimacy while I watched, warmed by the love that drew them together as I was later to be chilled by the anguish that split them apart.

There is nothing more destructive in childhood than a boy's sense that his father doesn't like him. It turns the boy into a craven creature, afraid to ask the questions he must ask of the only man he can ask, desperately longing for an encouraging smile that never comes, and always expecting, if not inviting, criticism he cannot answer. The man that boy turns into can seldom display genuine affection toward older men, and unknowingly locks himself away from those whose experience and generosity might offer support in times of bitter hardships. If I have come to any terms at all with the memory of my father, it is because I now have a son of my own. And I wouldn't dare have as many sons as my father had, because I suspect that one disliked and disaffected son (for the lack of feeling hardens into a mutual pact of distrust and contempt) cancels out the admiration and respect of all the rest.

My interest in other grown-up men was slight, in any case. When I left the one-room schoolhouse to go into the sixth grade in Longview, the school principal was a shadowy figure who, like my father, meted out punishment without inquiring into the nature or the motive of the offense. In the movies, men were only dim satellites in an orbit dominated by women. Warner Baxter, William Powell, and Herbert Marshall existed only to provide reasonable escorts and acceptable mates for Janet Gaynor, Myrna Loy, and Miriam Hopkins. My brothers, who also went

11

to the movies, driven in the car by my father on Saturdays to the Westerns and the "boys'" films, patterned much of their later behavior upon their favorites—George Raft, Edward G. Robinson, James Cagney—who seemed at home only with guns and gambling, racketeers and prison wardens. The women who appealed to such men (and to my brothers) were loud and vulgar in dress and speech—Jean Harlow, Joan Blondell, Barbara Stanwyck—not unlike the girls in the upper grades at school with whom my brothers disappeared in the late afternoons, into the woods and sheds. They were not the kind of girls I was going to waste my time with. As a matter of fact, by the time I was fourteen I knew what the main obstacle to my leaving home could be: it wouldn't be my parents, or my brothers and sisters; it would be a girl, if I wasn't careful. Already boys my brothers' ages were getting married and settling down to produce their own large families on neighboring farms. The conversations around the kitchen table, as I read behind the stove, hinted at the reasons. I determined to avoid any such entrapment. Like many adolescent resolutions, mine faltered now and then, and occasional furtive lapses in henhouses, corncribs, and haylofts afforded a mine-infested route I survived largely by luck.

One of my father's brothers worked for a railroad line, in I don't know what capacity. One Sunday afternoon, we drove to Crescent, where he lived in a detached railway car that was cheerfully furnished with cushions on narrow couches and flowered curtains at the windows. There I discovered, to my astonishment, magazines devoted totally to the movies. I spent the entire afternoon reading them avidly, and when we left, my uncle gave them to me. I hid them in the top of the silo. For several intoxicated summer months, I gazed heavy-lidded into the limpid eyes, in the full-page photographs, of Nancy Carroll, Dolores Del Rio, and Constance Bennett. I couldn't have been more than ten, but I remember an advertisement in which Metro-Goldwyn-Mayer boasted of "more stars than there are in Heaven," and there they all were: Jean Harlow, Joan Crawford, Clark Gable, Norma Shearer, Greta Garbo, John Barrymore, Robert Montgomery, Marie Dressler, and many more that I had never seen at all. I could steal away to Crescent without arousing curiosity at home only on Sunday afternoons, and the feature at the movie house changed every other day. So there was a vast population I was ignorant of, but could at least now read about, and I began to memorize the faces and read the gossip about them as if my life depended on it. I knew the names of Gloria Swanson's many husbands, and that Lilyan Tashman was Mrs. Edmund Lowe. I studied the cast lists of new films so attentively that I can still reel off the names of most of the players in the major motion pictures from 1932 to 1939.

My feverish mania for the movies led me into stealing the dime my mother doled out to me for the Sunday Mass collection plate and substituting a penny I managed to get my hands on during the week. Movies cost only a dime for those under twelve, and the wicked sensation of robbing my morning piety to pay for my afternoon pleasure made me so nervous that my mother thought for some months that I had the "call" to study for the priesthood.

We went to church in Longview every Sunday, except when we were snowbound. There were two Masses, one at nine and the other at ten-thirty, so that large families could attend in shifts, leaving someone at home to do the barn chores and cook the hearty midday meal. My father usually took Evangeline and the three oldest boys with him to early Mass, then came back and drove my mother and the rest of us in for the second service. Once the first group was on its way, Annabelle and my mother began preparing the younger children: dresses were fastened in the back, hair ribbons tied, ears and necks given a final check, and straightening of sashes followed last-minute adjustments of petticoats under skirts. The baby—whichever one it was at the time—demanded attention: some mornings, Annabelle rushed downstairs to find the oatmeal dish smashed on the kitchen floor and the little girls in hysteria because their freshly ironed dresses were soiled. The baby, fuming in impotent temper, beat his tiny fists against the tray of his chair while tears were wiped away and other dresses hastily put on. Once the young ones were all ready, Annabelle stood by the window waiting for a glimpse of her father's car on the road. Then, the church bells a mile away ringing us our warning, she'd run to the bedroom to tell her mother that we were going to be late.

The woman who emerged, pretty and pleasant, from her bedroom was firmly corseted underneath her Sunday dress, and wore unfamiliar silk stockings on her legs, high-heel shoes on her feet, and black leather gloves over the broken fingernails and chapped-skin rawness of her hands. Powder and rouge transformed the face we saw damp with perspiration and streaked with dirt on weekdays, and her one good silk dress replaced the rips and stains of her customary faded print house dress. Hushed with pride, I would brush her coat and hat before she put them on, and Annabelle would lift a cat hair from her dress or whisper that her stocking seams were crooked. Then, the collection envelope in her hand, and nickels and dimes distributed among us, my mother stood outside the kitchen door in the morning sunlight as we scrambled into the car to be driven to town.

Once a month, or sometimes less often, on Saturday nights, my father drove those of us who were over twelve into church for our monthly confessions. Kneeling in the curtained confessional, I squirmed as the invisible priest prodded me into inventing sins to replace those I couldn't remember. Then, leaving the darkened enclosure to my brothers (whose self-publicized sins were more lurid and various than my own), I knelt to make my penance before the fourteen depictions of Jesus on the way to his death, clutching my rosary and repeating the meaningless words over and over again. None of it, at that time, or since, was very real to

14

me. It seemed to have nothing to do with anything I knew or cared about. I didn't dare tell my parents, who insisted as I grew older that I continue to make the monthly confession, and that I kneel the following morning before the altar to receive the tasteless wafer which dissolved on my deceitful tongue and cleansed me, until the next communion, of my sins.

Our village priest often ended his sermons with exhortations against the films showing in Crescent. "That Mae West," he once intoned hoarsely to his openmouthed congregation, "is nothing but a wiggler." Mae West was, unfortunately, beyond my view, since her films were "for adults only." But many Sunday afternoons the main highway was lined with boys, most of them older than myself, thumbing rides toward the promised sinfulness of *Back Street* and *The Animal Kingdom*. I watched Irene Dunne and Ann Harding with more bafflement than enjoyment. If that was sin, why were the ladies so lovely? And John Boles and Leslie Howard so gallant? In the end, I decided to ignore the teachings of the Church in favor of the teachings of the movies.

One day after school, stopping in the stationery store to buy a pad of school paper, I went giddy with the discovery that movie magazines were sold there. For ten cents (the price of the paper tablet), I bought one. It was the first of hundreds, and it started me stealing paper from my sisters' notebooks and becoming the chronic borrower of other people's pencils and paper in the classroom. When I could, I cajoled my mother into giving me extra money. She thought I spent those nickels and dimes on candy bars, as other boys did. The stack of *Silver Screens* in the silo grew too high for safety. Somebody forking out ensilage below might glance up and see Mary Brian smiling down at him from a brightly colored cover and come up to investigate. I found new hiding places, under fallen trees in the woods in the summer and in secret recesses in the hayloft in the winter. There, my fantasy world peopled with bejeweled women and pomaded men, I re-

15

treated, leaving my brothers to satisfy themselves with what transitory pleasures they could derive from unwashed farm girls and opened bottles of whiskey stolen from my parents' supply, or from others.

Outside the silo was a noisy world of energetic people which, no matter how deep my preoccupations with the dream of Hollywood, enticed me now and then from my self-imposed isolation. My maternal grandparents, Gaston and Cécile Beaupré, still lived on the farm on the Indian reservation, and during my early childhood we could all squeeze into the car and drive off to see them. While my grandparents and parents, uncles, cousins, and occasional visiting aunts exchanged gossip in broken English and, to us, incomprehensible French, the children scattered through the fields and outbuildings to play. When my grandmother was not looking, we stole her dandelion wine from the cellar and cookies from the cookie jar in her sun-drenched kitchen, which looked out over a river, and, sitting under a shady tree in the pasture, we stuffed ourselves.

Eventually, my grandparents turned the farm on the reservation over to their oldest son, and moved to a small town nearby. My cousin Jean-Pierre lived with them. Jean-Pierre was my age, a physically active but taciturn boy. With that inexplicable chemistry of boyhood, we complemented each other, and I was fonder of him than I have ever been of any male my own age. We rode our ponies bareback together through the woods and over the fields and along the railroad tracks, whooping crazily at the engineers in order to persuade ourselves that we weren't as terrified of the steaming, whistling monster as the ponies were. He went to school in the town where he lived, but on Saturday and Sunday mornings and during summer vacations he would appear, scowling, at our kitchen door, and I would lay aside my magazines and books, and canter off with him. I accepted his limited responses to my constant, thoughtless monologues as something perfectly

16

natural, and was pleased when an ingratiating grin or a sudden spasm of merriment broke through his habitual, touching sadness.

His mother, my Aunt Leila, had divorced or been separated from his father soon after he was born, and she was now married to a man whose name, I think, was Krim, but he never accompanied her on her annual visits East to see her family and her son. My father said, behind her back, that she was "fast." She was a private secretary to a businessman in Detroit. I had seen private secretaries, of course, in the movies, but my Aunt Leila outclassed them all. She looked like Mary Astor, who, with a strong resemblance to the women in my mother's family, had become, in fleeting visions on the screen, my ideal of mature feminine beauty. Any woman who drew more than a passing glance from me had to resemble some movie actress or other, and Leila brought with her a glamorous exoticism of fur trim on her coats, marcelled hair, lipstick, and silk stockings, which defined for me (with my vast experience of fan-magazine photographs) the female nature. She was friendly and direct in manner, spoke with a faint huskiness that suggested cocktails and night clubs to me, and when, pausing in her animated conversation, she smiled at me, the most attentive of her listeners, I trembled. Plump and pretty, she explored the farmyards in her suède pumps, followed by a troop of admiring nephews and nieces. In the evening, she sat on the porch talking to my mother, smoking cigarettes and gently swinging her well-shaped legs, while my father hovered disapprovingly in the doorway. She swore mildly, with a casual, offhand ease, and told jokes that I later realized were more than slightly off-color. She was the first sophisticated woman I had ever seen. When she returned to Detroit, leaving us all presents (trinkets for the girls, a wristwatch, once, for me), I crept back to the silo, desolate and exhausted by so much exhilaration. Jean-Pierre, sullen and unpredictable, answered with an obscenity when I tried to talk to him about his glamorous mother.

Every summer, my father's younger sister, Maude Duncan, who lived in Providence, appeared with her stout husband and three pale city children. She, too, wore expensive, stylish clothes—velvet in the humid summer, once—and an abundance of jewelry, and makeup. Even though, with the strong, somewhat irregular features of the Lemays, she didn't look like any movie star I admired, I listened closely to what she said and watched carefully how she behaved. Her well-mannered sons and daughter were frightened by the animals in the barn, and must have been even more intimidated by their country cousins. Rudolph and Ambrose once got my cousin Neil drunk on dandelion wine and jeered him into jumping the pony over a barbed-wire fence. He fell off, with thin shrieks, and ran to the house with bleeding knees, while Frenchie and I raced behind him to assign the blame and watch the punishment. In the swimming hole, we smilingly invited Lucile to join us on the raft and then mercilessly stomped on her fingers as she tried to climb up to lie with us on it. After supper, the three Duncan children sat politely in the parlor, and we snickered behind our fingers at them. Aunt Maude sat down at the piano and accompanied my father in a dolorous, self-pitying song entitled "The Little Rosewood Casket." My mother sang loudly along with them, in the off-key monotone most of her children inherited, nodding her head and staring with thinly disguised ill-will at the back of her husband's favorite sister.

One morning, Aunt Maude and my father decided to drive off and see their father, a frail old man who had separated from my mean-tempered grandmother and lived in a county poorhouse some distance away. Late in the evening, they returned, visibly shaken: he had died some months earlier and no one had notified them. My mother, sitting on the porch in the summer darkness with a baby on her lap, turned away in outrage at the smoldering enmities in her husband's family. At his own funeral, years later, his mother knelt at the side of his casket opposite one of her other sons. They didn't speak to each other, as they hadn't (even though they passed each other almost daily on the streets of Crescent, and sat in the same church every Sunday) since the day over ten years earlier when the old lady had called her son's second wife whatever the French equivalent of "bitch" would be.

On the last day of the visit, Aunt Maude brought out her camera, and a sudden bone-crunching jostling of eight or nine children, all determined to be the single focal point of the group, produced vicious jabs and tears, frozen smiles, and unseen pinching fingers. To my knowledge, none of us ever saw the photographs. Or if we did, they have all disappeared, along with most of the memories they were meant to record forever.

When the Duncans drove off, waving smugly from the car windows, a suppressed hysteria sped us all in opposite directions. The younger children posted themselves at various windows throughout the house and waited for the final flash of sunlight on the black car disappearing down the dirt road that led to the main highway. Rudolph, Ambrose, and Frenchie went off to the barn to tease the cows and horses and, failing to arouse more than tail twitchings and warning kicks, turned their brutality upon each other. Evangeline, upstairs behind a locked door, stained her nails with scarlet polish left behind in a nearly empty bottle, and rouged her cheeks with cosmetics swiped from my aunt's dresser top. Annabelle sulked in the kitchen, washing the dishes, resentful that she had, as usual, to do the dirty work, and slamming cabinet doors shut because no one, in the entire two weeks, had once told her she was pretty—which she wasn't. She was, however, and still is, extraordinarily handsome, but being pretty and being handsome are in no way reconcilable to a ten-year-old girl with a boy's haircut (my father included her in the monthly kitchen barberings of his many sons) and a proud nature. In the winter, boxes of used clothing arrived from Providence, and were distributed by my mother with caustic remarks about the colors, style, and condition of the gifts. All one winter in the seventh grade, I sat at my desk with one too tight shoe masking the ripped seam of the other, locked in shame and flinching at the pain in my toes.

It was during one of these summer visits, when the other children were all off swimming, that, passing through the darkened parlor, I heard my Aunt Maude say, "Not another one! Jeanne, you can't keep doing this to Maurice!" My mother, flushing, shouted, "You don't think I'm the one who wants them, do you?" I tiptoed away, unseen. Of course she didn't want them. She didn't want me.

My wife finds it odd that all of us always refer to our parents as "my mother" and "my father." And Evangeline once said that we all act as if we were only children. Not one of us admits that we shared our parents with each other. As adolescents, we avoided the words "mother" and "father," and referred to our parents, in moments of affection as well as derision, as "Maurice" and "Jeanne"—never, of course, to their faces. Later on, Gabrielle and Marianne came to call their mother "Saint Jeanne," a half-endearing and half-contemptuous term which she accepted, sometimes, with baffled, good-natured smiles. The mother my younger sisters knew has little in common with the one Evangeline and I remember. When we were little, before we moved to the farm, she was still an energetic, pretty woman. When I was a twelve-year-old, hitchhiking to the movies in Crescent, I was occasionally picked up by a farmer who would say, "You're one of Jeanne Lemay's boys, aren't you? I can tell by your looks. Your mother was the prettiest girl who ever came to this town. . . ." I'd ride along, proud and yet embarrassed, for already she was the stout, red-faced woman of unpredictable tempers and sudden sorrows, the mother Gabrielle and Marianne, Vincent and Floyd grew up with. Unlike us, they ridiculed her sometimes, even to her face, and argued loudly and openly with her. But they also seemed capable of more genuine affection with her than we were, perhaps because they had not witnessed the gradual changes age, appetites, and unhappiness had brought to her.

20

What I saw then as unreasonable temper (she once hurled a hot flatiron clear across the kitchen at Ambrose, who still carries a scar on his handsome, saturnine face), I see now, with knowledge gained from being a parent myself, as unbearable anxiety. Life for us on the farm was a never-ending series of illnesses, accidents, and quarrels. Six-year-old Gabrielle, on a summer afternoon, went trotting off to the barn behind the boys to tease the animals. She now has, on either side of her mouth, what appear to strangers as two oddly placed dimples, but those of us who saw her stumbling from the barn after a well-aimed kick from a horse know better. Marianne, left alone for a moment when she was three, caught her arm in the washing-machine wringer. Now in her sleeveless summer dresses, her mottled, discolored flesh recalls the baby screams that brought us all racing into the kitchen. And Frenchie, stretching across the wood-burning stove to reach something or other, fell and braced himself with both hands on the hot griddle, acquiring the first of many ugly childhood scars. But bad as our family accidents were, we saw worse ones around us. A classmate of mine, helping his father with the fall threshing, lost an arm above the elbow when he reached thoughtlessly across the machine belt to retrieve a hayfork. Another boy, playing with us in his hayloft, leaped from a beam to the huge pitchfork suspended from the roof and slid, shrieking, across the sharp blades which mangled his private parts so badly that he became a falsetto-voiced curiosity to younger boys as he grew older. My mother watched it all, within her family and outside, and saw her beautiful babies grow into quick-tempered, unreachable strangers, as she became, before our humiliated and defiant eyes, a stranger herself.

We worked in the hayfields, in the gardens and the barns, in the pastures, mending fences, chopping wood, and spreading manure. Early in the morning, my father stood at the foot of the stairs and shouted us awake. Frenchie and I pulled on our pants and shirts and hurried, half awake, through the frost-brightened pastures in our bare feet to get the cows. Snarling at each other like the dogs that accompanied us, we herded them back to the barn, where we helped feed and milk them and clear the steaming manure out from behind them, before letting them out to pasture again. We went barefoot from May until October, from snow to snow, our feet as hard as the bark on the trees, and as dirty. I was nowhere near as useful around the barns and fields as the other boys were. My eyesight was poor and my attention was seldom fixed on what I was doing. Weeding the garden, I daydreamed of Ronald Colman and Loretta Young and pulled up vegetable plants along with weeds. One muggy afternoon, when a thunderstorm was imminent and my father and brothers were off on other business, my mother asked me to go out in the pastures with a halter and bring our mare, Snip, back to the barn. For what seemed like hours, I circled the playful horse, drawing close to her only to have her canter off again until, defeated, I sat on the wood fence and let the rain mingle with my tears of rage and frustration. Snip apologetically nuzzled me from time to time, but by then I no longer cared. When the storm was over, my mother came across the fields, haltered the placid mare, and led us both home. She promised not to tell my father, and she didn't.

We were becoming conspirators against him. In the henhouse, her apron pockets full of fresh eggs, she would brush my hair back from my forehead and smile vaguely at me. "You're too good for us," she told me once, tears trembling on her lashes. And I, without a moment of self-doubt, agreed with her. She used me against my father, I realize now, as he used Evangeline against her, as they each used their children, and their lives, against each other. Once when he didn't come home all night (he often stayed out without explanation), she switched on all the lights downstairs and yelled and banged pots and doors in the kitchen until we all got up. Frenchie and I went to get the cows. Rudolph and Ambrose sneaked away to the barn. Coming back through the pasture with the cows, Frenchie and I found our father, slumped in the front seat of the car by the meadow gate, with a strange woman asleep beside him. We didn't tell my mother. We didn't have to. She told us, as we fed and milked the cows, that he was an evil man and would be punished in hell, just you wait and see. By the time he came back, the morning chores were done. She narrowed her eyes and tightened her lips at the sight of him, but I don't remember hearing her shout at him as she had shouted earlier in the morning, moving like a mountain cat through the barn, accusing him not only of infidelity and thievery, but of other sins way beyond my comprehension. Staring at me with lost eyes over the rump of the cow I was milking, she said, "Don't grow up to be like your father, Harding." I had already determined that I wouldn't. By the time I was fourteen, the odor of the manure we followed in the cable cart from the barn to the manure shed every morning sickened me, and it didn't take much persuasion for me to embrace my mother's version of me as too good for the life my father led. Many years later, I realized that he, too, was too good for it, that almost any human being was too good for the life he led—or the life she led, for that matter.

The older girls became mothers to the younger children. In my case, it was Annabelle who became my guardian even though she was younger than I. After a beating in the woodshed for having talked back to my father, I'd be sent to bed without supper, and Annabelle would come upstairs with a piece of chicken or a saucer of blackberry pie. Sitting on the side of my bed as I ate, she would mutter, "You'll show 'em. Just you wait." I have seen her only twice in the last twenty years, but she is still the one I feel closest to. When Floyd was born, during my fifteenth year, it was I who fed him, bathed him (not very often, for none of us bathed very often), put him to bed, and sat with him under the trees in the front lawn and, holding him in my arms, sang him to sleep. When I left home—his father and mother, not his brother—he was talking baby talk. He still does.

When Jean Harlow died, I mourned secretly and inconsolably.

But the day Floyd was born I was no more, and perhaps even less, moved by that event than I would have been by one of the cows calving in the barn.

Most of my brothers and sisters were born at home. Only one —I think it was Marianne—was not. Trudging home from school one October afternoon, I stopped in my reveries as a car slowed down to give me a lift. Inside, pale but smiling, sat my mother, and in her arms, enveloped in blankets, was my baby sister. I rode home with them in silence, jealous of that sleeping infant, who, of all of us, had been born specially in a hospital.

Seven of the thirteen children were born in March, and March along the Canadian border was still harsh winter, with the roads all but impassable and the one town doctor often out on call for cases of pneumonia and virulent childhood diseases. Sleeping in the large room above the kitchen, in the double bed that I shared with Frenchie and Ambrose, I awoke to grunts and groans, and screams that pierced the chilled dark air, and hurried footsteps. Terrified, we all three made our way furtively down the back stairs and sat on the bottom steps until the screams ended and the footsteps subsided. In the quiet, we stumbled back into our bed and slept until morning, when we were led into my parents' bedroom, off the parlor, to see the new baby.

Birth on the farm was neither surprising nor unexpected. We watched colts and calves slide from the glistening insides of animals; and new litters of puppies and kittens, broods of chickens and ducklings, punctuated our daily lives. So did the deaths of horses, cows, and pets. When I was a little boy, no more than seven, my favorite white kitten was killed by a kick from a cow. I wept for weeks until my father, having to slaughter a cow for our winter supply of canned beef, chose the murderess and allowed me to watch the execution. Sometimes, though, relatives, not animals, died, and those were a surprise, at least to us children. My father, stamping snow from his boots as he came into the

24

kitchen from delivering milk cans to Longview, said, "Amélie died last night." My mother, at the stove, suspended her spatula in midair and turned away so we wouldn't see the tears with which she customarily greeted sad news. The next day, they drove us the ten miles to my uncle's farmhouse, where his four daughters sat numb in the kitchen as we took off caps, mittens, coats, and galoshes. One by one, we were ushered, unwilling and apprehensive, into the sweet-scented presence of death. Since Amélie was my godmother (although I don't remember hearing a kind word —or any other word, for that matter—from her), I was lifted, every muscle tensed in protest, to kiss her cheek. That touch of oily death against my lips, and the proximity to the lidded eye I was certain would flick open to stare into my deceitful face, provoked a fit of sobbing which my mother laid to grief for my departed godmother.

Grief was loud and full in those rural parlors where candles burned at either end of open caskets in which relatives lay, rosaries twined around their bloated fingers, surrounded by the ruffled satin of casket linings and the cloying smells of flowers and incense. Unknown aunts and uncles appeared, accompanied by strange little boys and girls just like us in suits and dresses just like ours, from farms across the border in Quebec and from mill towns in Massachusetts and Maine. Tears were interrupted only for prayers. When my father's oldest sister, Léonie, was brought home to Aunt Hélène's living room in Crescent, we were all shepherded in to see, for the last time, that legendary aunt who had founded her own personnel-counseling office in Fall River. She had always been much too busy with her office affairs to spend much time with us, but sometimes Maude had brought her along on a summer afternoon, wearing, as Maude herself did, fur trim on her coats, dangling beads around her neck, and glittering bracelets on her wrists. In the flickering light of Aunt Hélène's parlor, her dyed red hair displayed its last marcel and her painted rosebud lips were closed forever. But we were held up to stare at her, all the same, and then released by sobbing aunts who sent us upstairs to play with the other children.

Up there, huddled on the beds with cousins we had seldom, if ever, seen before, we heard Aunt Maude and Aunt Hélène screaming out below their hysterical confessions of sisterly acts of vengeance and malice. (My mother, riding home after the funeral, reminded her grieving husband that his sister Maude had once cut up Léonie's new silk dresses into little pieces, enraged because her sister had "made eyes" at one of her young men.) Assaulted by sounds of sorrow drifting up to us in French and English, we fell back upon the blankets, seeking escape, however fitful, in sleep, wanting only to be taken back to the security of our own beds and the fields and barns and silo where our lives were spent.

It must have been in the fall of 1934 that I entered the sixth grade in the Longview school, where Rudolph, Ambrose, and Evangeline had already preceded me. My memories of Frenchie's childhood, though he was only a year older and the most pugnacious threat to my daily peace, are even dimmer than of my own. I think, however, that by the sixth grade he had dropped back into my class.

Longview was a town of about five hundred people, mostly not French-Canadian. They seldom had more than three or four children to a family, and their names were Baldwin, Flint, Owens, Hamilton, Langdon, Rich. They were a different breed from us, as we were each to learn through the nicknames and doggerel insults of unthinking country prejudice. The fraction of Mohawk blood, however remote, was an additional stigma. Annabelle, who came to the town school a year after me, was chased home nearly every afternoon by little boys shouting "Squaw! Squaw!" One day, goaded beyond her usual stoic good sense, she turned and struck out at one of them with her lunch pail, and he had to have several stitches in his head. After that, they didn't bother her any more.

In good weather, we walked through the pastures behind the

barn and, hopping from slippery stone to slippery stone, across the stream at the foot of the hill and through the woods to school. In the winter, when the snow came, some of us put on skis and were pulled along by ropes tied around the waists of others, who were riding the three ponies. We stabled the ponies in a shed near the school, put our skis up in the loft above them, and hurried into the brightly lit warmth of the spacious classrooms of the Longview school, a palace of brick and glass and highly polished corridors. Fresh from the nestlike closeness of the one-room schoolhouse, we found ourselves thrust among children who were all, roughly, the same age, and we edged into competition and companionship with them. We were later taught by women of various ages and temperaments, but in the beginning all of us were introduced to the sterner discipline and higher standards of town education by the sixth-grade teacher, Agnes Clark, a neat, fragile little woman with curly blond hair and piercing blue eyes that never missed anything that happened in her room.

I lost my heart to her almost immediately, when she clasped her thin, pale fingers together and announced, "I am going to read you *The Prisoner of Chillon*, by Lord Byron. I love Byron." Only a moron or a woman so enveloped in a love of her own (which she certainly wasn't) could have ignored the adoration I directed unblinkingly at her all day long. It was no time at all before she was reading my compositions out loud to the class, primly articulating each syllable and smiling with conspiratorial pride as she handed the ink-scrawled sheets back to me. She corrected my grammar, widened my vocabulary, listened to my incessant conversation, and described the movies *she* saw nearly every night (she had a car of her own) in Crescent. I became that anathema of the classroom the teacher's pet, intent on her every word, my eager hand raised before her questions left her mouth, and smiling smugly as she praised me for my answers. I studied hard and happily at night, back of the kitchen stove, to earn the grades that put me, and kept me, at the top of the honor rolls (published each month in the Longview weekly newspaper) during all my school years.

In the schoolyard, quite understandably, I was nobody's pet. One particular boy, larger than I was, and older, taunted me loudly and unceasingly from the moment the recess bell shrilled through the building until we came back into the room, his face flushed with the gloating pride of the tormentor and mine with the shame of the victim. Months went by and I pretended I didn't hear his insults and dodged meekly and unsuccessfully the blows aimed at the softer parts of my body, until one day, enraged beyond all caution, I charged into him, head down. A crowing, cheering crowd surrounded us, and since I had started it, there was nothing to do but continue. He knocked me down over and over again, and over and over again I got up, my teeth rattling in my head, and charged him once more. My clothes were muddied and torn, my nose bloody, and both eyes swelling when he gave up and sauntered off. But he had waited just a little too long. For from three different directions of the schoolyard came three older Lemay brothers, who took turns in making him look even worse than I did. If anyone was going to bully the boy who at home they called "sissy," "bookworm," "squaw," and "doggie," it was going to be his brothers, not a stranger. Eventually, the school principal, his mild voice twittering in the sudden stillness, arrived to carry off the attacker and the defenders alike. The bully never bothered me again, nor did anyone else. The other boys kept their distance, and, in time, turned to me for help with their homework. In the flattering capacity of a tutor, I was invited into houses in town that my brothers and sisters were never allowed into, and for a while I enjoyed my social superiority. But one evening, walking home from a hard hour's wrestling with a classmate's inability to write a grammatical sentence, I suddenly realized that it was not I who was welcomed by the boys' smiling, anxious mothers but my mind. I was being used. I never accepted another invitation to accompany a boy home after school.

28

It was an indication of Miss Clark's perceptiveness that, having both Frenchie and me in her class, she put the entire distance of the classroom between us. From our earliest days in school, we had sat on the same double bench before the same double desk (probably so we could share the same schoolbooks), and several times each day I had to pick myself up from the floor where Frenchie shoved me whenever the teacher turned her back. Sometimes, I pushed him off the seat in retaliation. Once, the teacher spun around and snapped, "The next one of you two who pushes the other one off that seat is going to stand in the corner for the rest of the day." As soon as she turned back to the blackboard, Frenchie threw himself, bawling, to the floor.

Agnes Clark never for a moment pretended that Frenchie and I could be harnessed to the same whippletree. She taught me my way, and Frenchie his, but he—then or a year or two later—fell behind me and, like most of my brothers, never finished high school. They did not like school, and since I did, I can't take much credit for doing well in it.

Miss Clark held up her hand when I spoke too rapidly, and told me to speak with my mouth opened wider so the nasal tones that issued from between my clenched teeth would be softened. She grimaced at my dirty fingernails, and sewed buttons on my shirts as I stood, embarrassed and impatient, before her. Then, smiling, she released me.

When I passed from her sixth grade into the higher ones, I managed not to let go of her by becoming a sort of unofficial assistant in her extracurricular activities. She was the faculty adviser for the school newspaper, and she saw to it that some of my better compositions appeared in it. After classes were finished for the day, I stood in the cramped, airless closet helping her run the mimeograph machine and collate pages. As we worked, we talked. She seldom mentioned my brothers and sisters, though the younger ones turned up in her class year after year. Or my parents. I'm not even sure she knew who my mother was. One day, I told her

29

that I had a new baby brother (it must have been Floyd) and she smiled ambiguously, her mouth twitching slightly, before returning to the messy job of inking the roll in the machine.

Stapling the drying sheets of paper together, she fixed her grave eyes upon me and answered patiently those questions I had courage to put to her. There were many I didn't dare ask. I was fourteen by then, and the questions surging through my head could never have found their way into our conversations, so I skirted them by sharing my opinions of movie stars. I had somewhere in the preceding year discarded the gallant ladies who atoned so nobly for their transgressions and the romanticized mother figures in favor of women in love. While love could be tragic, as it always was with Garbo, it could also be slyly wicked (Carole Lombard lounging in silk pajamas) or archly mischievous (Claudette Colbert teasing reluctant Gary Cooper into marriage). Those adroit, scantily clad comediennes were leading me toward the answers my suddenly perplexing body was demanding.

My brothers, more observant about such matters than I, told me that Carole Lombard never wore anything under her dresses. How they could tell I never learned, but I took their word for it. They had discovered my passion for the movies, and, with typical brotherly inconsistency, sometimes tolerated it and sometimes ridiculed it. Behind the barn one afternoon, Ambrose demonstrated to me the use of a contraceptive, tried to teach me how to smoke a cigarette, and then discussed, with unfamiliar seriousness, his concern that Joan Crawford, a particular favorite of his but not of mine, was so alarmingly thin. Frenchie, who was more malicious, came racing to the barn one night as I was milking the cows and told me that Greta Garbo was dead; he'd just heard it on the radio. I dropped the milk pail and fled, sobbing, to the woods. At night, lying between them in the bed we shared, I dreamed of scented, velvet arms around my shoulders and soft, accented voices murmuring in my ear. I would wake to the warmth of my brothers' sleeping bodies sprawled carelessly beside me.

Agnes Clark defined, with subtle tact, the distinction between ladies and other women: a sour expression conveyed her opinion of Barbara Stanwyck's strident voice and vulgar dress in *Stella Dallas*; a nod of approval told me when my choice, Katharine Hepburn or Margaret Sullavan, matched the standards I should impose upon myself. One of her weekly chores was lining up the lower classes in the corridors for the Friday morning assembly. I used to stand and watch her as she went up and down the line of unruly children, her high heels tapping and a faint perfume preceding and following her presence. I was shocked when I heard boys whisper obscenities after her—as shocked as I would have been if they had been whispered after my own mother. I admired her poised pretense that she didn't hear, and I would gladly have risked my life to punch the boy in the nose, but she wouldn't have approved of that. "Gentlemen," she once told me, "never have to fight."

But what place was there for a gentleman in the kitchen at home, or in the barns and fields? And what kind of mothers and fathers do gentlemen have? Walking past the town barroom one afternoon with some boys from my class, I stopped with them to snigger when a woman, barely able to walk, was helped into a car by several boisterous men. As we passed the car, I saw, slumped in the seat, my drunken mother. The other boys, who hardly knew me, probably didn't know who she was, and I, her favorite of her many sons, pretended that I didn't either.

My mother drank. So did my father, and so did my brothers. One of them told me in later years that he was a confirmed alcoholic by the time he was fourteen. In the late afternoon, coming into the kitchen from school, I would see my mother sitting slackly at the table with the uncapped bottle before her and a loose-lipped apologetic smile upon her reddened face. But there were in those years, as there always are, pressing reasons for finding the solace of obliteration. The Depression, late in reaching the backward rural areas, had wiped out any possibility of supporting

31

twelve children adequately on a dairy farm when the price of milk dropped so low that it seemed pointless to deliver it to the local creamery. Our barn had burned, one spring afternoon, and from the smoldering ruins of the building the acrid stink of charred animal flesh lingered about the farmhouse in which my parents drank and cursed and fought. One by one, the boys were accused of smoking in the barn. Since I was the only one over the age of twelve who didn't smoke or drink in secret, my name was never mentioned in that heated roll call of shouted accusations and yelping denials.

The boys left home, to work in CCC camps or on neighboring farms, and returned, tanned and brazen, and too big to be punished by their parents. As each older boy left, a younger one replaced him in the double bed, and eventually I was the oldest of the trio. One day, in another upstairs bedroom, I was shown by a bright-eyed brother what a case of gonorrhea looks like. That sight stiffened my resolve not to tumble in the hayloft any more with girls eager to match yet another Lemay against the performances of his brothers. For I was growing up, too. My father, who regarded me as somewhat odd because I did not smoke or drink or use the scatological expressions which are as much a part of farm life as the matter they describe, insinuated doubts about my malehood. A knowing glance from my mother during one of his contemptuous baitings revealed who had opened, and quickly closed again, the door to the abandoned chicken house that had hidden me and a neighbor's daughter earlier that afternoon.

Once I was old enough to be out of doors late at night, I would hitchhike to the movies after supper, and coming home afterward I was exposed to casual encounters with women driving alone (the highway was a main route to Montreal) who picked me up and then parked by deserted or sleeping farmhouses and, with explosive ferocity, extracted payment for the lift. My lips bruised and my shoulders lacerated, I was dropped off in front of our porch and sneaked up the kitchen stairway to fall into bed, numbed by my evening's amorous variety, one as unreal as the other. Whiskey and cigarettes fouled my breath through the breaths of others, and the smell of rancid perfumes mingled with the smells of the barnyard, which never left my person, it seemed to me, until I had been away from home for months. Life on the farm, contrary to what my mother had believed, is not a haven for innocent growth into life. The inescapable confrontations with birth and death among the animals can brutally disclose the precious transiency of life and plunges the eager boy into whatever urgent pleasures are at hand. Rather than run the risk of venereal infection, I chose the back-seat embraces with women who seemed to know how to protect themselves (and me) by reaching into glove compartments that were traveling drug counters, and whom I never had to see again. I doubt if there is any easy way to enter manhood, and presumably there are worse initiations than mine.

Among Miss Clark's many extracurricular activities were directing the spring school play and coaching students for the annual prize speaking contest. The plays were rehearsed in the auditorium after school, and sometimes Evangeline, who was pretty and articulate, played the heroine. I was usually assigned character roles—grandfathers, comic Negroes, and sinister fast-speaking villains. I don't remember much about the performances except the overwhelming gratification of hearing the audience laugh at something I said or did, and sensing the acute attention that meant I was being watched with approval by every person in the audience. For the prize speaking contests, which I won every year, I wrote my own material. It cost a dollar, I think, to send away for the skits usually performed, and all the money I could steal or beg from my parents I spent on the movies. It may have been Miss Clark who suggested that I write my own. In any case, she helped me devise a piece about a white boy and a Negro friend coming home after dark and running into a ghost—a sheet flapping on the clothesline. Evangeline recited a monologue from *Anne of Green Gables* and won second prize. In her diary, which I habitually read standing behind her open bedroom door, I found that she detested me not only for having won but, in her unshakable (and possibly accurate) belief, for having stolen the idea from a book.

By the time I was fifteen, I knew that I was going to be an actor. I didn't tell anyone, not even Miss Clark, for the ambition to be an actor, in that community of storekeepers' sons and farm boys, would have aroused more ridicule than I could have faced. I read the few published plays that were in the school library, holding the pages up to the light to spell out the blacked-out words and phrases the English-teacher librarian had censored. On summer days, with nothing to do on the farm now that the barn had burned down, I hitchhiked to Crescent and spent hours in the public library there, reading plays, the *New York Times*, and national magazines. In *Theatre Arts*, I came upon names and faces totally unknown to me—Katharine Cornell, Alfred Lunt, Ina Claire, Jane Cowl, Lynn Fontanne, Tallulah Bankhead—and I was plunged into the distant world of Broadway. New York, seen in movies and read about in *Time* and *The New Yorker*, became the mecca toward which all my furtive ambitions were directed. I was going to be an actor. The applause I earned in high-school plays was my route to the approval I had always sought and so seldom found. I forgot about my schoolbooks, about my family, and about the wages of sin and fear of hellfire. I had found myself.

I began to study the techniques of Leslie Howard and Ronald Colman, and practiced speaking in a clipped English accent when I was alone. Then, with an enormous leap of ambition, I settled on Paul Muni, whose fussy gestures and eccentric postures, caught, as I practiced them, in the headlights of the lonely motorist, must have been an eerie sight. On the highway and in the silo I made faces in a hand mirror stolen from Evangeline's dresser, and recited snatches of poetry in other's people's voices, and secretly formed my plans.

34

After struggling for several years to earn a living on a farm without a barn or livestock, my father took a job in a creamery in the nearby town of Clairepont, and we moved there. I was the oldest boy still living at home. Rudolph, Ambrose, and Frenchie would be there for several days at a time, and then wander off again, to odd jobs and mystifying errands across the border, with unknown companions. Rudolph and Ambrose were extraordinarily handsome young men. Frenchie, with the long nose and narrow eyes of a Lemay, was not. My brothers would come home, change their clothes and take steaming-hot baths, shouting, cursing, singing, and laughing, and rush out again. They were not welcome in the houses of the more respectable families in Clairepont, especially those whose daughters looked after them with hot-eyed invitation. Occasionally, one of them would bring a girl home with him. My mother once broke down the bathroom door in the middle of the night to find a grown son naked in the bathtub with a swarthy, loudmouthed creature my younger sisters called "Black Beauty." Holding a scanty towel before her, she was chased from the house by my mother in her full-volumed rage. My brother dressed quickly and followed her, shrugging off my mother's curses.

Evangeline had gone away to normal school, and Annabelle had become the moving force in the household. She fed the children, made the beds, and cleaned the house, as well as attending school. I was in the senior class, quick-tempered and moody, indifferent to anything but the book in my hand and the fantasies in my head.

Clairepont was a bleak border town. Knowing I would not stay there any longer than it took to get my high-school diploma, I didn't bother to make friends. I had only six months or so to go, and nothing was going to stand in my way. But something almost did. The moment I saw Vina in the gymnasium, where the students danced to the high-school band at lunchtime, I fell head over heels in love. Her brother was in my class. A handsome, indolent boy, he sat next to me and openly copied my answers to test questions down on his own paper, and I encouraged him to do it. At first Vina ignored me as she glided by in the arms of other boys (I had never learned to dance), but then, wrenching up from the depths of my cautious nature more courage than I had ever called upon before, I succeeded in carrying her books home along the tree-shaded sidewalks, stealing unreturned glances at her averted face, and delivering, for her edification, all my half-baked opinions. Gradually, she came to tolerate my adoration. By midwinter, she talked to me with that halting, skittish confidence of the adolescent girl. We went to movies together. Clairepont was about double the size of Longview, and films were shown in the town hall. Sitting in the dim light, with her older brother behind us and my younger ones scattered throughout the hall, I held her hand and stared unseeing at movies I had seen the year before in Crescent. I sat on her porch in the early evenings, sometimes helping her brother with his homework and listening to her practice the piano inside. One night, alone in the house with her, I reached across the keyboard and took her hands, but she twisted them away from me and went on playing, her head high with pride. Finally, I gave up and went home. After that, she didn't speak to me again. I had, I can only suppose, revealed in some way or another that I would never marry her, or even give her the customary pleasures of a country courtship. In the weeks that followed, she crossed the street whenever she saw me coming.

The following winter, when I was in New York, Annabelle wrote saying Vina had married one of my classmates. Ten years later, Rudolph picked me up at the railroad station in Crescent to drive me home for the funeral of my father, who had been found hanging from a beam in the cellar. Approaching Clairepont, Rudolph stopped the car to pick up a woman floundering through the snowdrifts by the side of the road with sacks of groceries in her arms. As she got in the back, she looked at me, and I saw that it was Vina and turned away, unable to bear the sight of teeth missing in her mouth and the gray in her hair. She had, by then, six children, Marianne told me, and her husband drank.

When winter came to Clairepont, it was not winter as I had known it on the farm. The snow turned to slush and mud, and the houses in town seemed more isolated from each other than the distant farms had been. There was no silo or hayloft to read in secretly. There was nothing to occupy an unhappy sixteen-year-old boy except making trouble in a family that had already more trouble than it could manage. I refused to go to church on Sundays. It had been a long time since I had taken anything in church seriously, but I had always gone to Mass. Now, in a new town, with a new priest, I adamantly refused to accompany my family. My mother was distressed by this shift in me she couldn't comprehend, and received visits from the priest, who told her, and me, that I would return to the faith; Catholics always do. Rudely, I replied that I couldn't return to a faith I'd never had. My father—recognizing, I'm sure, that I had at last found the club to batter him over the head with—left the room whenever I entered it. Swinging my club with blinding cruelty, I followed him silently wherever he went, my contemptuous eyes watching as he folded his paper and retreated into another room, and I crossed that threshold, too, my book in my hand, to force him out again. However that harassed man coped with his other growing sons, he never found the clue to me. I was too big then to beat, and my mother would not have permitted it, anyway. Nothing in his parental experience supplied a weapon with which to turn aside my defiance.

In the spring, my youngest brother, Cyril, was born—a fair-skinned baby who whimpered but seldom actually cried. He died several months after I left home. My mother, who must have been in menopause, withdrew into the comparative safety of a mumbling insanity. Annabelle took care of the baby. My mother insisted that I be my youngest brother's godfather, and by tears and tight-mouthed, silent supplication she persuaded me to go to confession, take communion, and kneel before the altar again. A few months later, Rudolph woke me from a sound sleep and flung my clothes at me, and I dressed and went with him to witness his secret wedding to a girl my parents did not approve of. So my last two appearances in church were as a religious witness, one to a christening and the other to a wedding.

Floyd, then three years old, was my strongest link to the household. Babbling excited monosyllables and dribbling half-chewed bits of food, he stood waving to me as I left for school in the morning and raced to meet me when I returned in the afternoon. I loved him fiercely, with an unhealthy, premature guilt because I knew I was going to abandon him. That love, in the intervening thirty years, has been masked by irritation and cold anger, and was not fully acknowledged until I stood changing diapers once again, this time on my own son, the day we brought him home from the hospital. I can *look* at my brothers with some composure, but the *thought* of them, now that they and I are older, brings tears of rage into my eyes: rage at the waste of beautiful young men, driven by demons of lust, alcoholism, larceny, and outrage. One of them attended both my parents' funerals with a prison guard at his side. Another spent over a year in a state asylum because he shot up a bar where the woman he had been living with was sitting inside with her new consort, the bartender. But my brothers are not those deadbeats and jailbirds to me. Oh, no; my brothers are the slim athletes I envied as they rode off in brightly repainted secondhand cars with laughing, willing girls. In the middle of the night, they pulled themselves up and crawled through the window above the farmhouse kitchen to come to bed, smelling of musky female odors, and boasted to each other of easy conquests and sweet surrenders, while I feigned sleep, until, innocent in their exhaustion, they slept beside me. And I, of the three of us, appeared listless and spent the next morning.

My youngest sisters, Gabrielle and Marianne, were vivacious, pretty little things who squabbled with each other in the upstairs bedrooms after having exhausted their father's frayed patience or aroused my mother from her nodding lethargy downstairs. Evangeline came home on brief vacations from normal school, wearing lipstick and silk stockings like Aunt Leila and Aunt Maude (who no longer visited us), and peered disdainfully around at the kitchen and the dirty bedrooms before hurrying back to her classes.

At my high-school graduation exercises, I recited a poem I had written for the occasion, but my scholastic record would have been a disappointment to Miss Clark. The boundless misery of thwarted love, and my increasing impatience to get away, had driven me to reading books instead of studying them. But I graduated and put the diploma among those few personal effects that would accompany me out into the world. I knew, without being told, that it would help me get the kind of job I would need. After graduation, I worked in a summer camp on Clairepont Lake, with a classmate whose name I have forgotten. We peeled potatoes, mopped floors, washed dishes, and sneered at the city boys who were the counselors and the campers. Late at night, we swam naked in their lake and plunged from their diving board, and urinated in their recreational waters as a gesture against the enemy world of the privileged. I saved the money I earned each week for my escape into that world.

At the end of the season, I returned to Clairepont. The first night home, in the kitchen, my father and I erupted into a sarcastic quarrel over one of my brothers, who had been arrested for smuggling cattle across the border. My father had somehow scraped together the money to keep him out of jail. With all the moral fervor of my seventeen years, I told him that he was encouraging his sons to be gangsters. He replied that he'd rather have gangster sons than fairies. I knocked him down. Crouching over him, I pounded his head against the floor until, looking at him, I saw that I had broken his glasses. The anguish in his eyes lifted me to my feet and I ran upstairs.

Later that night, when they were all sleeping, I changed into

39

my graduation suit, took my high-school diploma and the hundred dollars I had earned that summer, stole a suitcase and a pair of black-and-white sports shoes my brothers had left in a closet, and crept down the stairs and out of the house. Hurrying down the driveway in the moonlight, I turned for a last look at the house, and there, in one of the front-room windows, was my mother, watching me. Was she pleading with me to stay? Or urging me to leave?

With the suitcase banging against my knees and tears streaming down my face, I walked toward the highway. Headed, this time, not for Crescent but for New York, I told myself that no matter what happened to me among strangers, it could not be worse than what I was leaving. And it hasn't been, ever.

PART TWO

...in the city... 1939–1942

Near our apartment in the East Village, derelicts sprawl sleeping against the fence of one of Manhattan's oldest churches. Sometimes, passing one of them, I wonder if he may have shared the shelter that housed me when I first came to New York thirty years ago. Does that heap of soiled clothing, aging bones, and battered history conceal a boy whose clear gaze and downy cheeks denied like mine the bloodshot eyes and the stubble yet to come? Was he one of us, birds of passage perched on the same roost, in flight from homes we thought we hated or hated us? And if he was, would I recognize him now? Or he me?

The boys who ate, slept, and showered with me have all, except one, blurred beyond recognition by now; the smutty jokes, the sudden friendships and the equally sudden enmities, the laughter and the quarrels echo fainter and fainter with each passing year. I have grown older while they remain locked within a building which has been replaced itself by a housing project. It exists today only in my mind, as they do, and only very occasionally there.

Manhattan has been my home since I first arrived here—the

same week Hitler invaded Poland—after hitchhiking two days and nights. Actually, it was my home long before: in movie comedies when Fred MacMurray courted Carole Lombard as I was to court my own girl, and William Powell and Myrna Loy led their tolerant married lives together as we were to lead ours. Probably only another country boy grown into city man can share the intensity of my affection or understand my irrational resentment at buildings being pounded into rubble and fixtures being ripped from naked walls. Walking down a once-familiar street dwarfed by sterile structures that have displaced the brownstones and tenements of my youth, I question whether simple human hopes can ever be fulfilled within those buildings. But then who knows? Perhaps my son, gravely watering his plants in his bedroom, dreams of country life as I dreamed, at his age, of life in the city. Perhaps he will find himself within those towers of glass and steel as his father found himself within the buildings of bricks and plaster that made way for them.

My first sight of Manhattan was from the back seat of a sedan, the last in a series of vehicles that had carried me, lift by lift, the five hundred miles from my family and my past. The elderly couple up front smiled at each other as they watched me shift from window to window in the back seat nearsightedly absorbing the stunning first vision of my destination: not the solid substance of bridges and skyscrapers, but an airy lacework of myriad lights dancing against giant shadows. As we drove into the city in the September dusk, I pressed my unbelieving face against the window, peering at the upper stories of buildings incalculably taller than the tallest silo back home and into faces that stared or smiled back at me from the sidewalks or looked up from behind newspapers in the trolley cars that clanged beside us. The couple dropped me, with best wishes, at a street corner, where I stood gripping my brother's suitcase with one hand and waving farewell with the other until they disappeared in a stream of traffic. Then I was on my own. I was on my way.

44

I wandered through the streets for an hour or two until a plump, dark-haired woman in a print dress surveying the passers-by from a stoop motioned me to join her. "You looking for a place to stay, kid?" she demanded in such challenging tones that I didn't dare deny it. In a moment, she ushered me, on a stream of pronouncements upon the heat, the neighborhood, and the traffic, into a room which I now realize her children must have vacated for a boarder; sullen eyes followed me from a rumpled mattress on the living-room floor when I went to the bathroom every morning. I paid a week's rent in advance from the hundred dollars I had saved that summer, slid my suitcase under the bed, and hurried out to locate the Broadway theatres. After buying tickets to six plays and gulping down a plate of spaghetti at the counter of the first restaurant I had ever entered, I sat in the balcony of the National Theatre as Tallulah Bankhead, her gleaming white shoulders bare above a low-cut black evening gown, strode with venomous energy through the fascinating melodramatics of *The Little Foxes*.

In the morning, my landlady served me juice, coffee, and doughnut-shaped rolls which seemed to glue my teeth together as I chewed them. Leaning her ample weight upon the kitchen oilcloth, she examined me closely with good-natured superiority. She interrupted me almost immediately to say she couldn't understand a word I was saying, but I was too intimidated to reply that I couldn't understand her very well either. She informed me, with haughty authority, that *nobody* wore black-and-white sports shoes after Labor Day, and asked how long I intended to stay, huh? Retreating from questions I couldn't answer, I went back into my room, tucked the five remaining theatre tickets inside my high-school diploma folder, and locked them up in my suitcase. On my way out to the street, I paused briefly to ask how to get to the World's Fair.

That afternoon, bored in the bleachers as the Aquamaidens splashed below me, I rose to find another distraction. At the gates to an exposition, I discovered my wallet had been stolen: the old,

old story, as shocking as if it had never happened before to anyone. The eighty or ninety dollars that was to support me during my first weeks in the city had disappeared. I decided against reporting the theft to one of the policemen stationed at various posts on the fairgrounds for fear of questions that would result in my being sent back home again before I had even begun my independent life. Back in my room, I dumped out loose change from my pockets onto the bed, and decided that those quarters, dimes, and nickels would have to sustain me until another week's rent was due.

Masking my agitation from the landlady's eye, I sauntered past her to buy apples and loaves of pumpernickel, which I carefully divided into daily rations and then hoarded in my suitcase before hurrying off to see Katharine Cornell in *No Time for Comedy*. If my landlady noticed the increase in my appetite in the morning, she didn't mention it. I got through the days as best I could, roaming through the streets, picking up discarded novels from trash cans to read in the park or in the suffocating closeness of my room, until I could blot out my growing panic in the presence of Fredric March and Florence Eldridge in *The American Way* or Katharine Hepburn and Van Heflin in *The Philadelphia Story*. Reluctant to leave those glamorous creatures, I took to loitering around stage-door areas, dashing from the theatre I had just attended over to the National to wait until Miss Bankhead slipped past, in furs and pumps, to her car, or to the Barrymore, where Miss Cornell came out, paused to greet her admirers, and then vanished, with dogs, maid, and gracious smiles, into the splendor of her limousine. Late at night, unable to sleep because of pangs of hunger and bouts of dismay, I stared at the ceiling and daydreamed of the future when I, like Francis Lederer, would move under bright lights with Katharine Cornell, the exquisitely dressed focus of a thousand eyes, velvet sounds issuing from my gifted throat.

The tickets became merely stubs, and the quarters, dimes, and nickels drained away, one by one. At the end of the week, I packed the Broadway *Playbills* in my suitcase, said goodbye to my landlady on her stoop, already surveying the sidewalks for my replacement, and walked jauntily away. Around the corner, I approached a policeman.

"Listen," I said, "somebody just stole my wallet."

"Tough titty, kid," he replied.

I started away, but he called me back and offered to help me. I wouldn't tell him much beyond the fact that I was far from home and absolutely penniless. After silently evaluating my situation, as well as my appearance and vocabulary, he referred me to the Traveler's Aid Society, who referred me to the Children's Aid Society, who sent me, referral slip in hand, to a shelter for runaway boys.

Saving the nickel supplied for my transportation, I walked downtown and stood, for a moment, under the protection of the vast, colonnaded Municipal Building, without a hat or coat in the September rain, watching boys scurry in and out of the shelter across the street. In groups of two or three, they dashed from doorway to doorway and, seeing me with my suitcase in hand, they shouted vulgar warnings ("Turn back, peckerhead, before it's too late!") which I pretended to ignore as I made my way past them through heavy double doors into the squat brick building between the Bowery and Brooklyn Bridge that was to be my home for over three years.

The Brace Memorial Newsboys' Home had been founded by a wealthy philanthropist as a haven for marauding gangs of homeless newsboys who had terrorized lower Manhattan some fifty years before I reached its doors. Newsboys had long since given way to vagrants churned up in the wake of the long Depression. In the brightly lit spacious lobby where I tried to shake the rain water from my hair and from my only suit, boys somewhat older than I were beached inside by the downpour. They lounged on the stairs and against the walls, casting impudent, challenging glances in my direction. I hastily presented my referral slip over a railing to an indifferent girl who directed me to a bench already occupied by two other newcomers whose suitcases and paper-wrapped parcels rested on the floor beside their leaky shoes. They looked me over with practiced eyes. One of them leaned across the other and jerked his thumb toward the closed door. "Don't tell that dame in there where you come from, unless you want to be shipped back." I stared at him. "Just give her your name. Let her guess the rest of it." I nodded. "What *is* your name, pal?" the other one asked. "Harding Lemay," I told him. This sent them into paroxysms of stifled laughter. Punching each other in the stomach, they invented variations of it until, blushing, I turned from them, determined that the next time someone asked me my name I would find one less susceptible to adolescent jokes. From that day on, most people who knew me well enough to use my first name called me Pete. Ignoring the snickering pair as best I could, I took a rain-dampened book from my jacket pocket, opened it, and used it as a shield behind which I could survey my surroundings. At the further end of the high-ceilinged lobby, I could make out a wide stairway going down to the basement and up to the floors above. On one side of the lobby, a door opened into a large dining room, and doors on the opposite wall led to various offices, into one of which I was summoned finally. There a pleasant older woman tried to find out where I came from. But I had not escaped from home to be shipped right back again: the only information she obtained from me was my name and age. Sighing, she changed the subject and urged me softly to write home to my mother. Then she filled out some forms and told me to come back the next morning and we'd talk about finding a job.

In the basement, we three new arrivals silently shucked off our clothes, handed them over to a surly janitor who flung them into a steam machine to kill the vermin presumably inhabiting them, and crowded together under the shower, a humiliated trio of bumping knees, flushing faces, and no-longer-secret body hair. We put on the faded coveralls and fresh woolen socks the janitor provided and followed him four flights up to the dormitory on the top floor, where he assigned a locker to each of us and watched us store our belongings in it. He handed us each a meal ticket with spaces to be punched whenever we ate in the dining room, and then sent us back downstairs.

Branded as newcomers by our coveralls and linked together by the coincidence of arrival, we three stood in line at a serving counter in the dining room where a motherly cook in a food-stained smock handed us plates of sandwiches and bowls of hot soup. We found a table by a window and quietly ate our lunch, avoiding each other's eyes as the regulars at neighboring tables loudly commented upon our appearance and speculated, with disconcerting emphasis, upon our habits. I ate most of my meals for the next several years in that dimly lit room which smelled of Lysol and cabbage. Although food has seldom interested me very much, I remember what we ate there as wholesome and abundant. I don't recall any complaints about the meals: few of us had ever eaten so well before. After lunch, the cook distributed rags, brooms, and mops among us, and we cleaned the tabletops, scrubbed the counter, and swept and mopped the floors.

After supper, I had the first thorough medical examination in my life. Behind a screen, a doctor listened to my heartbeat, tapped and punched and prodded and pinched, and then announced curtly that I was in good health. But, examining my eyes later, he snapped with obtuse exasperation: "Don't you even *know* that you can't see properly?" He dismissed my stammered explanations with a disdainful gesture and filled out a prescription for a neighborhood oculist to fit me for a pair of glasses in the morning. In another office, I endured the dentist's drill for the first time (my father had yanked our aching teeth out himself with the aid of pliers, curses, and shots of whiskey), and then I was free to spend the rest of the evening as I wished, but I was not allowed, that first night, to leave the premises.

The Brace Memorial Newsboys' Home was not a correctional

institution, although some boys may have been referred to it by family-court judges. Most of us, however, were sent there, as I had been, by social-work agencies. Others probably heard about it through the grapevine in boxcars or flophouses, on highways, and in fruit orchards. It was staffed and administered by the Children's Aid Society and was run pretty much as are the Y.M.C.A.s, although the regulations were somewhat stricter, since we were minors. We could check out any time we wanted to, but if we chose to stay, we had to be in bed by midnight when the front doors were locked. On the second floor was a large recreation room, with ping-pong tables, writing desks, and chess and checker games scattered throughout; there was also a small platform stage at one end, with a piano on it which was usually covered and very seldom played. Although strategically placed signs prohibited smoking, cigarette butts littered the floor under the tables and clotted the potted rubber plants in the corners. Too nearsighted to play ping-pong or even to watch others play with any pleasure, I buried my face in my book until ten o'clock, when the dormitory opened and I settled down with thirty other boys no more alien to me, and no more familiar, than my brothers had been.

Well over a hundred of us were living in the house, most of us sleeping in several open dormitories and perhaps a score or more sharing private rooms on the lower floors. The dormitories were illuminated all night by pleasant blue lights in the ceiling. Every hour or so, a floor counselor made his rounds with a flashlight, checking beds and washrooms to make sure we weren't smoking or quarreling or breaking other rules that had been explained to us when we were admitted. These young men were college students, for the most part, and were genuinely friendly and helpful. We reported thefts to them (my black-and-white shoes, carelessly left under my bed instead of in my locker, disappeared the first night but were located the next morning in another boy's locker), complained of colds and headaches and other ailments, and sometimes teased them about their earnestness or tried to divert their attention when we were doing something we shouldn't be doing, like playing poker between the beds or passing pornographic pictures from cot to cot.

Daily life at Brace seems vague to me now, little more than snatches of whistled songs and whispered jokes, but my existence, even during that first day, was freer from threats (real or imagined) than the seventeen years I had spent at home. My delight in having escaped from the home I had never been able to accept as my own blinded me to possible hazards of being alone in a strange city surrounded by boys of various and perhaps vicious habits. Thanks to my nearsightedness, even the noisiest of them were little more than shadows. I fell asleep quickly and happily each night in a bed of my own, with clean sheets and warm blankets, secure in anonymity at last.

Unlike me, few of the boys intended to remain in the city. They were transients, pausing to take stock of themselves before moving on. New arrivals appeared every day, and each morning faces just becoming familiar had vanished from sight. But there were some regulars who returned winter after winter, showing up with the first snowfalls and departing with the spring rains. From a boyhood among people mostly of my own kind, I was plunged into a clamorous fraternity with boys of all temperaments, backgrounds, accents, and nationalities. Some names were so ordinary that I could never remember them, and others so strange I despaired of ever learning how to pronounce them. Few of my new companions had gone very far in school. I seemed to be the only one who read books. During mealtime and washroom conversations, they spoke crudely and belligerently, sometimes covering ignorance and confusion with obscenity and insolence. Some of them were liars and petty thieves, bullies and troublemakers, but most of them were friendly ordinary boys with pleasant faces and modest manners. We paired off at the dining-room tables and as we polished dormitory floors or scrubbed toilet bowls, drawn together by the need for company. Years of distrust of my brothers had bred in

51

me a deceptive show of interest which hid a reluctance to enter into close relationships. I was much more of a listener than a talker, and from my new companions I learned of childhoods much meaner than mine, of parents more negligent and brutal than my own. Boys with trembling lips and clouded eyes blurted out incidents from their earlier lives in the safety of the evening lamps. In the cold light of morning, they usually greeted me self-consciously, turning away in humiliation at having exposed themselves to a stranger who revealed little, if anything, about himself in return. I had abandoned my brothers, as one of them lightly reminded me years later, forming ties more to my taste than those blood had formed for me. Or so it seemed as we sang our songs, swapped stories, washed socks and underwear in basement sinks, rinsed out contraceptives in lavatory basins, and muttered sleepy defiance from bed to bed, growing blindly into manhood together.

The guidance counselor interviewed us, and, matching boy to opportunity, referred us on to printing firms, restaurants, and stores for jobs, usually provided by shipping clerks, supervisors, and floor managers who had once lived at Brace themselves. Within a week, I was sent with a blond, cheerful newcomer, whose history was as unknown to me as mine was to him, to a stationery store in the forties between Madison and Fifth Avenues. We were hired that day as delivery boys for ten dollars a week; working hours were from eight to six each weekday, and from eight to one on Saturdays. During that first week, I was more often lost than not. I stood in doorways, drenched by autumn rains, sodden packages slipping from my hands, and sat, baffled, in crowded subway cars unaccountably roaring past stations supposed to be my stops. Once, I was carried along in a flood of noontime clerks and secretaries on Wall Street, crying soundlessly because I couldn't locate a building which turned out to be only a block or two west of me. But the week passed. I collected my pay envelope on Saturday and bought a map of the city. On Monday, I knew the streets and subway stops by heart, at least on paper.

Those of us with jobs paid three and a half dollars for room and board at Brace, which left me a fortune for theatre tickets and movies. To save money, I went back and forth to the dining room for lunch. After a childhood of riding on wagons, sleighs, and ponies, only occasionally in an automobile and never on a train, I took a childish delight in traveling by subway. Standing between the swaying cars and staring at the gleaming rails beneath us, I congratulated myself on having become, at last, part of the greatest city in the world. One day, I stood on the steps of the palatial library building on Fifth Avenue and counted the women passing by who wore fur coats: I, who'd never even seen a fur coat just several weeks before. Inexact carbon copies of Joan Blondell and Loretta Young smiled at me in elevators, and sleek imitations of Franchot Tone and George Brent stepped aside as I got off to make my deliveries. Their tailored suits, carefully barbered hair, and scent of after-shave lotion were proof of the distance I had come from overalls and barnyard odors.

But occasional elevator operators did catch my heel as they closed their doors; uniformed doormen at luxury apartments directed me with pungent insults to service entrances; and maids slammed doors in my face after snatching packages from my hands. It was easy to ignore such pettiness and rudeness, and to laugh off the condescension of receptionists who reserved their friendly greetings for men who wore expensive suits. I was bounced happily from delivery to delivery by the genuine concern of those who looked up from their typewriters to ask if I wasn't cold without a jacket or where my raincoat was.

After supper one night during my second week at Brace, killing time before a movie, I roamed through the corridors and open areas of the upper floors. Beyond the recreation room at the further end of the second floor, opposite the apartment which housed the Director and his wife, I came upon a small room. A neat, hand-printed sign taped on the inside of the window of the door proclaimed it as the library, so I entered. A slender blond woman seated at a worktable near the window glanced up at me as I stood in the doorway, and smiled. I nodded to her and hurried over to the bookshelves. A search through the Rex Beaches, Jack Londons, and James Oliver Curwoods revealed nothing to interest me, and I sighed heavily. From behind me, a low-pitched voice with an English accent spoke: "Have you read *The Grapes of Wrath?*" The woman at the worktable rose as I turned to her. "My name is Miss Bromhall," she said, and motioned for me to sit beside her.

I needed no further encouragement. We talked—or, rather, I talked and she listened. In a rush of indiscretion, I told her my story, and, smiling, she told me that she, too, had left her home in England when she was a girl and come to the United States a stranger: it had all worked out very nicely. Having established that in common, we immediately shared our opinions on Tallulah Bankhead and Katharine Cornell, who had replaced my movie favorites; on Greta Garbo (whom she resembled, I thought, and told her so); on books I had read or merely heard about. When it was time to close the library, she told me that it was open only every other evening, and promised to bring me the John Steinbeck novel next time. She locked the door, waved a gloved hand to me, and went down the stairs. I climbed up the two flights to my bed and smiled myself to sleep.

When I returned *The Grapes of Wrath* to her, she lent me *Look Homeward, Angel.* I sat up nearly all night in a washroom stall, my new glasses sliding down my nose, and read it straight through. The next evening, talking to Miss Bromhall about Thomas Wolfe, his mother, and my own, I burst into tears. She rose and arranged books on the shelves until I managed to compose myself. The next book she brought was D. H. Lawrence's *Sons and Lovers.* Three nights a weeks in that peaceful room, isolated from the laughter of the boys down the hall at the ping-pong tables, we talked about books and the men who write them, about the way people live, the choices they make, women and the men they love, and the lives we share with each other. She never ducked an answer to a question, no matter how impulsively or tactlessly put. Without implying the slightest judgment on me, she challenged vague opinions, forcing me to express and to defend ideas I had never known I held.

Her blond hair was dressed in what I later learned was called a "pageboy bob," and, except for lipstick, she wore no makeup, which set her delicately featured face apart from those I saw on my delivery rounds to offices and hotels. She couldn't have been more than thirty at the time, but her imperturbable grace made her seem, quite often, centuries older than I. She never discussed her personal life. I don't know where she lived or if she lived alone, but that had nothing to do with us. The life we shared took place beyond the door I unlocked for her when she appeared at seven o'clock every other evening, and which I locked behind her when she left at ten. She carried back to her apartment the book I had returned to her, and I carried upstairs to the washroom the one she had brought for me.

Quite predictably, it wasn't long before smirking boys loitered around the toilet stalls to make jokes about the bookworm in the shithouse. I was accustomed to the ridicule prompted by reading books, and usually managed to ignore it. Soon, however, the Director's wife, a plump, watery-eyed matron in silk dresses and fox furs who haughtily sailed past groups of sniggering boys, stopped me in the hallway to recommend the latest James Hilton or A. J. Cronin best-seller. I was becoming the ladies' pet at Brace, as I had been the teacher's pet in school, and knew I was headed for trouble. Not knowing what to do about it, however, I went on reading, dimly aware of the arguments swirling around the wash-basins on the comparative merits of Hank Greenberg or Joe DiMaggio on the baseball diamond, Joe Louis or Bob Pastor at Madison Square Garden, and Dorothy Lamour or Betty Grable in bed. My indifference to their consuming interests was bound

55

to be challenged eventually when one of them, having lost an argument with an equal, would turn his rage on me.

But I was saved from the impending confrontation. I suppose one of the counselors, or perhaps even one of the boys, told the Director that I read all night in the lavatory, for I was summoned to his office when I returned from work one evening. After some casual chatter, during which he told me that his wife thought I was a bright lad, he asked me if I would like to share one of the private rooms on the floor below the dormitories for five dollars a week. I could then, he said, read in peace as late as I wished. There would be a room available in a week or two and he would have my name put at the head of the list of boys who were waiting for private rooms. He regarded me for a moment over his horn-rimmed glasses. My expression must have conveyed the urgency of my situation, for he added abruptly that there was a room free at the moment if I had no objection to sharing it with a Negro.

That Saturday afternoon, I stored my belongings in a locker against the wall of a corner bedroom furnished with two narrow cots, two lockers, and a writing desk between the cots with a chair before it and a radio on it. Lying on one of the cots in his undershorts was Chester, my new roommate. I sat on my bed and returned his indolent gaze while the colors of our skins hung between us. We had seen each other in the lobby and the corridors but had never spoken. I wasn't sure I really knew which of the dozen or more Negro boys he was. Finally, he grinned and said, "Don't look at me like that, boy, or I'm goin' to think you're after something I ain't goin' to give you." Near-naked bodies hold few secrets for boys from big families, but, never having seen a Negro up close before except in the movies, I suppose I was staring. He swung his legs to the floor, pulled on a shirt and a pair of pants, and reached for his shoes. "Come on," he said. "It's Saturday. Let's get our asses out of here."

That afternoon, and during weekends and those evenings when the library was closed, Chester guided me through the streets outside. In the shadows of the Elevated, we scuttled up Park Row past flophouses, pawnshops, missions, and barber schools, through the turns and crannies of Chinatown, to the diamond displays on Canal Street. We skirted corpse-like men propped up in doorways, spit and urine and whiskey staining their threadbare trousers. Others, only slightly more animated, hoarsely offered to sell us the jackets off their backs so they could have just one more drink. "Don't you get mixed up with them bums," Chester warned me. "They'll rob you blind, and leave you naked as a baby in a garbage can somewhere."

I never saw anyone get any money from Chester, but he was a master at extracting it from others. Under the shelter of the Municipal Building, he panhandled with an ingratiating smile among the swarms of businessmen and secretaries approaching the subway entrance. Soon he had coached me in the techniques that had supported him across the country, he said, from coast to coast: "Always go up to 'em from the side, it scares 'em if you come on 'em head on; look 'em square in the eye; no matter how bad off they are, you gotta make 'em ashamed of bein' better off than you; don't speak too loud or clear, be humble, like a good boy down on his luck; and smile, keep on smilin', like there ain't nothin' but love in your heart; never look at what they give you till after they've gone, and always say, 'God bless you,' not 'Thank you.'" I was a poor pupil. Asking for money from anyone has always humiliated me (the prospect of wheedling a dime for the movies from my father when I was a boy made me vomit), and besides my weekly pay was more than enough for my needs. But I wanted to please Chester, so I did my best.

When we had collected enough change, we raced up the Bowery to the Venice Theatre. There Mazie Gordon, who became a celebrity among us that winter when Miss Bromhall posted a *New Yorker* Profile of her on the bulletin board in the recreation room, sat in the cashier's cage, her face caked with paint and powder, and welcomed us, or at least our nickels and dimes, to the technicolor charms of Priscilla Lane and Alice Faye. Inside the Venice, a steady hum of snores was punctuated by private laughter, curses, and quarrels; an acrid odor of urine, disinfectant, and the sweat of unwashed bodies stung our nostrils. But it was cheap and it was warm, so we endured, without complaint, the discomfort of pinching springs in cushions and insect bites. The projector usually broke down at least once during every showing; our raucous protests brought Mazie, movie magazines rolled into a club in her fists, among us to restore the customary lethargy. Whistles and catcalls greeted her entrance and hastened her departure.

Our noses and spines rebelled from time to time at the prospect of the Venice, and then we went to the Tribune, a higher-class movie house downtown toward the financial district. Chester never let me pay his way, and he refused to spend his own money, since the admission was much higher than at the Venice. I'd buy my ticket and go inside, then sneak out to the men's room and unlock an unguarded side door so he could join me, after loitering a few minutes among the urinals, down front to watch Greer Garson or Vivien Leigh.

We outraced cops who saw us sneaking from basement hideouts where we smoked the cigarettes and gulped down the cheap red wine Chester managed to locate. At nineteen, he had a network that supplied him with whiskey, cigarettes, clothing, and, too infrequently, stray and scrawny girls who passively permitted furtive intimacies. He spent more money than I earned, but I was too unworldly to speculate on how he got it. I didn't ask him what he did during the day while I delivered packages, and he never asked me what was inside the books he left me hunched over every night when he turned his face away from the light to go to sleep.

He was vigorous, strong, and healthy, with an open nature which seemed to hide nothing from me, and nothing had to be hidden from him. Only now do I realize that he never let me know anything more than what he wanted me to know. I never found out where he came from, if his parents were alive or dead, or if he had brothers and sisters. He lived, it seems now, cut off from the past and resisting the future: perhaps one was too painful to remember, the other too hazardous to anticipate. One night in the washroom, I overheard a coarse joke about that jerk with the book and his nigger friend. I came out of the stall, book in hand, to a dead silence which followed me out into the corridor, where a whining protest reached my ears: "You nuts? That boogie pal of his is goin' slice you up in the dark one of these nights!"

It may very well be that the Director had hoped that I might lead Chester into my habits, not follow him into his. Looking back on it now, it seems strange that that sensible, astute man would have thrown together two boys not only opposite in race, but in basic natures and interests as well. Perhaps he did it intentionally, believing that I required a more vital connection to real life than books and movies. Whatever his purpose in linking Chester and me, and whatever his response to the results, he never mentioned it in our brief and rare encounters in the lobby. His wife, however, was much less discreet. Pausing on her way out, she fingered her furs and avoided my eyes as she hinted that there were better ways to spend my leisure time: the museums, the concerts, the aquarium, the landmarks, the "cultural" life of the city. I nodded my head, implying promises of reform, until the lady we called "the Duchess" behind her back rustled off in her silks. Then I'd join Chester, lurking in a nearby doorway, for another exploration of downtown Manhattan, north to Canal Street, west to the piers, east to the warehouses, and south to the oceanfront at the Battery.

Too restless to stay inside, even during December weekends, Chester nagged me until we bundled up in jackets and roamed the streets side by side. Stopping at pawnshop windows, we rubbed our aching hands together and watched the clouds of vapor formed by our breathing as we inspected guitars, wristwatches, and binoculars we would never buy. The icy streets were filled with slush; derelicts as impervious to the winter winds as they had been to the summer heat stretched out trembling fingers from flophouse doorways. The basement hideouts of only a few weeks earlier were too damp and chilly for us now, although we did try to pick the locks on others that looked inviting. There was no place to go, usually, except back to our room and, eventually sympathetic to my complaints of wet socks and cold hands, Chester allowed himself to be persuaded to return to the warmth and quiet of Brace.

Spying upon our betters through the windows of a Chinese restaurant on one such afternoon, we heard the sound of voices raised in song. We traced the accompanying organ chords to a time-stained building just off Chatham Square, climbed the stairs to a loft, and entered a mission. Several men and women whose somber clothes emphasized the pallor of their earnest faces were leading a congregation of bleary-eyed vagrants in recitations of remembered sins and in off-key renditions of Christian hymns. Chester unbuttoned his jacket, picked up the hymnal from the bench ahead of us, and joined in the chorus of "Bringing in the Sheaves" with a loud, clear, confident voice which immediately dominated the hall. He had never sung in my presence and I was surprised and touched by the sincerity with which he gave himself to those simple melodies of faith and salvation. Fascinated, I watched the fluid muscles moving beneath the brown skin of his bare throat and, catching my eye, he winked. In mid-hymn, he shifted his beat to an irreverent syncopation which lifted the song from joyless guilt to a celebration of life. I joined in lustily, although I've never been able to carry a tune, and soon a timid little man wearing rimless glasses left the platform to come down and ask us to leave. We protested that we were enjoying the word of God, but we were ushered down the stairs into the cold again. On subsequent Sunday afternoons, we reappeared, grinning shamefacedly as the pallid faces on the platform went even paler at the sight of us. I followed whatever mood Chester set: if he was playful, I was silly; if he was earnest, I was fervent. There were times, however, in that cheerless hall when the unwavering faith on the platform prompted a grudging respect from us and we sang with a genuine feeling that lightened the bleakness of our surroundings and eased the pain we still carried from our childhoods.

Christmas scenes dominated the store windows uptown, and crowds of late-afternoon shoppers carried packages toward their homes as I returned empty-handed to the stationery shop. A few boys at Brace prepared for holiday visits home and, falling victim to a nostalgia for a home I never had, I finally wrote a letter to my family. I couldn't bring myself to write to my mother, so I sent it to Annabelle instead, knowing she would tell the others that I was working, and well and happy. She replied at once, but her penciled news of Evangeline at college, Rudolph's troubles with his wife, Floyd's new teeth, and baby Cyril's chronic illnesses did little to improve my spirits. The season bred in me then, as it does now, a foreboding of disappointment. I stayed at Brace for my first Christmas away from home.

Since the holiday fell on Sunday, stores and offices were closed on Monday. That day, the cook served the traditional meal to us at noon and the staff shared it, dutiful intruders among embarrassed boys on their best behavior. Late that afternoon, we all gathered for a party in the recreation room, which was transformed for the occasion with green pine boughs and colored ribbons drooping from the ceiling. Presents were heaped beneath a brightly decorated tree in the corner. Considerable effort had been made to create a pleasant time for us, but the hollow determination to force reality to match the myth just didn't work. We rubbed our backs, in thinly disguised boredom, against doorjambs as plump matrons, assembled by the Director's wife, stood like a row of full-breasted robins on the platform stage and caroled

61

tidings of joy at us. Later, they distributed the presents (neckties, probably bought, Chester whispered, wholesale from a onetime boarder at the house), peering at attached cards to trill out their versions of our names. We turned away with churlish bad manners: whatever we thought of our own mothers, we could not accept these well-meaning, synthetic substitutes. The Director's wife gave me a special present: a best-seller by C. S. Forester which seemed so perfectly suitable for boys that I couldn't bring myself to read it for months. Murmuring her season's wishes, Miss Bromhall slipped a small envelope into my hand as she was leaving. It contained two theatre tickets: one for Maurice Evans in *Hamlet*, the other for William Saroyan's *The Time of Your Life*.

By mid-January, even Chester had no desire to venture outside, and, cooped up in our overheated room, we were thrown back upon our own resources. He had found a mouth organ somewhere and spent hours playing songs of homeless cowhands and waiting mothers while I lay on my cot reading. Those songs my father and brothers had sung milking cows and pitching hay made the pages of James T. Farrell and Sherwood Anderson swim before my eyes. Chester would stop in the middle of a song, tap the spit from the harmonica against his knee, and put it away. Meeting his gaze over my book, I'd find him regarding me as my brothers often had. I sensed that I was failing to live up to some expectation he could not express and I could not define. We'd smile vaguely at each other, and I'd go on reading as he moved quietly on his bare feet about the tiny room, trying to occupy himself without disturbing me.

I was entering the life I had left home to find. During one of our early conversations, I had confessed my dreams of becoming an actor to Miss Bromhall, and in an uptown restaurant after work one day, she introduced me to a friend who ran a ticket agency. From then on, I picked up passes at box offices to see Pauline Lord, Grace George, Ethel Barrymore, Ina Claire, Florence Reed, and Ruth Gordon in plays whose titles I may be the only person who still remembers. When my deliveries were finished for the day, I rushed downtown to Brace for supper, changed my clothes, and rushed out again, uptown to a play, and came back to read in my room until dawn. I paid to see the popular hits, like *Life with Father*, or Gertrude Lawrence in *Skylark*. I even paid to watch John Barrymore, a suave legend from movie magazines read in the silo six years before, weave his drunken way through a comedy so trivial and vulgar that I was enraged at having spent my money to see it. I was beginning to spend money on other things besides plays and movies. I bought a suit for the first time, and a raincoat, and shirts, shoes, and ties. With a confidence bred by new clothes, I smiled at the girls in the offices and talked back to doormen who tried to bully me. Once, I delivered some stationery to Ina Claire in a hotel suite; she opened the door herself, a vision of smiles, satins, and vagueness. That evening, Miss Bromhall clasped her hands together and said, "No! What is she like? Tell me!"

For my eighteenth birthday, in March, Miss Bromhall gave me theatre tickets again, for Maurice Evans in *King Richard II*, and Ingrid Bergman and Burgess Meredith in *Liliom*. At her desk in the library, we analyzed the plays and the actors, and later compared our impressions of the Lunts in *The Taming of the Shrew*, of Laurence Olivier's Romeo and Vivien Leigh's Juliet. She brought her copies of the texts and showed me how the plays had been cut to suit the actors and described performances she had seen in London when she was a girl, Barrymore's Hamlet and Edith Evans's Rosalind. Our time and talk were so crowded with actors, plays, and novels that there was little room for other subjects. Although Miss Bromhall had relatives still living in England, she never mentioned the bombing of London. To me, the war in Europe was little more than a background for the heroics of Alfred Lunt and the elegance of Lynn Fontanne in *There Shall Be No Night*, and the Nazis were sinister obstacles to James Stewart's courtship of Margaret Sullavan in the movies I saw on those nights when Miss Bromhall was not scheduled in the library and her ticket-broker friend had nothing for me to see on Broadway.

When Chester was out, I read aloud from plays by Chekhov, Bernard Shaw, and Eugene O'Neill that Miss Bromhall lent me; when he lay smoking and staring at the ceiling opposite me, I read under my breath. I copied the words I didn't understand into a notebook and took them in to Miss Bromhall, who explained their meanings and taught me how to pronounce them. Then I would read *Saint Joan* or *The Cherry Orchard* all over again. Chester stayed out more and more, and later and later. After I'd fallen asleep, he'd come in, switch on the light, and I'd wake up blinking at the lipstick on his throat and chest, pretending I didn't notice that his face was drained of friendship, even of interest in me. In the dark, I heard him toss and turn in his sleep, mumbling words I couldn't make out. In the morning, he, who once had to be dumped out of bed, sat fully dressed staring glumly out the window when I opened my eyes. He spoke in grunts and shrugs when he bothered to speak at all. I know now, of course, that he must have been hurt. I know, too, that I was blind and selfish. But I also know that neither of us could have reached across the space that separated us. We continued to live side by side, unable to keep the distance from widening between us.

A distance was growing, too, between all of us at Brace, and, indeed, between us and the world outside, which could not be dismissed by switching the radio from Gabriel Heatter to "The Hit Parade," ducking into the men's room when the movie newsreels showed torpedoed ships and burning cities, and hurrying past newspaper headlines. Friendly teasings in the washrooms blazed into fisticuffs about the American Nazi Bund and Communists, about Jews and Negroes, unions and bosses, leaving blackened eyes and bloody noses in their wake, as well as threats of vengeance in dark alleys outside. Boys enlisting in the army grinned sheepishly over their coffee at breakfast. Others announced with slit-eyed belligerence that the bastards would have to come and get them. Books and plays provided an escape for me; Chester had the streets outside now that spring had come again; others patrolled the corridors looking for something to hit or kick or torture. Taunts of "kike," and "nigger," and "fairy," perhaps once whispered behind departing backs, were now spat out with contemptuous challenge by boys who, innocuous at best and crude at worst only a few months before, were now hardened, suspicious strangers. There were fewer new faces: unhappy or unwanted sons enlisted in the services from home instead of hopping freights or thumbing rides as we had done. The new arrivals often spoke with European accents and were too eager to make friends. Rumors of "foreign" habits dominated the lavatory gossip, and old-timers nudged each other slyly as timid newcomers entered to take showers or to use the toilets.

One of them, a year or two older than I, spoke with a sibilant accent and wore a thin mustache which made his pallid face suspect among our clean-shaven ones. His clothes were well made but fit tightly where ours hung loose. Desperate for companionship, he sometimes cornered me, as the Director's wife did, in bookish conversations, but his were about Thomas Mann and Marcel Proust, while hers were about Anne Parrish and Daphne du Maurier. Trapped in the corridor with him, being winked at by smirking boys who passed us, I avoided his pleading overtures, ashamed of my transparent rudeness but even more ashamed of being seen in his company. When he called one of my favorite movie stars "nothing but a Berlin streetwalker," I seized upon his casual remark as an excuse to brush past him whenever he approached me again.

He came into the washroom some weeks later when Chester and I were under the showers. We shouted coarse jokes about guys who hang around showers, and turned our backs on his

65

tentative smiles and liquid eyes. Drying our feet on a bench later, we heard thrashing noises and hoarse groans from behind the swinging door to a toilet stall. Having heard similar noises often before, we yelled encouragement to him until a muffled shriek, too intense to come from mere self-abuse, brought us to our feet. Chester swung open the door. The butt of all our ridicule was slumped over a toilet bowl, and drops of blood fell upon his shoes and socks and on his twitching hands, one of which held an open razor. We tried to stop, with towels and washcloths, the blood that spread warm from his throat to our hands and arms, but we couldn't. "Sweet Jesus," Chester whispered, and ran off in his shorts to get help. The Director and his wife soon appeared, then a crowd of gaping boys, and, finally, policemen and ambulance attendants. Chester and I were sent back to our room, where a policeman stood in the doorway and asked us questions we couldn't answer. We never found out if he lived or died, or why he did it, or what his story was. We may have never asked. Neither of us could find the words to talk about him, or about anything else.

When I came home from work one evening, Chester's clothes were gone, and so was he. No matter what new boy slept in the other cot during the months I lived in that room, it was always Chester's to me. I'd open the door each evening, hoping to see him there, sitting on his cot playing his sad songs on the mouth organ. Six years later, just discharged from the army, I ran into him on a spring afternoon in Washington Square. We threw our arms around each other and went off to have a beer. In a Greenwich Village bar, he lifted up his shirt to show me a jagged scar embedded on his smooth brown stomach by a Japanese bayonet. I reached across the table and ran my fingertips over the ugly tissue. Our eyes met, as fondly and as blindly as they had when we were boys, and then, as before, looked hurriedly away. Parting in the April twilight, we shook hands and promised, over twenty years ago, to keep in touch.

After Chester left Brace, Mortensen, who delivered packages with me at the stationery shop, moved in to take his place. A friendly blond boy with good manners and an open disposition, he carried me with him into casual comradeship with other roomers on the floor. Ray Masella and Johnnie O'Neill shared the room next to ours. Ray was part Hawaiian, an aggressive, cheeky street urchin, and Johnnie was a sly bigot from South Boston who often started arguments that his roommate ended with his fists. Ray worked in a printing press and Johnnie as a clerk in a department store, but they didn't reveal much more about themselves. Not friends, as Chester and I had been, but companions, we skirted personal confidences, demanding only each other's company as we gathered in our rooms for late-night bull sessions over the beer we sneaked past the floor counselor. Now the old guard, we inspected newcomers at mealtime and gossiped about them in private. On weekend evenings, we ventured uptown, further than Chester and I had ever dared to go, to Yorkville, where the American Nazi Bund held its rallies and stolid girls in beerhalls good-naturedly resisted our timorous advances.

That summer, the Director, probably prompted by his wife, decided we needed exposure to the social graces. Accordingly, we were instructed in ballroom dancing on Sunday afternoons in the recreation room by a tall, angular girl with long red hair who, I discovered some years later, was one of Martha Graham's dance troupe. We didn't know or care who Martha Graham was, and we didn't attend the lessons because we wanted to dance. All we wanted was the phone numbers of the girls we clamped in damp embrace as we circled the floor. Soon we were taking them to the movies, whispering nonsense into their delighted ears as we held their hands in the dark. We were introduced to sisters and friends and, now and then, to a glowering father and an anxious mother. A few of us even got invited for pasta and lasagna in cramped apartments in Greenwich Village.

Now we really had topics for our midnight sessions: which girls would and which girls wouldn't. We debated the probabilities exhaustively before dropping the subject, with the same thwarted potency with which we left the girls in their hallways, to resume our arguments about the Roosevelts, John L. Lewis, Lindbergh, and Hitler. The closeness of our rooms drove us out into the streets during the summer evenings. To take our minds off our failures with the girls, we'd decide to cool off in the presence of Linda Darnell and Ann Sheridan. On our way, we stopped to hoot at the maniacal orators in Union Square and, on our way back, we sat over cups of coffee in all-night eateries, loudly expounding our views of the troubled world. One night, I was left almost senseless on the floor of a White Tower restaurant after several burly workingmen, overhearing my opinions, tried to broaden my political understanding while my buddies looked on. They helped me down the street to Brace and put me to bed, where I lay considering, among other things, the advantages of keeping my mouth shut in public.

Exhausting her personal collection of books, Miss Bromhall sent me with a note to the Chinatown branch of the public library, where a brisk gray-haired woman took me firmly in hand. Each evening after work, I picked up a book she had put aside for me, and entered, never to leave it completely again, the world of the great nineteenth-century novelists. Most of what little I know about life in other times and other places comes from those abundant chronicles of detail and character. When I arrived in London several years later, during the war, I strolled through streets I had already walked with Pendennis and David Copperfield. Riding into Paris in a jeep full of soldiers on a late-spring morning, I did my best to hide tears of homecoming. The boulevards, the bridges, and the spacious public *places* were as much my own as they had been Balzac's, as much my own as Park Row and the Bowery had been mine when I first read *Père Goriot*, and much, much more my own than the dirt road leading from my father's farm to Longview before I had ever heard of Zola and his *Nana.*

When the store closed on Saturday, I usually walked uptown to an East Side movie house that played French films, in which actors resembling real people played monks and farmers, bakers and seamen, fathers and sons. The language of my grandparents opened doors I had tried to slam shut, and the actors who spoke it linked my interior world for the first time to the pastures, roads, and households of my childhood. When Raimu could not bring himself to complete a loving gesture to Pierre Fresnay, running away to sea, I wept for that father and his son and, without knowing it, inched away from the contempt that soured all my thoughts of my own father.

Another Christmas approached: I had been away from home for fifteen months. I believed I was immune to my family, but songs the boys sang in the washroom—"When the Work's All Done This Fall," and "Back Home Again in Indiana"—sent me inexplicably shaken back to my room. A phrase spoken behind me on the street reminded me, with a scorching intensity, of my mother sitting in our kitchen. A toddler on a stoop with smudges on his face and scabs on his bare knees halted me with unexpected concern for my forsaken little brother Floyd. I was, quite simply, homesick. I gave up resisting it and boarded a train to take me home for Christmas. Past the slush of back alleys and the brick walls of trackside factories, we reached the pines and snow of the Adirondacks. At Tupper Lake and Saranac, French-Canadian lumberjacks swung themselves up into the unheated railway cars. Shivering under my overcoat, I pretended to sleep, listening to familiar accents exchange ribald stories and sing the cowboy laments that seem to be the special taste of the Canuck woodsman.

I hadn't written to say I was coming home. I intended to surprise them, but they surprised me even more. My mother seemed not to recognize me: she didn't stop rocking in her chair by the stove when I bent to kiss her cheek. The baby, my godson

Cyril, had died early in the fall, and when I mentioned his name, she turned away and cried. My father was rarely in the house, and when he was, he moved with the precarious deliberation of the alcoholic. Evangeline was spending her vacation from normal school with a classmate. The older boys were gone, both married: Rudolph was a truck driver seldom at home with his quarrelsome wife, and Ambrose was a chef in Florida, where his wife was a waitress. Frenchie worked as a hired man on a nearby farm, but no one had seen him for months. My younger brothers, Clarence and Douglas, were growing too soon into handsome, energetic replicas of their older brothers. I shared their bed in a chilly upstairs room which hadn't been swept in weeks. We woke in the morning, shivering between the ripped and soiled sheets, staring at each other. My pajamas were as alien to them as their unwashed bodies, still reeking of cheap whiskey and cheaper perfumes from the night before, were to me.

Annabelle, a senior in high school, still took care of the younger children, cooked the meals, cleaned the house, and tolerated her mother's whining and her father's indifference. I stayed for a day or two, more homeless at home than I had ever been away from it. I left, after obviously invented excuses, the day before Christmas, the presents I had brought still unopened on a table in the parlor. My father drove me without a word to the station in Crescent. When I turned to wave goodbye to him, he had already swung the car around and was headed back to the home that he, unlike his sons, was not free to leave. I went back to what I could cope with: delivering packages of office supplies, reading the novels of Émile Zola and Turgenev, and to Gertrude Lawrence and Ina Claire in the Broadway theatres.

At Brace, I rented a single room, and gave up the afterhours companionship with other boys. They didn't seem to miss my company and I was too busy to miss theirs. Every night, I sat at the desk by the window writing a play in longhand in a school composition notebook. In two weeks I had finished it, and much of that time was spent trying to think of a title. I finally settled on *The Young and the Weary*. It was a very sad, very poetic play about a runaway boy coming home to his loved and loving mother, with a father conveniently dead, or otherwise disappeared. I liked it so much that I immediately wrote another, but I can't remember its title, plot, or characters. Having written them, I had no idea what to do with them, so I stored them on the top shelf of my locker with the *Playbills* I had collected. They rested there for several weeks before I took them in to Miss Bromhall. Several evenings later, she told me she thought they were quite good, but she had bought me an anthology of dramas by popular Broadway playwrights. Before I was halfway through the volume, I asked her to return my manuscripts, but she had lent them to a friend. I stalked out of the library and didn't go back again.

A couple of weeks later, she stopped me in the corridor and, after some casual conversation during which my continued absence from the library wasn't mentioned, inquired how I liked my job. Never having thought of work as anything but a means to keep alive, I asked why she wanted to know. She told me to see a lady at the New York Public Library the next day: the friend to whom she had lent my playscripts. They had both agreed, Miss Bromhall reported, that I might be happier, and far more useful, working with books instead of delivering packages.

I was hired the next day as a page in the library's cataloguing department, at a salary slightly higher than what I had been earning. The work was undemanding, and it liberated me from the snow and rain and constant colds that had plagued me for over a year. I rolled heavy trucks of new books from the shipping-room elevator, sorted them into heaps on worktables, stamped each one with the library marker, pasted pockets for borrowers' slips inside the covers, and then rolled them on to another department, where they were prepared by librarians for the branches that had ordered them. I performed my duties at first somewhat

71

in a daze, moving within a book reader's paradise of popular best-sellers, new editions of classic novels, scholarly works, poetry, essays, and plays, as well as manuals on how to upholster furniture, feed cats, and train oneself to be a mechanic or a wireless operator. In the stacks beyond us were the "closed shelves" for those books considered too daring to be displayed openly in the circulation branch on the floor below. I took one home with me each evening, gulped down my supper, and locked myself in my room to plunge into the verbal forests of John Cowper Powys, Radcliffe Hall, and even James Joyce. Undismayed by obscure phrases and unfamiliar words, I didn't linger over what I didn't understand, but just kept on reading.

I gave up going back to Brace for lunch, and spent the hour in the library cafeteria getting to know my fellow pages and clerks. I quickly became friends with one of them, Bill Johnston, a tall, gangling clown a year older than I, with a biting wit somewhat softened by a Southern drawl. We sat together telling jokes and teasing the girls before separating to go back to work on different floors. He invited me to dinner after work in the apartment near Columbia University he shared with his mother, a handsome, kindly woman who was either widowed or divorced. She wrote poetry which was published in magazines I'd never heard of, and had once written a novel about her native South which, next morning, I could not find listed in the library's files. It was the first time I'd ever been in a home like theirs, with expensive furniture, bookshelves lining the walls, a typewriter uncovered at a desk in the corner, and an air of tolerant confidence between mother and son. I was tongue-tied in the presence of such easy affection, and terrified that I might knock some precious object from the coffee table or spill my water glass upon the spotless tablecloth, but I survived the evening, which was the first of many.

Bill intended to be a writer, like his mother, and went to school in the evening. After work, we'd sometimes stop with a couple of girls for a drink before they hurried back to families in the

Bronx or upper Manhattan; then he departed whistling, his hands in his pockets, for a quick meal with his mother before his classes, and I rushed back to my room to read Aldous Huxley. At lunchtime, as I talked earnestly to lonely older librarians, he'd rise to get a second cup of coffee and wink lasciviously in our direction. He called one of them "the Black Widow Spider." A nervous spinster named Miss Potter, she worked in my department but didn't seem to have friends among the women her own age. She wore horn-rimmed glasses and pulled her hair straight back into a bun; she also wore long white gloves to protect her hands from dust and germs. I wasn't aware of her interest in me until she stopped me on my way out one night to reprimand me for reading "forbidden" novels from the closed shelf. I defended myself politely but firmly, and she abandoned the subject with a sigh.

Soon I was one of a group of boys she befriended whom Bill called "Potter's impoverished protégés." She didn't hide the fact that there were others, but she never brought us together. Bill said she collected only artistic types, and implied that she used us for some bizarre purpose, but since she was always quite proper with me, I assumed he was making another one of his odd jokes. A highly opinionated lady, she signed her name, "H. W. Potter," and later, when we knew each other better, she confided peevishly that her mother had christened her Henrietta Winifred, but she didn't think the name suited her. When she discovered my interest in the theatre, she took me to Saturday matinées, fitting me into her busy schedule. She'd leave me, after Ethel Barrymore had liberated Richard Waring from the Welsh coal mines in *The Corn Is Green*, to join "Martin" at an art gallery, or meet "Douglas" for supper before taking him to a Lotte Lehmann recital.

Bill and I also went to matinées together. He sat, I remember, nudging me with suppressed laughter as matronly Jane Cowl hovered over young Kent Smith in *Old Acquaintance*. I pretended

73

I didn't know what he was driving at, even when he took me to see *Pal Joey*, a rowdy depiction of the uses older women put young men to, and young men put older women to. He ridiculed, with gleeful high spirits, Miss Potter's interest in me, but nothing in her behavior had led me to doubt the sincerity of her generosity. And since Bill had a mother who showered him with affection and attention, I chalked up his reaction as merely another example of his outrageous sense of humor.

Miss Potter sometimes invited me to Saturday afternoon cocktail parties in her cluttered apartment on the lower East Side. There she introduced me to artists and women who seemed to be their mistresses, to fragile poets and boys my age who seemed to be their lovers, to modern dancers, unpublished novelists, and assertive strays who claimed to be actors. We sat on the floor in the candlelight, poets reciting their antiwar verses, painters maligning art dealers, and novelists slandering publishers. Miss Potter watched me with proprietary pride, encouraging any opinion on art and writing I cared to venture as she paraded me before garrulous strangers who may very well have assumed that I paid for her attentions as I assumed their companions paid for theirs.

I spent much less time with Miss Bromhall, stopping by only for brief chats before continuing out on my way uptown. Politely pretending not to listen to our conversation as they glanced through magazines at the table, youthful refugees from Europe waited for her to come back to their assistance in building new lives and learning a new language. Ironically, although that once-deserted room was now seldom empty, there were so few new arrivals at Brace that one dormitory on the top floor was closed down and the dining room no longer served lunch. For my birthday in March, Miss Bromhall gave me a ticket to Katharine Cornell's lavish production of Shaw's *The Doctor's Dilemma*, and even as she handed me the envelope, we both sensed our relationship had changed. I may not have been the sophisticate I thought I was, but I was no longer, and never would be again, the country boy she had befriended. If I didn't know how to pronounce a word, I looked it up in the dictionary Miss Potter had given me. In opening the door to a life with others who shared my interests, Miss Bromhall had made herself, perhaps intentionally, less necessary to me. She accepted my new-found independence with the same imperturbable grace with which she had accepted my dependency only a year before.

But if Miss Bromhall withdrew gracefully from my life, Miss Potter dominated it with a somewhat heavier hand. During the summer, she sent me off on appointments she arranged with personnel directors in large corporations. In offices overlooking the city, they told me that a bright boy like me could go far in their firms, especially with so many young men being drafted, and offered me jobs, usually in the mailroom, where, one of them told me, everyone begins his career in business. I didn't want to leave the books I handled at my worktable; I didn't want to leave people who talked about books and authors for anonymity in vast corporations. I returned each time to Miss Potter and told her I wasn't right for the job and the job wasn't right for me. She'd glance at me sharply, sigh, and send me back to my book truck. Gradually, she gave up trying to improve my situation.

One by one, boys left Brace for the armed services and pages left their jobs at the library. Bill Johnston registered for the draft, and his mother, interrupting herself at the supper table, gazed over his head into some unsettling future. He, however, didn't mention the unavoidable induction as we sat watching Gertrude Lawrence sift out the men in her life, with the help of psychoanalysis and Kurt Weill songs, in *Lady in the Dark* and Paul Lukas defy the enemies of freedom in *Watch on the Rhine*. His mother, trying to cheer him up—or more likely trying to bolster her own spirits—took us out to dinner and then on to see *Blithe Spirit* on a Saturday night. On the way to the subway afterward, she impulsively asked me to spend the night with them. When I got back to Brace the following afternoon, one of the boys greeted me in the lobby with the news that the Japanese had bombed Pearl Harbor.

The next day, normally cheerful women stood without expression in the library corridor as President Roosevelt announced over the radio that we were at war. Their ashen faces and trembling hands made me realize that in those lives that had never concerned me before were brothers, nephews, and an occasional son in uniform. What they had all dreaded had happened. When we met for lunch that day, Bill left abruptly to go off alone somewhere, his narrow shoulders hunched, no longer whistling the piercing melodies that usually accompanied him whenever he walked. I, who had hardly bothered to follow the news of the war in Europe, was filled not with anxiety about the future but with rage at having wasted the past.

I had run away from home to become an actor, but had not even tried to take the first steps. My daily life had been an envelope within which I carried a secret dream I didn't have the courage to pursue. I had wasted precious evenings and weekends watching glorious creatures in a world I longed to enter, substituting that narcotic practice for the action that should have led me into it. Bill was drafted in the spring. After his departure, I moved miserably through each day until Miss Potter, seated beside me at matinées of *Macbeth* and *Candida*, noticed that my attention was halfhearted even there. She nagged me until I confessed the reason for my depression, and then, as usual, she acted, quickly and effectively.

In her apartment in May, she introduced me to one of the most legendary of the glorious creatures, "a friend of a friend." I sat on a sofa with Pauline Lord, a dumpy little woman with gray hair and enormous sorrowful eyes. Her great Broadway successes were years behind her, but I had read the plays and studied reviews and photographs of her performances in *Anna Christie*, *They Knew What They Wanted*, and *Ethan Frome* in old issues of

Stage magazine and *Theatre Arts*. Much more important to her, however, I had seen her two most recent vehicles, trivial failures which she explained were "too special for today's audiences." She listened to my stammered hopes of becoming an actor, fixed her haunted eyes upon my own, and told me if I was quite, quite certain I wanted to join "the profession," she would arrange an audition for me with a friend who ran an acting school.

A few days later, Miss Lord sent me a note to Rita Morgenthau, the director of the Neighborhood Playhouse School of the Theatre, but I didn't have the courage to use it immediately. For some weeks, I carried it with me every morning to work, fully intending to call Mrs. Morgenthau that day, but I could not face the prospect of being rejected. Finally, in a surge of self-generated bravado, I confided to several women friends at the library that I would be leaving my job in the fall because I'd been given a scholarship at a drama school. Within a few days, I had no alternative but to call Mrs. Morgenthau, who set up the necessary auditions for me. I appeared, awash with perspiration, in the dimly lit library of the school and was interviewed first by Sanford Meisner, who wasn't interested in the recitations I had prepared but asked instead unanswerable questions about why I wanted to be an actor. He left me, and Martha Graham glided into the chair across the table and talked about painters, musicians, and novelists with an unblinking scrutiny which excited and repelled me at the same time. I left my appointments absolutely certain that Miss Lord's kindness had been useless and wondering how I would tell my friends at the library that I was not going to drama school after all. But, a few weeks later, Mrs. Morgenthau wrote me I had been accepted as a scholarship student. It seems clear to me now that the scarcity of young men during that first year of the war probably had more to do with my acceptance than any aptitude for the theatre I had displayed to Mr. Meisner or Miss Graham.

I kept my job in the library until classes began in late September, and then, in exchange for room and board and a token salary,

I became a counselor at Brace. The work demanded little beyond my presence all night on the single floor of dormitories and private rooms still occupied. The services Brace had provided for over half a century of vagrant boys were obsolete in a nation of eighteen-year-old soldiers and sailors; consequently, the services to the remaining boys were sharply curtailed. During the summer, Miss Bromhall was discharged. We spent our last evening together in that little room, equals at last, each beginning a new life. She spoke for the first time of her work as an illustrator of children's books and listened to my enthusiasm for teachers who had not yet taught me, and for a career I had yet to begin. She switched out the lights, and I locked the door behind her for the last time and accompanied her to the subway, where she wished me success at school before disappearing from my life as unobtrusively as she had entered it three years earlier.

I registered that summer for the draft, but my wretched eyesight and a heart murmur revealed by the medical examination required before my classes began convinced me I was in no danger of ever being drafted. Miss Potter, whose faith in my future stardom exceeded even my own, gave me a make-up kit, volumes on acting techniques by Russians with names as incomprehensible as the contents of their books, and theatre tickets. She even escorted me, by subway, to distant Brooklyn to see Martha Graham in a modern-dance recital.

September came: I joined twenty-five other hopefuls on two crowded floors in a midtown office building. All but four of us were girls, and several of them, like all four boys, were on scholarship. Jo Van Fleet, slightly older than the rest of us, had been a schoolteacher briefly; before that, she had been the star of a West Coast college campus. Determined, hard-working, intelligent, she was by far the most gifted actor in the class. Elizabeth Wilson, a tall, rawboned girl, had played in stock, and Adeline Hiatt had been at the Cleveland Playhouse. An intense, wiry girl with flashing black eyes named Ethel Craft was one of a dozen children of an Ozark mountain family. The others were mostly pretty daughters of indulgent parents, recently released from finishing school, who wore expensive clothes, jewelry, and bland expressions. The boys, unlike me, were sophisticated and self-confident. Richard Hylton and Frank Latimore were to have brief careers in the movies, and Bill Hunt is now an off-Broadway producer. Débutantes and campus stars, boys and girls alike, we threw ourselves into the camaraderie of shared ambitions and were trained in acting, speech, ballet, modern dance, fencing, make-up, and theatre history.

We were taught speech techniques by Mary Barnett, who drilled us relentlessly to rid us of what she called "sectional" speech. Crouching on the floor before me, she peered into my mouth to trace the origins of the sounds issuing from it, and inserted a pencil between my back teeth to keep my jaws open while I spoke. Sound by sound, she freed me from the nasal north-country accent which distorted nearly every word in the language. In another room, Van Machlin, an earnest Scotswoman, listened to our recitations and analyzed, with brisk common sense, our inadequacies in enunciation, voice projection, and breath support.

Late at night, in my room at Brace, I held a mirror before my face to practice correct positioning of lips and tongue for Miss Barnett's approval. I copied long speeches from plays into a notebook I carried with me every working hour, and read them out loud on the subway and during walks in Central Park. Boys passing the recreation room peered in through the door, shook their heads, and left me shouting nonsense verses and lyric poetry into that dim expanse of unused ping-pong tables and writing desks. But no matter how hard I worked, the results discouraged and humiliated me. One morning, by some miracle of inspiration and application, I read straight through a long Yeats poem to the somewhat astonished admiration of teacher and classmates. Startled at what I knew was a breakthrough, I slumped back in my chair with a self-deprecating remark. Jo Van Fleet, seated next to me,

79

turned upon me in a fury. "Stop belittling yourself!" she shouted. "You'll never be any good if you don't know when you're doing good work."

In classes she called "movement" rather than dance, Martha Graham led us through exercises on the floor and at the barre. Dressed, like a priestess in some mythic ritual, in a long black jersey gown, she moved imperiously among us, straightening elbows, adjusting wrists, tapping knees, and slapping slack buttocks. After the first class, she told me to return to the practice room at five o'clock. Standing at my side at the barre, her accompanist at the piano in the corner, she taught me with fierce determination how to anticipate the beat. Several years later, disembarking with my army unit in Scotland, I was the right-hand pivot man in the formation. That night, I wrote Miss Graham thanking her for teaching me how to keep time, saying that if it hadn't been for her kindness, I might very well have led an entire company of soldiers right back into the Atlantic. She answered with a friendly, cryptic note which said, in effect, that she had not done it out of kindness but because she believed that every human being should be in control of his body.

Late in the afternoon, her long-time colleague, Louis Horst, taught us ballet composition. Rotund, white-haired, and with skeptical blue eyes blinking behind pale-rimmed glasses, he was the very image of the jolly German music master. We were tired and irritable after a long day, and his elfin, usually bawdy humor lightened our self-consciousness as we performed, to bits of Chopin, Mozart, and Erik Satie he played on the piano, creations we entitled "Escape!," "Trauma!," and "Ecstasy!"

Sanford Meisner, who, along with Lee J. Cobb, Franchot Tone, Stella and Luther Adler, John Garfield, and Elia Kazan, had been in the recently disbanded Group Theatre, was our acting teacher. We weren't allowed, in our first year, to speak during acting scenes. That would come later. For the time being, we enacted mute improvisations of lovers pouring poison into cocktails, spies

80

rummaging through diplomats' desks, and prisoners trying to escape from concentration camps. Quick-witted and analytical, Meisner jeered at our inadequacies. He terrified me, which hardly helped me relax in his classes. Acting was proving much harder than it appeared to be when Alfred Lunt and Fredric March were doing it. In our wordless exercises, we sought to establish principles of human behavior which Meisner insisted are the basis for truthful acting. To that end, I read Stanislavski's *An Actor Prepares* and endlessly discussed the theories it expounded in dressing rooms and over cups of coffee in the neighborhood Automat. Actors' terms dominated our conversations—"improvise," "immediacy," "intention," "beat," "sense memory"—and before long I was using them with unassailable authority. I had, indeed, joined the profession.

Too vain those first few days to wear my glasses, I could hardly follow the dance exercises demonstrated for us on the little stage at the far end of the rehearsal hall. The boy next to me at the barre whispered that I should do what he was doing. During our lunch break, I treated him to soup and coffee. He told me, with amiable condescension, not to be a fool; to wear my glasses: Leslie Howard wore them, so did Gertrude Lawrence, and Paul Muni. Drawn together by similarities in our backgrounds, Richard Hylton and I quickly became friends. We had both come from poor families, run away from home, and were alone in New York, and were both scholarship students. But, more important, his path into the theatre had started, like mine, through the movies with which we'd blotted out the humiliations of unhappy childhood. On the other hand, it may have been the differences between us that linked us together, as is often so with young friends. Ric was quick and impulsive, I was cautious; he was handsome with a febrile animal grace, I was clumsy and ordinary-looking; he was energetic, a doer who quickly became the favorite of the teaching staff, and I was a watcher who refused to expose myself to criticism and ridicule. I talked about actors in terms of their talents and the roles they played; he gossiped, with feline familiarity, about their personalities and sexual habits. Although he often went to the theatre, he seldom read a play unless he had to rehearse a scene from it. Slightly older than I, he had developed a poise which I envied as he moved through the classrooms, smiling at teachers, teasing girls, ignoring the other two boys, and winking with cool amusement, from time to time, at me. I happily ran errands for him, lent him money, asked Miss Potter to obtain library books for his use, and arranged for rehearsal space at Brace for him. For three months, we worked on scenes and speech assignments, ate, drank, and went to plays while other boys our age, including my brothers, were drafted to fight the war which didn't touch our lives.

The summons for my army physical arrived in mid-December. Ric advised me to pretend, as he said he had, that I was a homosexual. That deception was out of the question for numerous reasons, not the least being three brothers in the service. "Do you want to be an actor or don't you?" Ric asked. "I do, I do." "Then be an actor," he said, "not a goddam patriot!" I didn't argue with him: I couldn't tell him that being an actor wasn't worth cutting oneself off from the life others our age were living, and losing. The differences between us were obviously much wider than the similarities. "You'll never be an actor," Ric announced, his usual friendliness turned sour. "Never!"

I was inducted into the army on New Year's Day, 1943, myopia, heart murmur, and all. Miss Potter, seething with outrage at the waste of such a rare talent, took me to see *The Three Sisters*, in which Katharine Cornell and Judith Anderson languidly lamented their rural lives in nineteenth-century Russia, and *The Skin of Our Teeth*, in which Tallulah Bankhead and Fredric March assured us, all evidence to the contrary, that we would, we must, survive. Miss Potter and I had coffee at Childs, where, with tears swimming behind her glasses, she hinted at a tragic romance ended during the First World War. Nothing in her appearance or manner supported that vision of distant tragedy and, sensing my embarrassment, she brusquely paid the check. I left her at a subway entrance and went on to a farewell party Ric gave for me in the rooms he shared with an older actor. A Negro folk singer sat on the floor in the candlelight and strummed a guitar, and a flamboyant actress of uncertain years nearly choked me with a mouthful of champagne she released between my teeth during what I had assumed was to be merely a friendly kiss.

Ric and I met for drinks occasionally on my furloughs and he sent me postcards while I was overseas. When the army discharged me in 1946, he was between engagements, having made his Broadway debut several seasons earlier. We had dinner at a popular theatrical restaurant but his eyes barely rested on me as celebrities came and went. He had become the actor he always knew he would be. I was starting all over again in the fall, returning to the school that no longer interested him. After that, movie contracts and star billing separated us, but he came to my first wedding with a party of noisy friends and usually telephoned when he was "in from the coast." One morning, I saw him on the other side of Fifth Avenue and crossed over to speak to him. He was on his way to have his teeth capped; he'd just signed for a movie that would make him a star, he told me, playing the part of the son in a Negro family passing for white in a New England town. He glanced pointedly at his watch while I tried to find some common ground between us, then nodded and hurried away.

I hardly ever saw him after that, and then only from a distance, as he escorted Jane Cowl or Dorothy Gish to opening nights, or was part of a group of exquisitely dressed men at Martha Graham's recitals. At a dinner party some years ago, I caught sight of a bloated, once-familiar face disappearing into a bedroom as we entered the living room. The hostess, a business acquaintance who prides herself upon her theatre connections, told me that Ric wouldn't come out of the bedroom until I left: he could no longer tolerate reminders of his youth.

83

Dining with my wife at a restaurant, I recalled a story he had told me ten years earlier. When he was twelve, he said, his mother often locked him up in the garage while she went off on weekend trips with men friends. He tried to run away, and from then on she roped him to the wall, leaving food for him on a plate on the floor as she might have done for a dog or a cat. He stood in the corner one evening while his young uncle shot himself in the shadows. My wife, somewhat dubious of the recollected traumas of my actor friends, did not believe it. She may be right: perhaps Ric did invent that story, but if he did, it surely masks another as damaging, if not more so.

Over the years, I heard news of him from mutual friends. A distinguished character actress, once a classmate, said he had come around to her dressing room to borrow twenty dollars. Another former classmate, now a suburban housewife, told me she had run into him on the street while shopping with her children, and he had burst into tears at the sight of them. Several years ago, I saw his photograph in a Greenwich Village newspaper. The paragraph below it reported he had been found dead in a West Coast hotel for transients, shabby, forgotten, and broke. He had come to the end of the dream that had linked us together, for a little while, twenty years earlier.

But dreams do end. Mine have. Tallulah Bankhead died in 1968; Pauline Lord died long, long ago. Katharine Cornell no longer appears on the stage, and neither does Ina Claire. The obituaries in the morning papers remove, one by one, the glorious creatures who peopled my dreams. Putting the papers aside, I am content to look into the faces of those who have made such dreams unnecessary.

I left the Brace Memorial Newsboys' Home behind me in the cold January dawn to entrain, with hundreds of others, for Fort Dix. Ten years later, after applying for a marriage license in the Municipal Building, I stood with my girl under the colonnades where Chester had coached me in panhandling. Across the street,

84

a large sign proclaimed the familiar building to be "THE NEW YORK LAW SCHOOL." Hand in hand, we approached it. The brass plaque identifying the building and its founder, against which we had stubbed out our cigarettes and scratched our defiance to the world and those who run it, had gone. Inside, boys not much older than we had been wore neat business suits and preoccupied expressions as they prepared themselves for futures as attorneys, senators, judges, and, who knows, perhaps even Presidents. The young receptionist nodded blankly when I asked her if I could show my fiancée what had once been my home. When we left, we walked up Park Row to Canal Street and chose our wedding rings from display trays Chester and I had gazed at so many years before.

The last time I passed the site, on my way to jury duty, an enormous cavity littered with broken laths and shards of glass was all that was left. The boys and the building are gone. Gone, too, are those who led us from adolescence into some measure of maturity. But rubble does not, cannot displace them or totally efface the building they worked in; not as long as boys it sheltered still survive, whether they are middle-aged family men or anonymous derelicts sleeping in the cold, sprawled against the fence of St. Marks-in-the-Bouwerie.

...in the army... 1943–1946

The train that carried me from New York City to Fort Dix took me to a life that was no worse, if not somewhat better, than what had preceded it. It isn't fashionable to admit it today, especially in the circles we move in, but I enjoyed being in the army. I wasn't a good soldier; I was hardly a soldier at all, for, looking back from a distance of twenty-five years, the army consists mostly of the books I read and where I read them, which actors played which parts in the plays I saw on leave in New York, London, and Paris, and several men who became the only close friends I'd ever made. Seventeen years in an upstate backwater and three among runaway boys had prepared me for anything the army could offer, an advantage shared by few, if any, of my fellow recruits.

Barracks living was no novelty after the dormitory at Brace, nor was making my own bed every morning, or sweeping the floors. The food served in mess halls was no worse than what I'd eaten all my life and, an early riser since my farm childhood, I was awake long before the sergeants burst through the doors shouting, "Drop your cocks and grab your socks." The vocabulary that sent us to bed at night and got us up in the morning may have seemed raw to some recruits but none of it was unknown to me. Open toilet stalls and showers had long since diluted the embarrassments of communal nakedness. All of it—roll calls, indoctrination lectures, inoculations, short-arm inspections, the bullying of sergeants and the condescension of officers—was familiar territory I'd lived within, in one form or another, since birth.

Daily army life is little more than waiting for something to happen; soldiers spend idle hours brooding upon what lies ahead and what they've left behind. Except for clothes worn on the train, I'd sent everything home for my younger brothers, and Miss Potter was safeguarding books, manuscripts, and *Playbills*, which, like herself, would wait for my return. The only thing I regretted leaving behind was my barely begun training for an acting career, but I was determined to continue that on my own. Ironically, the army provided more free time to study than I'd ever had while attending classes. The loose-leaf notebook of speeches begun at Brace was hidden at night beneath the socks and underwear in my footlocker, but during the day it seldom left my person. Sitting apart from the others between formations and after chow, I memorized speeches later recited on solitary guard duty. There, pacing briskly in the cold with my rifle on my shoulder, Henry V exhorted his yeomen at Agincourt, Marchbanks pleaded for love and understanding, and Kurt Müller said farewell to his children before returning to a martyr's death in Nazi Germany. The derision of my companions didn't reach me: I'd been in that territory, too, in the barnyards at home and in the corridors of Brace.

A sergeant in my unit was an alumnus of Brace, and he wangled a weekend pass for me before we were shipped out to training camp. Back in Manhattan, I didn't call Miss Potter or get in touch with my classmates of a month before. No longer

90

a civilian and not yet a soldier, I checked into a hotel in the theatre district, polished my shoes, brushed my uniform, slicked down my hair, and joined the flood of servicemen outside. But the uniform did not transform me into an irresistible attraction for the girls patrolling the streets, and from doorways and under theatre marquees I watched the techniques employed by other soldiers, but could not bring myself to use them. Abandoning any hopes of that diversion, I fell back upon a familiar one and went to see the Lunts in *The Pirate*. Sunday morning was spent with a crossword puzzle, the afternoon at a movie, and most of the night with a book. What returned to Fort Dix on Monday morning was a little more of a soldier, a little less of a civilian.

We were transferred for basic infantry training to Fort Bragg, North Carolina, where I did what I was told, moving unprotestingly from calisthenics to parade field, from chow line to rifle practice, to gas-mask drills, ten-mile hikes, bayonet practice, to kitchen and guard duty. My father, brothers, uncles, and cousins were all good huntsmen, but I'd never held a gun in my hands. On the rifle range, however, I won a marksman rating. The hikes and drills and exercises which exhausted sturdier boys were child's play to me after Martha Graham's dance classes. Months of delivering packages in all kinds of weather had immunized me from the coughing spells and runny noses that infected the barracks after outdoor hikes in rainy weather and overnight bivouacs. Not particularly competent at polishing shoes, organizing a footlocker, or the art of making a bed, I was gigged each Saturday morning at inspection and confined to the post on weekends, a punishment totally without effect, since I preferred staying in to read the books Miss Potter sent to me from New York. The sergeants boasted, with uncouth glee, that "our asses belonged to the army," and I handed mine over without protest, reserving the more essential parts of myself for my own use.

Whatever our pretensions of maturity during the day, at evening mail call we became only boys again, stretching out on our bunks to read and reread letters from mothers, sisters, and sweethearts. Annabelle, who still managed the household at home, found time to write round-robin letters to her brothers in the service. Ric Hylton and other classmates occasionally reminded me of the world I'd lost by hastily written postcards of news of their progress in school. Bulging envelopes from Miss Potter spilled out clippings of Broadway openings and new best-sellers, with long pages about plays she'd seen and books she'd read, advice on choosing friends, warnings about promiscuous girls and the diseases they carry, and maternal inquiries about the state of my health and happiness. Her letters indiscreetly confided secrets she would never have mentioned in person: family troubles long past, a fiancé killed in the First World War, and the embittered loneliness of a life without fulfillment, which mine could not, would not, must not duplicate. Each letter concluded with lavish praise for my talents and fervent belief in my future, not in the army but on the stage from which the stupidity of those who ran the country was keeping me.

Every week, a package of books arrived from her, a present which could not be shared with my barracks mates, who unfailingly watched me unwrap the packages and then shared their own boxes of candy and cookies with me. A soldier who reads books instead of playing cards or shooting crap is, of course, the barracks eccentric. But to some he is more than merely eccentric: he is the enemy. After all, rural mortgages are foreclosed by educated men, teachers who ridicule slow boys and preachers who harangue fast ones are book readers, too, and so are Communists, Jews, and fairies. In time, though, the bookworm found his place with irascible sergeants, brusque inspecting officers, mountain boys who had to be forcibly held under showers, the virgins and the lechers, the bullies and the victims. Bashful country boys asked me to compose letters to girls back home which they painstakingly copied onto ruled paper and sent off to Kentucky and West

Virginia. Blustering crapshooters and poker players looked up to my bunk for verification of historical facts and definitions of words. Crowded together where none of us wanted to be, we made the best of it, and if the life itself held few surprises for me, the men who shared it with me held even fewer.

In anger, malice, or cheerfulness, they'd all been encountered before. Braggarts boasting of future bravery under fire and of last night's triumphs in local beds echoed my brothers behind the barn; timid boys shielding their pubic areas in the showers echoed newcomers at Brace. The sounds of snores and muffled sobbing, of frenzied self-abuse and words spoken in sleep after the lights were out, were all familiar and often comforting. I'd seen boys sneak out of bed to kneel at prayer in the moonlight before, listened to songs of distant mothers and sweethearts, and heard heated denunciations of unions, Jews, and the goddam President before.

Past experience had taught me, if nothing else, the security of retreating into books during the afterhour activities of boys my own age, and after chow I usually lay on my bunk, where no one paid much attention to me. One night, a bellicose loudmouth threw down his poker hand in disgust and began to bait two Bronx Jews who shared a self-imposed ghetto in a far corner. Irritated more by their acceptance of his taunts than by his bigotry, I slammed my book shut and told him to lay off. As surprised by the vehemence of my objections as I was, he turned his frustrations upon me. With no choice, I swung down from my bunk wondering how to handle the situation I had started. As we moved toward each other, a sandy-haired man I'd seen but hardly noticed before stepped between us with his rifle butt grasped firmly in his hand and a tight, grim smile on his face. My menace picked up his poker hand again, and my savior, whose name turned out to be Eldor Mainville, took me off to the post exchange for a beer, where he told me that it's more important to know what one believes, and why, than it is to flaunt it like a red flag before those who can't understand it. People like you, he said amiably, have enough trouble in life without inviting more.

I can count on the fingers of one hand the men with whom I've maintained friendships for more than several years. Memories of my head being held in a toilet bowl by one brother while another repeatedly flushed it may help to explain why friendships with other men have been almost impossible for me to establish and to keep. In any case, only a few have ever reached beyond the surface ease with which I deal with people. Eldor Mainville was not only the first but by far the most important. We had passed each other in latrines and on chow lines but had seldom spoken; he confessed later that he usually avoided men like me who speak before they think. Whatever our original opinions of each other, we were soon inseparable. Since the others in our unit had buddies of their own, they made space at mess-hall tables so we could sit next to each other, parted ranks in formation so we could march side by side, and assumed that we'd share the same tent on overnight bivouac. We were, as buddies usually are, like a well-matched husband and wife, comfortable in each other's presence, essential to each other's contentment. Men without women regard their mates with an inexplicable mixture of tenderness and toughness. My good luck was in finding a man whose innate decency and secure view of himself and the world made him not only a friend but a tutor and a guide as well.

Older than I by five years, and, like me, of French-Canadian extraction, Mainville was a good-looking, serious, self-educated man. He was appalled by my ignorance of all literature except novels and plays, and he sat in deserted drill fields or wandered through pastures with me explaining economic, philosophical, and psychological theories I'd never heard of before. He lent me books by Veblen, Henry George, William James, Spinoza, Freud, and Jung, and quizzed me about their contents when I'd finished reading them. He'd gaze at me thoughtfully with shrewd blue eyes and

94

then explain once again the single tax, or the relationship of the ego to the id. Although he never derided my ignorance, he unfailingly rebuffed the frivolity with which it was always masked. He expanded my view of favorite playwrights—Shaw, Ibsen, Chekhov, and O'Neill—as critics of an imperfect society rather than as mere vehicles for acting talents I admired and hoped to develop in myself. He was the first man who'd ever treated me as if I had a mind; because he took me seriously, I began to take myself seriously.

Fastidious and practical, he also taught me how to clean my rifle thoroughly, to organize my footlocker properly, to polish my shoes, and to keep my uniform neat. I was no longer restricted to camp on weekends, and sometimes, since Mainville's tastes did not run to hill girls with nasal drawls, I mewed around back porches and trackside shacks with other fellows. Late Sunday nights when we returned to the barracks, Mainville nodded as he looked up from his bunk, stubbed out his cigarette, and took up his rifle, or mine, to see if it required further attention for the morning inspection.

Basic training was over in June. I was now a soldier who could plunge a bayonet unflinchingly into an enemy belly, sight along a rifle barrel at a moving target, and drop to the ground at the sound of planes overhead. I knew how to fire not only a rifle but a Browning automatic, a pistol, and a machine gun, and could dismantle them piece by piece, identify the parts, and put them back together again. I could keep step in parade drill, stand at attention for hours in sun, snow, and rain, present arms, salute the colors, run double time over dirt roads and across fields, and crawl upon my stomach over obstacle courses while machine-gun bullets whistled in the air above me. I hadn't dropped dead in my tracks or shot anyone by mistake. I was a soldier, ready for combat.

There were some things the army didn't teach me. During one morning roll call, my name was shouted out for duty at the motor pool. My repeated protests that I didn't know how to drive were unheard, unbelieved, or merely brushed aside, and I was assigned a jeep to drive and a nervous young lieutenant as my first passenger. Somehow the jeep got into motion, but the only way it could be stopped was by ramming it into the corner of the orderly building, which dumped the lieutenant out unhurt in some surprise, and probably more relief. After a colorful display of language and temper, my sergeant grudgingly allowed that perhaps I really couldn't do what any other red-blooded young American can do with his eyes closed, drunk or sober.

Before the orders came that we were sure would send us into combat, we were given our first two-week furloughs. Mainville went home to Rhode Island and I went back to Manhattan. In the mornings, I lingered in the lobby of my Broadway hotel watching elderly actors inquire for messages at the front desk. In the evenings, I eavesdropped on smartly uniformed young officers escorting smiling girls to pleasures upstairs that were denied to me, a lowly private. My dates were with Miss Potter, who, although she did allow me to pay for my own dinners and theatre tickets, refused to let me pay for hers. After her incautious confidences in letters to me, she seemed somewhat ill-at-ease in my company, and every now and then a gesture of impatience warned me that my apparent restlessness annoyed her. She made up a schedule of recitals, lectures, and art-gallery showings to occupy my days while she was working and on those evenings when other young men required her company. But art and music only quickened my restlessness. My classmates at drama school were too busy with their own affairs to pay more than token courtesy to the phone calls I made to them. The city seemed alien and foreign for the first time, and the Broadway theatre seemed to have lost its hypnotic power: during the tuneful ebullience of *Oklahoma!*, the transparent melodrama of *Tomorrow the World*, and the saccharine facility of Helen Hayes playing Mrs. Stowe in *Harriet*, my mind drifted back to Mainville's lean, reflective face explaining

Henry George's theories, to my barracks mates' gambling, wrestling, joking, cursing, and laughing while I read.

I just couldn't go back to Fort Bragg before my furlough was over, although the thought did cross my mind. I went home to visit my family instead. Five service stars hung in the porch window overlooking the puddles in the dirt road: two more would join them before the war was over. By a coincidence, Ambrose and Frenchie were also on furlough, the first from a paratrooper unit and the other from the infantry. We hadn't seen each other since they'd left home before me, and, brothers in uniform as we'd never been brothers in overalls, we swallowed whiskey straight from tumblers in the kitchen, our feet propped up against the wall, and swapped stories of the army. My father, who was now running a liquor store around the corner, poured whiskey into a glass for me for the first time, probably more in tribute to the uniform I wore than to any maturity it may have clothed. But back at Bragg, unpacking my duffle bag, I found a pint of brandy he had slipped into it for me.

Annabelle, past twenty, had left home for a wartime job in a factory town some hundred miles away. Fourteen-year-old Gabrielle had replaced her in running the household. Clarence had left school at seventeen to enlist in the navy and, except for one or two postcards, hadn't been heard from since. Douglas, at fifteen, was as tall as we were and by far the best-looking in a family of handsome boys. From across the room, his dark eyes rested upon us with an unfathomable mixture of admiration, envy, and contempt before he vanished on secret excursions of his own. The younger boys, Vincent and Floyd, both under ten, were adoring slaves who located cups in the sink for our morning coffee, ice for our drinks from the pantry, and towels to dry ourselves with in the tub. We took Gabrielle and twelve-year-old Marianne dancing at the Clairepont Inn, where their schoolmates watched them circling the floor in the arms of soldier brothers and my father's friends stopped us to shake hands and wish us luck.

Confused by so many grown-up sons in her kitchen, my mother called us by the wrong names and cried softly to herself when we stopped to talk to her in her rocker by the stove. Leaving her, we avoided each other's eyes and drove through fragrant back roads to border bars in drunken, noisy fraternity. Frenchie had become, not surprisingly to me, a contentious, bantam-sized troublemaker, and Ambrose concealed a streak of meanness under a flashing smile and watchful eyes. Overhearing the accents of English pilots at the next table in a roadhouse, they provoked, with mounting hostility and vulgarity, a chair-throwing, bottle-breaking brawl during which I ducked under a table. Ambrose pulled me out. "Goddam it," he roared, "you don't have to fight, but don't hide under a fucking table!" The limeys took to flight, routed once again by their Canuck adversaries, but the bar was a shambles of broken furniture and shattered glass. We roared ourselves back home to the bed we had shared as boys, kicking off the sticky sheets from our naked bodies as we had ten years earlier on humid summer nights. A couple of days later, we grinned our farewells, returned to our companies, and forgot all about one another.

Our unit was broken up when we returned from furlough. A group of us, including Mainville and me, was attached to another company and transferred to a Coast Artillery post on an island off the coast of Maine. Awakened every night by sirens, we stumbled out of bed and made our way blindly to gun positions overlooking the harbor to fire into the damp, cool air. During the first week, a part of my machine gun fell into the Atlantic while I was dismantling it. Since the gun seemed to operate just as efficiently without it, its loss was never reported. During the day, we tried to keep awake at our captain's briefings on coast-defense tactics, took turns at guard duty along the howitzer emplacements facing the ocean, ran our daily hikes around the island, and performed light forestry duties devised to keep us from attempting to swim or hitch rides from passing fishing boats to the fleshpots of Portland. There wasn't much to do beyond clearing away underbrush between tree trunks and planting infant pines in various locations. Soon it seemed that trees were planted on one side of the island one day and dug up and replanted on another side the next. Grateful that the captain hadn't found anything more onerous to occupy us, we performed our duties with languid good humor. After chow, while the others wrestled, played softball, volleyball, or touch football, or went swimming in the chilly summer waters, Mainville settled back against a tree trunk to lead me deeper into economic theory and philosophical concepts.

The summer evenings sent us down dirt roads to homesteads where girls whose sweethearts and husbands were off in the service invited us up onto porches, into kitchens, and, not as often as we wished, into bedrooms. At Saturday night dances in the village hall, plump girls with glowing eyes danced in our arms, perspiration glistening on their foreheads and staining their summer dresses. The island families were mostly French-Canadian, as Mainville and I were, and in the language of my grandparents I was ingratiating myself with the dark-haired bride of an absent sailor when we were unexpectedly confined to the barracks area. The elders of the inbred community, whose eyes followed us on the roads with the same burning distrust we were to see later in northern France, undoubtedly complained to the captain. From then on, the girls waved at us when we double-timed past their porches and vegetable gardens. The summer fog and rains shrouded us in gloom, and normally cheerful men turned surly and belligerent. Good-natured teasings exploded into spiteful feuds and sudden assaults: one evening, a hand reaching for a shovel to terminate an imprudent argument about Catholicism was intercepted by Mainville. Once again, he cautioned me about foolish opinions, and then, dismissing the incident with a sigh, returned to his explanations of William James until the night grew too cold for us to remain out under the stars.

Our commanding captain was no more than three years older than I, and somewhat younger than most of the men in his company. One morning, he summoned me to the orderly room and flipped an open letter across his desk to me, saying, "How do you suggest I answer that?" Miss Potter had written to say that my letters indicated an impending nervous breakdown. In a long, passionate plea for my release from service, she revealed secrets I'd kept to myself in the army: that I'd broken off all family ties and was alone in the world, a gifted actor whose country could use my talents more effectively by letting me return to the theatre which so sorely needed me. "Well?" the captain insisted.

I told him Miss Potter was simply an old maid trying to be my mother and urged him to ignore her letter, saying quite truthfully that I was not unhappy in the army. Putting the letter away in a desk drawer, he gazed at me thoughtfully for a moment, then dismissed me. I wrote several indignant letters to Miss Potter but could not bring myself to mail them. The captain must have answered her, however, for a bitter note revealed that I had thwarted a plan she'd formed with an attorney friend which would have freed me. My outraged reply accused her of meddling in my life and making me a laughingstock in my company. She insisted that she was trying to help me: if I wouldn't fight for my talents, then she'd have to fight for me. We gradually exhausted the subject; she resumed her extensive reports on books and plays and sent me peace offerings of candy that was shared with my barracks mates and books that were kept for myself.

The work details soon bored me, and I slipped away into the woods as I had sneaked away to the silo to escape childhood chores in the fields. Entire days were spent stretched out under the pines memorizing speeches from plays and reading novels until, one afternoon, a slight noise behind me revealed the captain watching me with a bemused smile. Closing the book, I started scrambling to my feet but he put a restraining hand on my shoulder. "What are you reading, Private?" he asked. "*Crome Yellow*, sir," I told him. "I like *Antic Hay* better," he said, and sat down beside me. As shovels struck stones and soldiers shouted and laughed just beyond the trees, we talked the afternoon away, discovering mutual admirations in Aldous Huxley, Virginia Woolf, and E. M. Forster. He'd been a sophomore in college when he was drafted and was going to be an English professor when the war was over. We maintained the distance between officer and enlisted man by separating to return to the barracks, but from then on some of the books I read beneath the trees belonged to him and some of those he read in the privacy of his quarters were mine, sent on at my request by Miss Potter. From time to time on the parade ground, I'd catch his eyes resting on me reflectively. When he strolled by Mainville and me talking outside the barracks in the evening, he'd return our salutes and then tentatively touch the trim mustache he cultivated to appear older than the men he commanded.

Finally, he called me into the orderly room. He had been studying the army files of my I.Q. scores, educational background, and other records, and had recommended me for a crash program for intellectually gifted enlisted men at the University of New Hampshire. He would miss our talks about books, he confided, exposing the lonely boy beneath his superior rank, but my potential was being wasted on a desolate island with men the army could find no better use for. When Mainville heard the news, he snapped out laconic contempt for everyone who ran the world, in the army and outside of it, and warned me I was being sucked, through my susceptibility to flattery, into the ranks of men he despised, the users of others. But he dolefully agreed there was nothing to be done about it. We said goodbye a week later.

Classes and drills at the university left me no time to read and very little time to think. I'd been graded high in linguistic aptitude and assigned to classes in Japanese language and culture. Without books to read or Mainville to talk to, my spirits plunged into despair. Nightmares of death in Asian jungles woke me screaming in the cell-like room I shared with a meticulous, ambitious boy who seldom spoke. If I had to die far from home, it should be where my ancestors had come from, not off some-

101

where in the South Pacific. The captain had misjudged me. Being an officer held no attraction for me: a private's peculiarities of taste and manner are easily absorbed within the ranks and, more important, his spare time is his to spend as he wishes. The army was entitled to everything but my mind. Mainville was wrong, too: there was something to be done about it. Deliberately and quickly, I flunked each of my classes in turn and was sent back to the island, where Mainville greeted me with buoyant smiles and the captain eyed me in a quizzical silence. A week later, he transferred both Mainville and me to Camp Shelby, in Mississippi, for Field Artillery training.

Mainville was assigned to a different company at Camp Shelby, and although we made our way from opposite ends of the camp to carry on our discussions, we never again shared our daily lives. When I was shipped overseas a year later, he'd already preceded me. We never met in Europe, but we wrote long letters, and even from a distance his precise handwriting and logical thinking calmed my irrational fears of certain, sudden death. We grew past mere friendship into a sustaining attachment. By a lucky coincidence in military orders, we returned to the States on the same small troopship when the war was over, and he took me home with him for a weekend, where his mother and married sister regarded me with the same consideration and deference they paid him. His high-school friends stayed up all night to drink beer with us, and we, veterans all, argued about what we had done, and would do, with our lives. That was the last time we saw each other. I returned to acting school and he enrolled in a Western college. For almost ten years, we continued writing long candid letters, but candid letters are a hazardous means of maintaining friendships. We'd both been married a few months when I wrote that my wife and I hoped to have children right away. His reply, brutally contemptuous of bringing children into a corrupt world, ended with the gratuitous comment that he could only assume my wife was already pregnant. I wrote back that I could only assume his was sterile. He didn't answer.

102

But surely we invite the termination of friendship just as we invite its initiation. Perhaps I wanted to be free from the critical eye of a mentor. Perhaps he wanted to be free at last from the boy who, after years of tutoring, still didn't seem to be growing up. Whatever the reasons for our rupture, a sense of having betrayed him, or having provoked him into betraying me, nagged me for almost fifteen years. Then, last year, a postcard from the Southwest was in the mail one morning: "I'm sorry about the way I said it, but what I said still goes." He signed it "Love," a word I can accept without suspicion now as I could not have fifteen years ago. We are writing long candid letters to each other again.

My second year as a soldier found me, like my new companions, an old-timer shouting "Watch the hook!" to recruits being marched past to their first inoculations, and sending trusting replacements in our barracks off on fools' errands to orderly rooms and supply sergeants. Our lives revolved almost exclusively around the mammoth eight-inch howitzer that we dug into position under simulated combat conditions, loaded with shells it took two men to carry, fired over the Mississippi landscape, and then moved quickly to a new position in anticipation of enemy retaliation. Trained by Regular Army sergeants, we worked in groups of ten or twelve, relying upon each other for survival as well as for companionship. I was promoted to corporal and put in charge of eight men in a communications patrol. Traveling in a small truck containing all our gear and large wheels of coiled wire, we laid concealed telephone lines in the woods, spliced broken or cut wires, and set up switchboards and connections between our gun positions and forward observation posts. We were soldiers, at last, whether we liked it or not, bound together in the shadow of that giant weapon to be pointed toward the soft underbelly of the enemy.

The closeness of our duties in the field brought us closer together during our leisure. My days of reading beneath the trees and lying on my bunk waiting for something to happen were over. My squad

103

saw to that. I held Wilson's trembling head over the toilet bowl in the latrine as he retched up a long night's drinking, answered Glennon's wife's letters for him and lent him five bucks to take his Mississippi girl out dancing, made sure Merejekowski was treated by the medics when he came back from shacking up down the road, and covered up for Mansard's many and varied derelictions of duty. I became fond of men who would never have interested me in civilian life, and they grew fond of me, a boy whose interests would have aroused their contempt under any other circumstances. Two elfin buddies from South Boston, named Donnolly and Doran, decided, after hearing me sing in the showers, to teach me how to carry a tune. No one, they insisted, was tone deaf, and hour after hour they started me off on the right note and hummed me back into the tunes of the simple Irish melodies they sang as easily as they breathed. But their efforts failed: I sing today as badly as I did then, as my brothers and sisters all do, as my mother did before us. Occasionally, in the chow line, a pair of eyes rested on me with disbelief: anyone who seemed so bright about so many things should be able to learn such a simple thing. Today, listening to our children sing with the talent they inherit from their mother, if I close my eyes, I can envision my two buddies, now middle-aged, side by side in a Donnolly or a Doran parlor in South Boston, singing in effortless harmony and with utter sincerity their songs of Irish eyes and darling mothers.

Side by side at the post movie theatre, we groaned rapturously at the sight of Betty Grable, Alice Faye, and Rita Hayworth, hooted when Alan Ladd, Errol Flynn, and Robert Taylor single-handedly won our wars for us without changing expression, shrieked fake sobs of sympathy for Bette Davis and Greer Garson, and offered to trade places with Gary Cooper as Ingrid Bergman slid into his sleeping bag, and with Humphrey Bogart as Lauren Bacall advised him to "pucker up your lips and blow." Back on our bunks, we speculated on the accessibility of the actresses and the potency of the actors. When someone said he couldn't imagine, ever, Hedy Lamarr taking a crap, a mountain voice drawled from a bunk in the shadows, "Yeah, sure, but jes' reckon what she'd look like if she didn't!"

Like nuns, we went in pairs on weekend passes to New Orleans to take up positions in the French Quarter in front of balconies where mysterious females lured us inside with promises that could never have fulfilled our fervid expectations. We raced from their squalid rooms to military prophylactic stations and winced as yawning medics injected medication into our aching organs. Meeting each other afterward, we may have grinned and boasted of the times we'd had, but deep inside we swore to ourselves never, never to risk it again. But still, during heavy Mississippi evenings, we sneaked under fences and over stiles like stray tomcats to farmhouses or shacks on the outskirts of town where we were sometimes permitted entrance and sometimes chased away.

Point-two beer in the post exchange was rejected for homemade whiskey sold at outrageous prices by thin-lipped farmers from their back porches. Delta rural life was as alien to us as Burma would have been, or Algiers. Coming back alone one night from some rendezvous, I was picked up by a mean-spirited man in overalls who whined a stream of colorful obscenities as we careened over the unmarked dirt roads. He screeched to a halt outside a tar-paper shack, told me to wait up, sprang out of the car, and disappeared inside. Through an open window, I watched in numb fascination his hurried copulation with a fully dressed, heavy-limbed woman on a kitchen table. A moment later, he swung back behind the wheel and, still cursing with a deadening hatred of life, drove me to the gates of the camp. Nothing I've read in newspapers or in fiction about Mississippi has ever surprised me since. We Northern soldiers may have joked among ourselves about the legendary Southern hospitality, but we shuddered when old men sitting on courthouse steps spat as we passed and their narrow eyes followed us until we were out of sight. When we fell out on hikes to fill our canteens from kitchen faucets,

105

wheyfaced women slammed screen doors in our faces without a word. The enemy abroad, we told ourselves, could be no worse than the enemy at home. Drawing together for security, we trusted no one but ourselves.

A soldier's strongest security is his buddy; without one, he is only half himself. In a few months, Mainville's place had been taken by Ernest Cahn. My senior by ten years or so, Cahn carries a slight accent from the Germany he fled in the thirties with his older brother and widowed mother. A man of tact, grace, and rare tolerance, his knowledge of books, painting, music, and the theatre inevitably brought us together in that group of men who cared nothing about such things. On our first leave together in New York, he introduced me to his mother, a fragile little woman who smilingly accepted the fate that had swept her from bourgeois comfort in Frankfort to a job in a button factory in Queens. He introduced me also to Evelyn, the witty widow he was to marry after the war, who assessed me with shrewd directness before accepting me as his friend and hers.

Cahn was more faithful to his Evelyn than most soldiers were to their wives, which meant his company on passes precluded the bedroom haunts other buddies might have encouraged. In compensation, however, he introduced me to a style of life known only in movies and novels. After an *haute-cuisine* dinner of bouillabaisse and crêpe suzettes in New Orleans, he shrugged off my outrage at the check, paid it, and took me to listen to a jazz pianist at a night club. Mainville's economists were put aside for Cahn's favorite European novelists—Thomas Mann, Colette, and Proust; and he read Melville, Hawthorne, and Willa Cather at my suggestion. Our conversations about books were far less analytical than those I'd had with Mainville; Cahn was less interested in shaping or influencing my mind than in exposing it to a variety of stimuli. Letters to Miss Potter in New York about my new friend and our sybaritic diversions brought a warning from her that,

106

among other things, "The Jew is more erotic than the Gentile," which was contradicted by Cahn's celibacy in a barracks of promiscuous men.

On furlough, Evelyn cooked dinner for us in the apartment she shared with her mother, and sometimes Cahn's mother put me up for the night in her living room and served us breakfast before she left for her factory work. Cahn took me to museums and tried to explain why he admired the Klees and Tchelitchews that confused me. At a matinée of a thriller starring Elisabeth Bergner, he described her performances as Ophelia and Saint Joan in the Germany of his youth, and seeing Paul Robeson's Othello, he recalled with specific details Alexander Moissi's performance in Max Reinhardt's production a generation earlier. We heard Lotte Lehmann sing lieder, Traubel and Melchior sing *Tristan und Isolde* at the Metropolitan Opera House, saw the Ballet Russe and Martha Graham; his knowledge ranged over topics and celebrities of several generations on two continents, exposing me to a wider and more subtle culture than anything I'd known before. He expounded no theories, having learned, probably, that there is little chance of improving life but many occasions to enjoy it. When I brought him together with Mainville one weekend at Camp Shelby, they didn't seem to like each other. Cahn was a skeptic to Mainville's idealist, a sybarite to the other's ascetic. Fond of them both, I drew from each what my unformed nature required.

The combination of the men in my squad who needed my attention and a buddy to give me the attention I needed made the daily routines at Camp Shelby tolerable, if not enjoyable. Daydreaming boys swung from their bunks on Sunday afternoons to display photographs which were the secret centers beyond the profanity, bigotry, and stupidity they usually exhibited, the muted aching beneath rages, spiteful pettinesses, and sour depressions. The only photograph in my wallet was of my sister Annabelle. My bunkmates assumed, with my tacit encouragement, that the frequent bulky letters from Miss Potter were passionate outpourings from a desolate sweetheart. While other footlockers were decorated with pinups of Ann Sheridan and Rita Hayworth, mine boasted a studio portrait of Eleonora Duse, twenty years dead, and another of Martha Graham in a stark dance pose. Upon inquiry, Duse was identified as my grandmother and Miss Graham as my mother. Whatever their private opinions of my bizarre relatives, my bunkmates extended the same courteous respect they gave to all women relatives. I never mentioned my actual relatives to others and, in time, built up the pretense that I was the only child I'd always wanted to be. Without Mainville's presence to restrain me, I started spinning a net of lies around myself that was not broken through for ten years. At dinner in our apartment years later, Cahn told my wife that he'd never met a liar as brazen as I was. He is right. An entirely fallacious life, constructed over the shame I felt for my family, began in the army and flowered during the years that immediately followed. It was not until my first marriage collapsed in a sea of mutual deceits that the structure that had grown from thoughtless inventions was acknowledged and eventually examined.

Yet, on leave in New York, my eyes followed Marlon Brando with fraternal empathy as his followed every movement Mady Christians made in *I Remember Mama*. I could accept that Norwegian immigrant family of thirty years before and three thousand miles away, but nothing made my own—French-Canadian, only five hundred miles from me—acceptable. Cutting off whatever was detachable from my past, I refused to take out life insurance, because there was no one I wanted to profit from my death (or life), and I refused, too, to wear the dog tags the army issued to me until the initials on them that identified me as a Roman Catholic were removed. When my company marched off to the chapel of their choice on Christmas or Easter morning, I was washing dishes in the kitchen or clipping a hedge on the commanding colonel's lawn for refusing to attend compulsory church

108

services. Embracing anonymity, I didn't go home on furlough, didn't write to my brothers, who didn't write to me, either. Annabelle joined the SPARS to become the sixth service star in my mother's window, and her occasional letters could not bring my family from the limbo where they'd been assigned. The army was a sanctuary from the reality that had always shamed, or frightened, or overwhelmed me, and any story served to answer questions about the folks back home.

During my summer furlough, Miss Potter, concerned about the rumored laxity in army morals, introduced me to a "nice girl" —Alice, who was a student actress. All through my two-week furlough, I escorted Alice to dinner and to lunch, to the theatre and movies, to public beaches and to open-air concerts in the Park. Returning to her apartment one night after the theatre, we kissed in the kitchen while her two roommates waited for us to join them for coffee and cake in the living room. For the first time since high school five years earlier, the promise of love opened up before me, and instead of evading it this time I plunged recklessly into it. But Miss Potter, unfortunately, was right: Alice *was* a nice girl. Pretty, graceful, and high-spirited, she was protected beneath a pliable surface by the inner steel impetuous boys often find in well-bred Southern girls. She glowed with sentimental approval as Margaret Sullavan accommodated Elliott Nugent on *his* weekend passes in *The Voice of the Turtle,* but in the dim light of her apartment she moved my hands firmly from secret places and I held myself face down in an agony of arousal next to her on the sofa while Frank Sinatra crooned of love on her radio. Her roommates served as chaperones, continuing the sorority closeness begun in the obscure girls' college they'd all three attended in the South. One was training for the opera; the other writing her first novel. Without men friends of their own, they returned home at the most inopportune moments from singing lessons and part-time library work and greeted me with genteel but scarcely disguised suspicion. I left them—virgins all—to return

109

to Mississippi and release my frustrations with strangers in tawdry bedrooms.

Alice even denied me a photograph for my wallet, probably suspecting, and quite rightly, that it would be shown off as evidence of a conquest never achieved. However, she did write frequent letters of cheerful news of her career, her friends, and her ambitions. Upon this flimsy connection, another dream was spun: the life we would share when the lights went on again all over the world. Her presence, sweeter in its imagined compliance than its reality would ever have been, followed me on top of weapons carriers, across the Atlantic, even into rooms entered to find temporary solace.

In the autumn of 1944, I was put in charge of two other soldiers and assigned to a Coast Artillery station on the Massachusetts shore. The sole inhabitants of an isolated lighthouse flashing signals out to sea, we cleaned and operated the light, cooked our own meals, maintained guard duty, and endured each other's idiosyncrasies as best we could, which took some doing. Rizzo, a sulky Italian in his thirties whose wife was apparently playing him false in Brooklyn, shouted curses all night in his sleep. The draft board had interrupted Brown's career in amateur tennis, and he alternated between monomaniac practice sessions against the whitewashed walls and staring despondently out the window at ice and snow. And for me the interior of the lighthouse proved an ideal setting for acting exercises: Romeo's lyrical longings echoed up the winding staircase, and Iago's machinations were hissed from the landing into the cavern below.

As we were going about our usual activities one Saturday morning, the door opened slowly. A young lieutenant, fresh from Officers' Training School, had come to inspect our quarters. Behind him, his jeep rested in icy ruts and his driver shivered within it. His eager face froze into dismay at the sight of me shouting Elizabethan verse full-voice into space, Brown perfecting his backhand against the wall, and Rizzo pounding his fists against the cement in impotent Sicilian rage. Noiselessly closing the door,

110

he crept away to report to his superiors. I don't know what happened to him, or to my fellow lighthouse keepers, but in a few weeks I was transferred back to my Field Artillery unit in Camp Shelby and shipped overseas to Europe.

In the predawn darkness of early December, Cahn and I filed with thousands of others across the gangplank into the great gray *Queen Elizabeth*. Rumored to be capable of outrunning German U-boats, the liner made the Atlantic crossing in four days without an escort. We left our fusty quarters only to take positions on the sea-swept decks for nightly lifeboat drill. There, vast wintry skies above us and mammoth ocean waves slapping against the rolling ship, we rehearsed lifelessly for survival at sea, then returned below decks where we slept cramped face to face or feet to face in a wretched stench of flatulence, halitosis, unwashed socks, and unbathed male bodies. During waking hours, huddles of boys played poker and shot crap while I, suspended in a hammock-like cot, read whatever I could get my hands on, including even the communications training manual issued to me months before but which had always been put aside for more stimulating matter. From the next cot, Cahn's voice reached me above the steady hum of the engines in conversation about novels, art, music, and the theatre—everything except what we were being carried into. The first day out, my mind blanked out the name of the girl in *Twelfth Night* who falls in love with the disguised Viola. All through the crossing, the name eluded me no matter what associations Cahn and I conjured up to bring it forth. We landed in Scotland, and as we filed out across the gangplank into fresh air and onto solid land, a large poster across the quay advertised a Hollywood film. "Olivia!" I shouted back the line to Cahn; other voices picked up the name and shouted it to him. From beneath his duffle bag, rifle, and pack, he grinned acknowledgment to me while the rest of the men cheered with no idea what that variation of their own "Kilroy!" or "Geronimo!" was supposed to mean.

A quaint railroad carriage transported us from Glasgow through

111

tidy villages and neatly groomed country estates to Wallasey, a seaside town not far from Liverpool, where we were billeted in the local inn, four or six to each room, with no heat and no hot water. Through the fog that blanketed our immediate surroundings, we heard rapid, high-pitched voices of occasional passers-by making their way through the wartime blackout. Chilled to the bone that first night, we glanced sheepishly away from each other as buzz bombs screamed overhead and were answered by anti-aircraft fire from nearby Liverpool.

We were indoctrinated by harassed young officers in our new roles as unofficial ambassadors abroad. In spite of what might appear hostile condescension, the English were our friends and allies. We were not to start arguments about comparative courage, politics, their royalty, or our leaders; we were, in short, to conduct ourselves like the gentlemen our commanders knew we were. Most important, we were cautioned that more G.I.s ended up in hospital wards because of action with English girls than with the enemy, and we were issued packets of contraceptives and mimeographed directions to army prophylactic stations, and informed that short-arm inspections would be held every morning rather than once a week, which had been the custom in the States. Then we were dismissed to perform our ambassadorial functions.

My communications squad met for daily sessions in splicing wire, setting up switchboards, and memorizing the code with which we would identify ourselves to observation posts in combat. Cahn was appointed company clerk; we saw each other only in formations and as we double-timed through cobblestoned streets in the fog that was the English substitute for air. The giant pulse of the sea put us to sleep at night and woke us in the morning. In between, our routines were pleasant and undemanding: we were waiting to be used across the Channel. We polished our shoes, cleaned our equipment, and wrote endless letters to buddies and to family. The knowledge that military censors now read our letters before they were mailed inhibited some of us and spurred others into outlandish fictions to shock or intrigue the unseen eyes that uncovered our secrets.

In the evening, we investigated the life around us. Fish-and-chips stands sold us masses of heat and grease which we swallowed without tasting before entering pubs where workingmen threw darts at a board in the corner. English 'alf-and-'alf replaced the point-two beer of our post exchanges. The men smoking their pipes at the tables could have stepped directly from the pages of Thomas Hardy and D. H. Lawrence, and I eavesdropped shamelessly on their sporadic conversations, but they paid no more attention to me than they did to the cats under the table or the insects in the cracks of the wall.

At midnight, boys burst in from the fog with incredulous accounts of being accosted from doorways and hedges by girls only too eager to receive what we were eager to give. Cahn smiled tolerantly at their stories, and made no comment when I bundled up to go out into the evening mists. But doorway and garden pleasures were not my goal. A poster on a street kiosk lured me to the Liverpool Repertory Theatre, where Eileen Herlie glided through the outdated morality of *The Second Mrs. Tanqueray* in exquisite costumes and a flamboyant red wig. The following week, Sheridan's fastidious wit in *The School for Scandal* flew past my uncomprehending ears for the entire first act until they accustomed themselves to hearing the words spoken as they should be. Several years before, I had seen the mature Ethel Barrymore play young Lady Teazle in a Long Island summer-stock production, and the great star's baritone authority had left me somewhat confused about the May-December marriage around which the comedy revolves. The excellent cast in Liverpool, including Mary Ellis as the pert, slim country bride and Miss Herlie as spiteful Lady Sneerwell, gave me my first genuine understanding of actors serving a play instead of distorting it to serve themselves. During our last week in Wallasey, Miss Herlie played Anna Christie, O'Neill's waterfront prostitute, with skillful virtuosity far beyond that of

113

my Broadway favorites who played not characters in plays but merely themselves. During five short weeks far from the classrooms in which I had prepared to be an actor, my education for the theatre began.

The lessons that began in Liverpool continued in London. During our first leave, Cahn was obliged to visit family friends outside the city, so my companion was Cermak, a modest man in my squad whose conversation seldom strayed from his wife and their cat back in Brooklyn. Never having seen a play before, he went with me to a matinée of Shaw's *Arms and the Man* and watched Ralph Richardson's ironic Swiss mercenary and Laurence Olivier's Balkan peacock with no discernible response, either to them or to the unrestrained excitement they aroused in me. That evening, he smilingly rejected my invitation to see John Gielgud in *The Circle* and went off to watch, as he put it, "real people." During that leave, my real people were Olivier's Richard III, Gielgud's Hamlet, and Richardson's Peer Gynt. The glamorous women who'd always attracted me to the theatre were dismissed forever in five days during which I watched three gifted actors play eight roles in six famous plays. On the train back to Wallasey, Cermak tolerated my incoherent enthusiasms as long as he could and then tried to bring me back to earth. I didn't want to be on earth; I wanted to be on the stage. If Olivier and Gielgud could be there, then so could I. On future passes, Cahn attended the opera or the ballet, listened to Myra Hess play at noontime for bomb-weary Londoners in the Tate Gallery, or went off to retrospective showings of modern painters. My time was devoted totally to the theatres, watching everything being presented, from silly thrillers and placid domestic comedies to the outrageous innuendos of a Hermione Gingold revue and the polished bawdiness of John Gielgud's production of Congreve's *Love for Love*. A miraculous conjunction of military timing and an English theatrical renaissance placed me where the greatest acting lessons in the world were being given; nothing short of a direct hit by a German

114

bomb on the theatre or on me would have kept me from them.

Profuse letters went off to Mainville, Miss Potter, and Alice, describing the indescribable glories of my discoveries, but they seldom provoked the responses I expected. Mainville, stationed in another part of England, wrote that all this was "grand" but that the world was going up in flames all around me and it might be wiser to turn my attention to that since that's where our lives are lived. From New York, Alice countered my extravagant praise of Olivier's Richard III with extravagant praise of Fredric March in *A Bell for Adano*; my marveling at the talents displayed by Margaret Leighton and Joyce Redman in classical roles in the Old Vic Company brought news from her that a mutual acquaintance had just scored a personal triumph in *Dear Ruth* on Broadway. Only Miss Potter seemed to share my spirit: she sent me copies of the plays I'd seen, so I could study them, and matched my descriptions of actors with memories of John Barrymore's Hamlet, Jane Cowl's Juliet, and Walter Hampden's Cyrano de Bergerac.

The world Mainville urged upon my notice obtruded upon my preoccupations whether I wanted it to or not. On my way to matinées, I could hardly avoid seeing bombed-out buildings which had only recently housed families and office workers, now unpopulated shells containing rubble, exposed bathroom fixtures, and suspended floor beams. After coming back from early-evening performances through fog and blackout, I stretched out apprehensively in the room I always took near a small park, to await the sound of the buzz bombs. Shivering urchins on the back streets of Liverpool piped, "Yank!—'ey, Yank! Go 'ome, Yank," wrenching my attention to bare blue knees and grimy feet tucked for warmth under patched trouser seats on icy stoops. Rancorous eyes returned my stares with a malignity bred in the stunted and deprived by the sight of the well fed and the well clothed. Cahn and I, dining at the luxurious Hotel Adelphi, ignored the lofty disdain of the elderly waiters who served us. Outside in the wind, derelicts shouted Anglo-Saxon epithets in our faces, and ancient prostitutes, reeking of gin and cheap perfume, employed identical words in futile efforts to entice us into shadowy doorways.

No matter how blasé or experienced we were, or pretended to be, most of us were startled by the open sexual traffic in wartime England. Returning from a local spot they'd nicknamed (for good reason) "the Gonorrhea Race Track," our bunkmates boasted of sharing "the greatest glory England has to offer." We knew from Mississippi and Maine that women whose men are dead or absent are hardly inaccessible to soldiers, but what surprised us was the lack of discretion in people supposed to be reticent about all personal matters. From the window of my London lodgings, I observed a girl in school uniform take her position every morning. On my way to buy tickets for a matinée, I approached her. The face in the harsh sunlight was ten years older and twenty years more experienced than the virginal costume she assumed for her profession. "Five pounds, Yank," she murmured. Five pounds! That was more than it cost to see ten plays. We stared at each other; from that face of artfully applied innocence issued promises of sado-masochistic gratifications so explicit that my knees went weak. Repelled by her avidity more than by her inventory, I managed to turn away. "You'll never forget it, Yank," she shouted after me, "only five pounds!" When I returned to my room an hour later, she was gone.

A limited number of seats for the evening's performance were sold each morning at the New Theatre, where the Old Vic played, and at the Haymarket, where Gielgud's company appeared. Queues of shivering theatre fans, mostly elderly women, formed before dawn to either stand in line or buy a stool to take one's place in line until the box office opened at ten o'clock. An American soldier was a rarity in the group, and voluble ladies struck up acquaintance with me to while away the time. One morning, a handsome, mature woman behind me invited me to have coffee with her. As Londoners began to bustle about their daily business

116

in the morning light, we talked of the Lunts, who had just opened in a new comedy, of Olivier and Gielgud, and Peggy Ashcroft's Ophelia, of the war, the bombs, of my America and her England. We picked up our tickets and spent the rest of the day in her bed. Her husband was an officer in Egypt or Burma or some other vaguely defined outpost of the Empire. Her children, nearly grown up, were away at school, safe from the bombings, except for the youngest, whom she'd kept with her and who attended a day school in the city. She was kind and womanly, intelligent and humorous, and the activities we enjoyed in her bedroom were neither sordid nor furtive. Seated across from me at the kitchen table for tea in the late afternoon, she glanced at the clock on the shelf: her son was due back from school shortly. I dressed and left. That evening, at the performance of A *Midsummer Night's Dream*, she smiled and nodded to me, as a casual acquaintance might, from the row ahead.

The pleasure we took in arousing English women to unabashed sexual abandon was heightened by the derision with which their men usually scrutinized us. In theatre lobbies, graceful, articulate young men accompanied each other or their mothers and glanced in my direction indifferently at best and contemptuously at worst. Choking back the inherited bigotry of the Canuck for the limey, I became the gauche, self-conscious intruder they scorned. Our officers could insist that the English were our friends, but they seemed to view us as servants imported to perform a particularly nasty job. The then current joke that the only trouble with American soldiers "is that they're overpaid, oversexed, and over here" was reflected in glacial stares in restaurants and theatres, as well as in shouted oaths from workingmen along the docks and muttered insults from tables in the pubs.

On the bulletin board in the orderly room, one afternoon, a handwritten note appeared inviting us to spend Sunday afternoons with a local mother and her two sons, aged ten and eight. Cahn and I tucked chocolate for the boys and cigarettes for their

117

mother into our pockets and set off. A plump, cheerful woman ushered us into a tidy little parlor where, after serving us tea scraped together from her rations, she mended socks while we wrestled with her sons on the floor. We went back often, sometimes together and sometimes separately, to sit in stuffed armchairs while the boys did their homework and she played scratchy records of Marian Anderson and Paul Robeson to make us feel at home. While her sons spent "quiet time" in their room, she told us of the Liverpool bombings when the children, one of whom had a severe nervous tic, had slept for weeks in the shelters. She shrugged off our sympathy: that wasn't why she was telling us their experiences. She merely wanted us to know what it had been like. She would have been embarrassed if we'd said so, but she was the plucky spirit Ed Murrow eulogized in broadcasts and Greer Garson sentimentalized in the movies. Her bountiful nature provided not only the "home away from home" her invitation had promised but a life away from the life we led, boys without mothers, men without women. On Christmas Day, we were the men at her family dinner. For the rest of my army term, her chatty letters followed me. When I returned to the States, she wrote that her husband had come home at last and they were living again in Liverpool. For several years, she sent Christmas cards with greetings from all of them, including the husband we'd never met; then they disappeared into their lives as I disappeared into mine. Now, when someone says England to me, my memories swing between brilliant actors on brightly lit stages and that sensible mother, darning holes in her sons' socks as she told us of the bombing raids on Liverpool.

Early in 1945, we were ferried across the Channel to Le Havre, where torpedoed ships still hung half submerged on the glassy waters of the harbor. We put up our tents in wind and sleet that ripped the canvas from our benumbed fingers, and crept inside to sleep in each other's arms within flimsy shelters that stretched mile on mile through the blasted orchards of Normandy. The months that followed dissolved the remaining vestiges of that singular inner core in each of us and locked us into a common identity that had no room for differences. Wearing identical battle fatigues, eating identical K rations, subject to identical orders and hazards beyond our control, we became identical ourselves. There wasn't one among us who wouldn't have preferred being anywhere else in the world with anyone else under the sun, but there wasn't one of us, either, who, in leaning down to pull another up into a truck or from a foxhole, didn't grasp that other hand as if it were an extension of his own.

Cahn's duties in the orderly room removed him from my sight unless I sought him out after hours. My life was my squad out on patrols, splicing wire, setting up switchboards, crouching on the ground to eat our rations, read our letters from home, and tell our foolish jokes to each other. Although, officially, they were my charges, they took care of me more than I took care of them. Only now can I acknowledge, too, that they were the bridge over which I crossed to understand others, the bridge which in time led me back again to my brothers. The oldest was Cermak, who'd gone with me to the play in London, and would often accompany me on later leaves to Paris and London. His unruffled masculinity was a bulwark on Channel crossings and in cafés during passes, as it was in combat. Glennon, a short, stocky redhead from Chicago, was the squad prankster, but his quick reflexes and marksmanship were our most reliable protections on patrol. Later, when we were stationed in a German village at the close of the war, Glennon approached a mannish-looking *Gräfin* to ask with devilish innocence if she wasn't possibly the wrestler he'd been matched against some years earlier in the Loop. Donnolly and Doran, having long since given up hope of teaching me how to sing, entertained us by sitting on top of the weapons carrier and harmonizing "I Had a Dream, Dear," and "Sweet Genevieve," with a sweetness of voice and nature that never deserted them.

119

Wilson, prematurely gray and with a cultivated New England accent, prowled the countryside for whiskey to deaden a personal sorrow he never confided and we never mentioned. We would come upon him passed out in the woods, slap him conscious, and pull him with us on our patrol. One night when planes strafed the barn we'd taken shelter in, he sobbed in my arms and then turned his tear-stained face to the wall to sleep, his exhausted body trembling against my own. Merejekowski, an energetic ugly Pole, prowled the countryside, too, but his search was for the "gash" he'd promised himself to screw wherever we spent a night. We lost him for days at a time to venereal-disease wards behind the lines, but he always came back, accepting our jokes with sheepish blushes and slipping away in the dark for yet another exposure to infection. Finally, there was Mansard, a French-Canadian buffoon from the woods of Maine who had to be forcibly restrained from dashing out from cover to challenge enemy planes with his pistol. Fond of all of them, I was fondest of Mansard; he was like my cousins on the reservation, a primitive set loose within the idiocies of civilization. These men were my squad. They retrieved me at last from the influence of older women, forced me to regard bodily functions and sexual habits without prudery, shame, or disgust. During our one week in France, Merejekowski shook each of us awake to take our turn with farm girls gathering dowries from sleeping bag to sleeping bag. One night, we all gathered in a sergeant's tent to watch a sturdy, naked girl couple over and over again with a large dog, as the visibly aroused soldiers egged her on in the flickering lamplight. Wilson leaned blankly at my side, hardly able to stand, and Glennon, punching his fist into my shoulder, said, "Hey, Shakespeare, what d'ya think a that, huh? This is France, huh? How about it?" Moral judgments of a mere month earlier proved not only narrow but irrelevant in this society where vigorous bodies could be maimed and burned and frozen within a few days. Whatever form it took, sex was only another, if not the strongest, mani-

120

festation of the life we were determined to maintain. Eventually, I could sleep undisturbed by frantic intercourse in the sleeping bag next to mine.

We advanced slowly east in the track of the Battle of the Bulge. Awakening in sleeping bags in the fields (once, a stray cow nosed me awake in the frosty morning), we opened our eyes, groaned, lifted packs and rifles to aching shoulders, and climbed again into vehicles that moved us through darkened forests, smoldering towns, and desolate farmlands. Cermak winked at me from his corner of the truck, Wilson blinked in morning-after passivity, Donnolly and Doran sang softly under their breaths, and in the growing light of dawn and the fading twilight I read *Gulliver's Travels* and *Moby Dick*. The landscape moved past us as I found oblivion from the hazards of our journey by burying myself in the satiric and symbolic voyages of years ago. Looking up from the book, I saw a nun cycling frantically beside our truck, her black habit flapping irreverently in the breeze, and then looked down at the page again.

Our own howitzers sent shells over our heads as we traced telephone wires through the forest brush, and German artillery sent their shells over us from across fields and forests. We inched forward, dirty, tired, anxious, and numb. One night, slumped over a glass of wine in a Belgian café, I left Cermak and Wilson to the stench that nauseated me to go outside and sit on the cobblestones. But the odor had followed me out. Finally locating its origin, I stripped off my boots and socks, separated my gummy toes, and scrubbed them clean with snow, then washed the stiffened socks themselves and put them on again, moist against my skin, before going back inside to finish my wine.

When Merejekowski was invalided in a hospital near Brussels with his usual complaint, Cermak and I stopped off to see him during a weekend pass. As we were leaving, a voice shouted from a cot, "Hey, Lemay!" I walked over to a stranger. "Hell, I'm

121

sorry," he said. "I thought your name was Lemay." He was in my brother Ambrose's paratroop company and had recognized the walk we Lemays all share, bouncing back on our heels with each step. Riding back with Cermak to my unit, I was unusually quiet, unable to find words to express the thoughts that were struggling beneath the surface of my mind, or to express others which might have displaced them.

The main force of our company positioned, fired, and defended our howitzers from enemy planes and artillery; my squad, under the cover of night, maintained telephone contact between them and forward observation posts. We were engaged in very little actual combat ourselves, but shelled-out houses, burnt-out tanks, and occasional corpses of men and animals littered the terrain we traveled. Pausing to drink from my canteen one morning, I threw up my breakfast at the sight of a young villager lying in a culvert with a bullet hole in his head, an uncorked bottle of wine under his arm, and flies making a meal of his face in the brilliant sunshine. He was my first sight of a war casualty. In time, corpses, enemy or ally, no longer distressed me, but I never got used to the sight of cows lying dead in their pastures, bloated testimonial to the insanity of human affairs.

We entered houses where food was still warm on plates left behind by German families fleeing approaching American troops. Occasionally, Wehrmacht soldiers younger than the babies among ourselves came out from behind tree trunks waving handkerchiefs over their heads and begging us not to kill them. Grouping them together, one of us would walk them back to our command post to be sent further back to stockades. From time to time, my rifle was fired at noises in trees behind me or into village windows where shadows threatened, but if an enemy died because of me, I never saw him. My combat experience was mostly ducking shrapnel from exploding artillery shells, once not quite quickly enough, as an almost invisible scar on my left knee still testifies. Like the others in my squad, I declined the purple heart that

122

medics offered, along with their aspirin, for any wound, however slight. Such tokens of courage were for combat soldiers who were fighting the real war ahead of us on foot and in tanks. We were merely cleaning up behind them.

Planes swooped down over us in the daylight, or rattled the windows of sheds we slept in at night, but they hardly punctured my thoughts. Crossing the Rhine, our motorcade of army vehicles stalled as German planes attacked it. From the top of our weapons carrier, I admired the pretty pattern made by colored tracer bullets in the twilight while my men dived beneath the truck or jumped over the bridge into the river. The planes were driven away, my men climbed back onto their perches, the motors started, and we moved on. Donnolly and Doran shook their Irish heads, teasing me about my bravado. Cermak unsmilingly told me that someday I'd wake up dead. But it was neither fatalism nor bravado. I couldn't have been killed; I wasn't really there.

I floated through the physical geography of the war supported by visions of John Gielgud haunting the battlements of Elsinore and Ralph Richardson peeling the onion to its barren core in *Peer Gynt*. Glennon, or Wilson, or someone shouted warnings as a sniper's bullets zinged past my ear from a German doorway or a forest tree, and my body fell instantly to the ground, no matter what my mind was involved with. Surrendering Wehrmacht heroes whistled Mozart melodies as we herded them back to imprisonment, and G.I.s answered with ribald barracks ditties and bawdy jokes. In midwinter, the entire company was rounded up into trucks one morning and driven back to a town where we were treated, ten at a time, to hot showers, issued clean uniforms, and marched into a theatre to watch Katharine Cornell and Brian Aherne in *The Barretts of Wimpole Street*. The Broadway of my Manhattan daydreams had followed us to Germany. My men, more inflamed by the sight of young girls in pretty dresses speaking English than they were impressed by New York's leading star, were vociferous in response. Only I had reservations. Now, after

123

Gielgud's Hamlet and Olivier's Gloucester, matronly actresses playing young girls no longer impressed me.

In April, my reading of Ahab's soliloquy, in Olivier's falsetto from *Richard III*, to Cahn at the other end of the line was interrupted by a voice saying, "Break it off, soldier, the President just died." We thought it was one of the pranks with which idle switchboard operators amused themselves, but the strange voice broke into sobs. I cut the circuit and slammed the book shut. Crouched before my underground switchboard, I remembered my mother, years before, reading a newspaper account of Eleanor Roosevelt's going right inside a mining family's shack while her companions remained outside in their limousine. My mother's voice cracked when she put the paper down on the kitchen table, saying, "Why, that woman really cares about people like us." Far from my mother and her kitchen, bereft in the Germany of concentration camps and fourteen-year-old soldiers, I covered my face and wept.

Over his martini, Cahn recalls precise dates and the exact names of towns we passed through following the infantry into a storybook landscape that revealed horrors grimmer than any ever found in fairy tales. He knows the facts; who knows the truth? Surely not I. Were there really naked human bodies splayed out like dummies in abandoned boxcars or heaped in trenches, soft as fallen fruit in the spring sunshine? Which were the sights my eyes looked upon, and then away from, and which those read about or heard about much later? Did my rifle butt break through the slats of a wooden door to a Bavarian shed to find within it not the cringing S.S. guards we expected but row upon row of shoes from the feet of children long since disappeared up into smoke? Was that I, whose stomach can withstand any sight or smell, vomiting my insides out against a tree trunk as men I ate and slept with emptied machine guns into any German male unwise enough to come within their sights? Did it really happen? To me? To them? To the world? Or have I invented dream upon dream upon dream, unable to look at or listen to anything outside myself?

As we roared into a village in southern Germany, our motors and shouts startled a team of horses hitched to a farm wagon with an old man and a little girl on the plank up front. The child whimpered and the old man reined his team, but the horses reared and started down the steep hill leading into the countryside. An attractive gray-haired woman stepped from the knot of motionless onlookers, reached up to the bridles quickly, and brought the horses under control. Murmuring softly to the horses, she looked beyond us to the mountains as we cheered and applauded, then walked rapidly up the hill toward the enormous structure of stone and glass which overlooked the valley. The villagers identified the building as a château and the woman as the countess who owned it and most of the land that could be seen from it.

We evicted her, along with female servants and relatives, from the château that afternoon, since its rooms were needed for hundreds of survivors from the neighboring concentration camp. We hastily organized temporary care and shelter for emaciated wrecks who could not explain any more than we could absorb the nature of the lives from which they'd been freed just the day before. Not knowing any other way to console them, we handed out concentrated chocolate bars and K rations and then ran aghast to their sides as they collapsed retching from food too rich for them to digest. We settled women into cots, arranged for baths and the treatment of bruises, sores, and insect bites, and assigned light duties to occupy the younger, healthier ones, burying ourselves in activity to escape evidence of warfare more brutal than the snipers' bullets we'd ducked and the artillery shells exploding around us. All night long, bullets ricocheted in the woods where

125

bands of G.I.s searched out the German caretakers of those who listened without response as we tried to find some words that could connect us to each other.

Late in the evening, the countess knocked on the door of the orderly room and asked permission to see the captain. I ushered her into his improvised office and he motioned for me to remain. In excellent English, she protested her "banishment to the game-keeper's shack" and complained that gowns from her closets were being distributed among the women, to replace the threadbare garments her government had issued them. Having endured an exasperating day, the captain at first contented himself with derisive grimaces as she catalogued her grievances. Then, with a shout of rage, he instructed me to take the "old bitch" back to her quarters and keep her out of his sight.

We walked to the gamekeeper's house, she nursing her humiliation in silence and I half expecting a bullet in my back from the leaves of a tree or from the upper window of a house we passed. But no bullets were fired. Only night animals and owls stirred beyond the trees and, like a refrain from my remote boyhood, a child's sweet voice sounded within a house. At the door of the gamekeeper's "shack" (which turned out to be an imposing eight-room house), we were met by a gnome-like woman the countess introduced as Fräulein Muter, her secretary-companion. From among the others who crowded into the hallway, the countess introduced just two: her sister, a refugee countess from Hungary, and her niece, another countess. They spoke for a moment in rapid German which I could not follow, and then, with a wry smile, the countess invited me inside to share their after-dinner coffee.

Sometime during those weeks, the war ended. Hitler was found dead in his bunker in Berlin, the Russian troops met ours in the east, and we halted where we were. Germany was kaput, but we had survived. A photograph of Cahn, Cermak, and me drunk on a mountaintop, unscarred, untouched, proves it. Ten or twelve of us were detached from our unit and it moved on. My squad was disbanded: Glennon, Wilson, Cermak, Donnolly and Doran, Merejekowski, and Mansard rode off to new assignments in the weapons carrier that had brought us from Normandy to Bavaria. Cahn and I shared the countess's study, falling into lifeless sleep after long days of asking questions in several languages, typing up forms, giving orders, making arrangements for cots on the ground floor for those too weak to climb upstairs and for meals to be served in private for those too unstable to eat with others.

Late every afternoon, I shaved, slapped lotion on my cheeks, and combed grease into my hair to escape into life again by join- ing the countess for after-dinner coffee in the garden behind the gamekeeper's house. There, under the flowering trellis, conversa- tions continued that had begun with Miss Clark when I was twelve, continued with Miss Bromhall when I was seventeen, and with Miss Potter when I was twenty. Leaning back against the stone bench, her silver coffee service on the table by her side, the countess spoke of Beethoven, Rembrandt, Goethe, and Schiller, and of her admiration for Thomas Mann, whose novels she had gone right on reading in spite of the regime's proscriptions against them. She spoke of her dead parents, aunts, and uncles, of her own girlhood with her sister on another estate much like this one, where they had been prepared for futures on the thrones of Europe, and of her children growing up on these grounds, one daughter now married to a Scandinavian nobleman, another to a stranger in England, and her only son dead or perhaps a prisoner in Egypt.

She was a gentle, quiet woman, released at last from abhorrent years when her Germany of literature and music had become a charlatan's hell of goosesteps and barbarism. She smiled (echoes of Ann Harding) at me over our coffee cups (Candida to my eager Marchbanks), and questions I'd been determined to ask lost their urgency. Eventually, however, they were asked and her explanations seemed reasonable. She didn't know about the con- centration camp, or the broken women who slept in her bed-

127

rooms now. She had lived a quiet life with her few companions, never leaving her estate, and the world had gone its way. Ask my sister, she suggested, the Hungarian countess who had walked with her daughter across the mountains to escape the Bolsheviks. But the Hungarian countess did not speak to me. She watched her daughter slip off into the woods with American soldiers and come back with chocolate bars, cigarettes, and silk stockings, but she did not acknowledge our presence. The countess shrugged slightly when I blurted out that you'd have to be blind and deaf not to know about a concentration camp ten miles away. "You are young, you Americans," she said, not unkindly. She was right: she had endured so much more than I (the destruction of her beloved Germany, an only son dead or captured in Egypt!). I believed her.

Most of the refugees in the château were Jews from France, Belgium, and the Netherlands. Cahn said that others were probably political prisoners, removed from more infamous camps to the east as the Russians advanced upon them. Fräulein Muter, the countess's companion whose grotesque appearance was married to a spiteful tongue, said they were all Communists. Perhaps they were, or had been, but few of them seemed to have strong convictions about anything any longer. To fill out forms required before they could return to their interrupted lives, we prodded them for personal information, but many had no idea where they'd been born, or where they had lived before they came to Germany, where their relatives were, or if indeed they had any at all. Some could not summon up anything even remotely resembling a coherent past, so we pieced together what we could, or invented what was needed, filled out forms and forwarded them to headquarters, where the wheels of repatriation were set in motion.

More docile than the women, the men turned their lackluster eyes away from ours, only twitchings below the mouth and the trembling of fingers giving animation to otherwise deadened faces and hands. The women, more resilient, seemed to come out of a

128

deep sleep, and stretched again toward the sun, toward life, toward home. The most vivacious of them was a once well-known Parisian actress, who sat with me on the lawn after lunch and spoke of her theatre and mine, of the Comédie Française, of the Sarah Bernhardt and Lucien Guitry of her girlhood, preferring older memories to those of the immediate past. She confided that she had often escaped into Saint Joan or Phèdre when her body or mind could no longer endure her existence, much as I had escaped from the irritations of my mild military life into Hamlet and Peer Gynt. When the truck took her off with a dozen others to a train for Paris, she waved goodbye with theatrical abandon, and I turned back to the château to deal with others taking her place.

The Autobahns that summer were clogged with displaced people. American military vehicles picked their way through hordes of liberated laborers the Germans had rounded up from conquered villages to work their factories and mines. They flooded from the east, carrying sacks of personal belongings and leading small children by the hand, stopped by the roadsides to eat or rest, and squatted in the fields to relieve themselves, a transient mass of strangers suspended between the wretchedness of the past and the uncertainties of the future. Indomitable old men, cheerful boys, young girls with babies in their arms, and crones with cooking utensils roped to their waists trudged through our stone gates to occupy beds just vacated by others now riding by truck and by train to their homes to the west.

Through my window one afternoon, I watched a well-built brunette girl approach the château. From a distance, she seemed no different from most of the women already with us, but as she came closer, I could see she wore an expensive tailored suit, high heels, and silk stockings, and carried a smart leather suitcase. Sitting across from me in the orderly room, she answered my questions in good English, glancing around the room with quiet assurance while unaccustomed perfume scented the air between us. She told me her name was Lucie, she was in her late twenties,

129

and that she had been deported from Brussels to Germany to work as a governess in a Nazi officer's household. Her fragrant hair brushed against my cheek as she leaned across my desk to show photographs of herself with two handsome blond children. When she returned them to her purse, I could see that it was well stocked with cosmetics, cigarettes, and other luxuries seldom seen among us. I took her next door to the captain, who smiled broadly and winked at me before dismissing me.

After supper, Lucie asked me to repair the lock on the door of the room the captain had assigned her. Although it was on the top floor, remote from the other women and from the soldiers' quarters below, she was afraid that one of the men might find his way to her. Even the captain had molested her, she told me tearfully, when he escorted her to the room. With a vehemence that surprised me as much as it did her, I turned on her. We spent our waking hours with women whose bodies hadn't known perfume for years, whose faces hadn't known lipstick, who were little more than mutilated ghosts barely retrieved from death. And she came strolling in from nowhere, flaunting freshly bathed flesh, perfume, fingernail polish, and shampooed hair. Of course the captain had molested her. Turning to the door, I jabbed the screwdriver into the wood to hide my tears. She put her arms around me and drew me back to face her. I fixed the lock and secured the door behind us. The next morning, the captain, passing me in the hallway, stopped to grin and say, "After you, Corporal! Keep her warmed up for me!"

Afternoon conversations with the countess about Bach and Goethe, followed by Lucie's embraces at night, diluted the anguish spilled into my ears by mothers who would never see their children again and children who had long ago seen the last of their parents. Grateful for any diversion that drained my body or filled my head, I buried myself in the trivia of record-keeping, safe from dry-eyed confessions as, ten years earlier, I'd kept safe from my mother sobbing in her bedroom. Or so I thought. In August on

130

pass in Paris, I sat on a bridge with nothing on my mind and burst into hysterical tears. A couple of M.P.s hurried me to a hospital, where the brusque attention of army nurses put me on my feet again in a few days. My captain, also on leave in Paris, came to see me in the hospital, extended my leave an extra two weeks and lent me some money, patted me on the shoulder with a grin, and left on his own excursions, during one of which, a few days later, he was struck by an army jeep as he wandered singing drunkenly at the top of his lungs in the middle of the Champs-Elysées.

For once, a city attracted me more than its theatres did. I looked up the actress refugee from the château, and she took me to see Françoise Rosay, whose first entrance in a trivial domestic comedy was hailed by a deafening ovation of applause and cheers. Before taking me backstage to meet her, my friend explained that Mme. Rosay was a heroine of the Resistance, having spirited underground fighters marked for Nazi retaliation out of France to England and Switzerland. The woman herself, with flashing eyes and vivacious smiles, was far and away more exciting than the actress or the play in which she starred. As a matter of fact, everything I saw on the Paris stages seemed drab beside the Parisians themselves. Watching a modern-dress Antigone defy authority, or a melodrama of espionage set in an asylum, a stately biographical drama of Charlotte and Maximilian, or even beruffled men prance like goats through *The Misanthrope* and *Tartuffe* at the Comédie Française, I squirmed in my seat until I could go outside again where the people were more theatrical than their actors.

Back in the château, I slept badly. Creeping upstairs to Lucie's room after Cahn had fallen asleep and back again before he woke up no longer seemed worth the furtiveness it required. I'd wake in the moonlight to find her staring at me, like a fox, with slackened jaws and glistening eyes. Out in the woods one day, I examined closely a photograph she'd given me and discovered faint traces of a Nazi uniform which had obviously been cropped

131

out. Sickened, I tore it up and scattered the pieces under the trees. That night, I resisted going to her room. Within a week, she had found another soldier. I slept better.

In a faded Munich newspaper, Cahn read a report of an official Nazi banquet. One of the guests listed was the countess's secretary, in *"der Blüte der Jugend,"* which, considering Fräulein Muter's appearance, was either a cruel Teutonic joke or servile flattery aimed at an important personage through her insignificant companion. During our afternoon conversations, the countess's recollections warred with those told by Parisian widows and by the women we were sending back to their homes. Sensing a duplicity in her and a complicity in myself, I ransacked her study one afternoon. In her locked desk, among letters from the dead count, documents of childbirth, and marriage settlements, were signed receipts for labor details she had requested from the concentration-camp commandant. Holding the papers in my trembling hands, I faced her: "You told me you knew nothing about it! You told me you didn't know!" We looked at each other for the last time (Marchbanks to Candida, American to European, human being to human being) before she said, with no particular emphasis, "I owe you no explanations."

The château and its occupants were taken over by UNRRA officials, and we were transferred to Salzburg, where Cahn was retained in some cultural capacity while I went outside the city to a château which housed Russian, Polish, and Baltic workers trapped between pasts under their Nazi captors and futures in homelands many of them did not want to return to. The new château was a handsome modern building set back on landscaped terraces, with well-planned bedrooms and many bathrooms. On its spacious grounds, hastily constructed compounds encircled the château itself like the tents of besieging armies. Within the compounds in amiable disorder, infants suckled unwashed breasts, lovers pleasured each other in full view of indifferent refugees

132

and incredulous G.I.s, and matrons with gold-capped teeth pressed alien food into our hands during our morning rounds. Outside in the sunlight, laughing boys leaned against the fences playing musical instruments and picking lice from each other's hair. Like me, some of them had picked up enough German to carry on simple conversations and we exchanged views of home, of life, of the future, of girls, wives, and mothers. In the communal latrine, a vibrant youth confided in broken English that he was from an enormous farm family, but didn't know where his parents were, or what had happened to his brothers and sisters. When he had been deported at the age of fourteen, his older brothers were already in the army and one sister was training for medicine, as he intended to do himself when he returned to Kiev, if he ever did. His blue eyes filled with tears and then cleared again at my assurances that we'd get him back home again. We parted outside the latrine, me to go on with my inspection, he to work in the garden patch he cultivated.

The men in my unit didn't like the Russians any more than they had liked the English and the French. Only the obedient, industrious Germans, whose neat farms and tidy kitchens resembled those back home in North Dakota and Kansas, gained the unqualified trust and admiration of G.I.s who, like most people, prefer hearing "*Jawohl*" in response to a command than "*Pourquoi?*" But then foreign people mean little more than foreign girls to men away from home, and the Fräuleins were easily the most willing partners we had ever found.

Since the château was a mere two-hour walk from Salzburg, I joined Cahn on weekends. The Salzburg Festspiel was revived during that first summer of the peace, and he took me to a spirited performance of Mozart's *The Abduction from the Seraglio,* and to a leaden one, in German, of Shakespeare's *Twelfth Night.* Symphony concerts and quartet recitals excited Cahn but, exposed too late in life to serious music, my attention was never more than halfhearted. Cahn's patient efforts to awaken an appreciation of

133

Mozart's genius was doomed from the start, and I soon longed for more compelling diversions during weekends in Salzburg.

Hundreds of thousands of soldiers now had to be prepared for civilian life again; the army instituted a series of courses for us in Salzburg. With the compulsion to learn what I have no talent for, I elected to study singing. In a practice room in the conservatory named after Mozart in the city in which he was born, a plump blond girl named Frieda tried to unravel the mysteries of the tonal scale for me. She shook her head in despair at my vocal ineptitude but laughed so merrily at the jokes with which I hid my embarrassment that she soon became my Fräulein. Our weekends were spent in the one inhabitable room of a house otherwise destroyed by allied bombings. She had come to Salzburg from Linz to study for the opera and had been caught there when the war ended. A seemingly uncomplicated girl, pleasant, sensible, and conscientious, she tolerated, with phlegmatic forbearance if no discernible pleasure, the lovemaking I required to remind me I was alive. Once all that was done with, she turned her back on me to slip into her clothes and then insisted, with Germanic obstinacy, that we take long walks in the hills outside the city. She refused to waste time teaching me what I would never learn to do, and suggested instead that, since opera singers must know how to act even if actors don't have to know how to sing, we work on scenes from Shakespeare's plays together. So we walked hand in hand as the snows fell on the nude statues in the Mirabel Platz and murmured lines from *Macbeth* and *Romeo and Juliet* to each other and then went back to her room where, after taking care of whatever urgencies possessed me, we rehearsed murder, love, and jealousy as 1945 slipped into 1946.

On a holiday in Bad Gastein, I sneaked Frieda into the room Cahn and I were sharing. For three days, he tactfully wandered about the wintry landscape to allow us continuous hours together. She left for Salzburg the day before we did and, sitting across the breakfast table from me, Cahn glanced at the bruises

134

on my throat and said, "It isn't worth it, is it?" He was right, and he could afford to be, with daily letters from his girl in New York. My letters were from my actress fantasy-sweetheart, Alice, who never mentioned love, let alone sex, and from Miss Potter, whose exclusive concerns were my mind and talent. Sharing Frieda's submissive body, while never distasteful, became incidental to rehearsals of Duncan's murder, Othello's rage, and Hamlet's woe. Cahn's friendly comment, however, nagged at me: how could he be so content in the absence of sex, and I so morose in the practice of it?

Passes to London and Paris became more frequent, and the cozy provincialism of Salzburg was left behind for rooms of paintings in the drafty Louvre and café counters among articulate, gesticulating Frenchmen. Across the Channel, London was returning to life like a giant insect emerging from hibernation. Street lamps burned through the fog at night and the theatres blazed with brilliant performances. If the Parisians were more theatrical themselves than their actors, the opposite was true of Englishmen, who transformed themselves into peacocks when they impersonated others. At the Old Vic, Olivier's Oedipus emitted three short harsh cries from some atavistic source when he discovered Jocasta was his mother after all. During intermission, he discarded the tunic, curls, postures, and rhythms of Greek tragedy for the satins, powdered wig, sibilant speech, and effeminate gestures of Sheridan's *The Critic*. The next night, Falstaff's unsated appetites raged through Ralph Richardson's thickened speech and bloated figure in ironic counterpoint to Olivier's Hotspur, stammering his final "w," before being left "food for worms" on the field, a relic of forces that have wasted beautiful young men in wars since the beginning of history.

At the Haymarket, Peggy Ashcroft's Duchess of Malfi, netted in John Gielgud's incestuous snare, died with the nerve-deadened sweetness of a concentration-camp victim while, down Piccadilly at the Criterion, Edith Evans plunged her parasol through the bird-cage veiling of her hat to elicit, with perfect timing, three laughs on Mrs. Malaprop's famous line "Lead the way and we'll precede!" If Webster's Jacobean melodrama cautioned us that the innocent are victimized throughout the ages by the depraved, Sheridan's comedy restored our faith in survival by its creation of that singular English phenomenon, the female eccentric. In a teashop, one such woman took me under her wing after we'd shared a table at breakfast. Middle-aged, stout, a combination of garish colors in dress and hair rinse, she pushed me before her into a taxi. Her husband and son were both returning from the service that week. "Just your age, 'e is, too, my boy," she said, patting my knee with a mittened hand. She was searching for a new dress to welcome 'im 'ome in, and she pulled me behind her into the shops, demanding my opinions and ignoring my suggestions. We lunched in a co-op restaurant on food that tasted like stale soft toast, and had tea in the afternoon in another. In the drizzling twilight, she rode off perched inside yet another taxi, as indestructible in her way as Edith Evans' Mrs. Malaprop, surrounded by the parcels I'd carried for her throughout the long day.

Back in Salzburg with Cahn, Frieda, and the displaced persons, there was nothing to do that hadn't been done before, over and over again. We settled down to wait until the point system of priorities for discharge from the army would end our occupation of a country none of us wanted to be in. After a month or two of sullen aloofness, Frieda, one night in her room, burst into sobs, demanding that I take her with me upon my return to the States. Grasping my arms by my naked sides, and pleading with tears I'd never seen before, she promised that after we married she would divorce me so I'd be free of her. I broke away from her and struggled into my clothes, and then walked through the ten miles of snow to my own bed in the château. Several weeks later, she sent me an invitation to a recital, during which she sang directly at me, before hundreds of smirking American soldiers and their Fräuleins, the accusatory refrains of "Plaisir d'amour." With unrelenting persistence, she wrote me for months after my return home, begging me to help her escape from a country and a life I'd never heard her complain about.

During my last week in Europe, Cahn and I drove from Salzburg to Rome on an errand for his company commander. We passed a woman sitting in a dressing gown outside an automobile trailer. On a table beside her, a phonograph played while she carefully polished her fingernails in the afternoon light. We—or probably only I—shouted lewd endearments to her but she didn't look up. Although I didn't see her clearly, or perhaps because of it, she is the image carried most strongly from that country I never want to see again to this one I never want to leave again: a faceless, anonymous woman, dressed for bed, indulging in a private ritual, oblivious to our presence as she must have been to the shames that had stained her people. It was years before it even occurred to me that she may very well have been one of the victims, not a passive observer, of her country's horrors.

A few days after my twenty-fourth birthday, Mainville and I stood on the deck of our troopship, which was being met by gaily decorated tugboats in New York harbor. From their open decks, vigorous girls in uniform sang "Sentimental Journey" and "Don't Sit Under the Apple Tree" above the cheers, tears, and laughter with which we greeted Manhattan's skyline. At Fort Dix, where my army life had begun, we were issued the necessary papers and monies and sped back into civilian life as we had been hustled out of it. After spending a weekend with Mainville and his family, I checked into a Broadway hotel to settle my immediate future.

First there was the career interrupted three years earlier. At the Neighborhood Playhouse, I was welcomed back from the great world beyond Stanislavski and enrolled once more for the two-year course starting in September; this put me back where I'd been at the age of twenty, except that now the G.I. Bill of Rights supplied a subsistence allowance as well as paying my tuition.

Ric Hylton met me for dinner at Sardi's, but he was too involved in his own pursuits to pay any more than cursory attention to my accounts of other actors' triumphs in London. Then there was Alice, who was replacing the young star of a Broadway hit. Between rehearsals, she allowed me to take her to dinner at an expensive restaurant. Her eyes avoided mine during my tentative overtures, and rapid little twitchings beneath her smiles warned me that if she had not succumbed to a soldier going into combat, she was not likely to surrender to a restless veteran with no foreseeable future. We remained friends for a year or two, but the dreams constructed on the flimsy basis of kindly letters painlessly vanished along with the possibility of sudden death, the essential cameraderie of buddies, and the tight discipline that had defined each day for me.

That left Miss Potter, whose free time was entirely at my disposal. As if the intervening years had never passed, we sat side by side again to watch what Broadway had to offer, and very little of it engaged my admiration: Katharine Cornell's stately Antigone was unbelievably decorous after the fiery young actress who'd played it in Paris a few months earlier; Maurice Evans' carefully enunciated Hamlet, set for some reason in a nineteenth-century European court, was a pale shadow after John Gielgud's eloquent hero; and Gertrude Lawrence substituted a facile charm in *Pygmalion* for the craft of comedy I expected after having seen Edith Evans and Yvonne Arnaud. Only two actors seemed connected to recognizable aspects of life, one beginning his career, the other near the close of hers: Marlon Brando, with an immediacy of behavior that was once his greatest talent, bending over to tie his shoestrings during one of Miss Cornell's more earnest speeches in *Candida*; and Laurette Taylor, incandescent with foolish pride and maternal obstinacy in *The Glass Menagerie*. I went back to see Tennessee Williams' play twice again alone, to be free for the tears that purged me of my chronic dejection, whose key seemed somehow buried in that drama of dependent mother and rebellious son. Returning to my hotel room after a matinée, I impulsively changed into my uniform, slung my duffle bag over my shoulders, and took a train home.

Somewhere between Albany and Crescent, a girl settled next to me in the chilly coach and spread her fur coat over both of us. She was on her way back to a convent school in Montreal after spending a holiday with her family. Through the night, we shared cigarettes and the flask she carried in her purse. She got off with me at Crescent, where, passing the movie-theatre mecca of my boyhood, we found a cheap hotel and registered as man and wife. After two days and nights of exclusive intimacy, one of us a truant from school, the other a truant from life, we could no longer tolerate the sight or sound of each other. Picking our way through the icy streets toward the railway depot, we ran into my father. He gazed from behind his glasses noncommittally during my mumbled introductions. (Years later, hearing the story, one of my brothers guffawed and said, "What the hell do you think *he* was doing in Crescent at that time in the morning?") "Your mother's been wondering when you'd be coming home," my father said shortly. The girl, relieved to be free of me, made her way alone up the hill to the station. My father went back with me to the hotel room, where he sat on the rumpled bed and watched me pack my duffle bag before driving me silently through the snow-crusted roads to Clairepont.

Nothing had changed, in the family or in my response to it. My mother turned beseeching eyes in my direction, but when I bent to talk to her, she abruptly looked away and shook her head impatiently. Gabrielle and Marianne washed the dishes, cooked the meals, and made the beds, glancing at me with embarrassed smiles when I entered the kitchen. Vincent and Floyd happily ran errands and followed me from room to room. My father pretended, as he had throughout my boyhood, that I wasn't there.

My army uniform was hung in an upstairs closet, and khaki shirts, socks, ties, handkerchiefs, and underclothes rested on the shelf beside it. Through the years, the clothing I'd worn in Europe shielded, with shabby incongruity, the growing flesh and bones and manhoods of my younger brothers. Waking sixteen-year-old Vincent for our father's funeral three years later, I found him shivering beneath the blankets in khaki shorts and undershirt left behind when I turned my back for the second time on the miseries of my mother and the mystery of my father, hitchhiked to Crescent, and took the train to New York, which has been my home ever since.

PART FOUR

...in the theatre... 1946–1951

Miss Potter welcomed me back to New York without inquiring into my reception at home. Through friends in social work, she found me a summer job as a recreation counselor in a camp for underprivileged city children. When I returned to the city in the fall, she had located a room for me in a once-fashionable mansion off Fifth Avenue, from which I walked twenty blocks downtown each morning to the cramped quarters of the Neighborhood Playhouse.

The dressing rooms, rehearsal halls, and practice studios seemed to have remained the same while the war had altered the natures of young people and disrupted the world they lived in. Sanford Meisner and Martha Graham still headed the teaching staff, but there had been replacements among the others, including Jo Van Fleet, my classmate of four years earlier, who was marking time before embarking upon her Broadway career by teaching acting improvisations as Meisner's assistant. The most apparent change was in the nature of the students themselves. Pampered boys had given way to toughened veterans, supported by the G.I. Bill of

Rights, who brought from shipboard and battlefield habits of loyalty, discipline, and perseverence. In the locker room, Jan Merlin's recurrent attacks of malaria and the jagged scar left embedded in Maury Hill's back by a Japanese bayonet were reminders of the life that had preceded our daily sessions at the dance barre and in acting classrooms.

What we had learned in army drills was applied to dance exercises (usually rooted in the pelvic regions of the body), which Martha Graham explained with a bluntness of language somewhat at odds with her soft-spoken, precise enunciation. Sitting primly before us, she analyzed not only her own art, which surpassed all other contemporary drama in range of insight and sheer theatricality, but that of James Joyce and Henry Moore, Stravinsky and Euripides, with the single-minded intensity with which she conveyed every thought and gesture on stage. Then, as her assistants, Nina Fonoroff, Ethel Winter, or Marjorie Mazia (then Woody Guthrie's wife, now Arlo's mother), demonstrated techniques of contraction and release, she moved among us, firmly correcting postures and whispering sometimes devastating personal criticisms: "Don't hold your hand like that," she told one of our more languid débutantes; "it means you can not give yourself in love." One autumn afternoon, her accompanist broke into the buoyant strains of *Appalachian Spring*, and she flashed a dazzling smile as we followed her across the floor, leaping like satyrs and nymphs to the music of her great dance drama. Later in the season, she parodied, with a monkey-like mischievousness, how we had moved in our first class, bare toes turned up away from the floor, and then, switching within the beat, how we had grown from awkward boys, self-conscious in our near nudity, to men glorying in the use of their bodies.

Sandy Meisner, impassive as an owl behind dark-rimmed glasses, interrupted our improvisations of domestic squabbles and espionage plots, leaning forward with a faint smile to inquire with unsettling sweetness of tone just what we thought we were doing.

144

Once, impersonating a lawyer quarreling at breakfast with a neglected wife, I used the word "case" with deadening repetition. Fixing a gaze on me that demolished what little confidence I brought to the classroom, Meisner spent a good five minutes ridiculing the meagerness of my vocabulary, the paucity of my ideas, and the limitations of my talent. I shifted in my seat, staring at the floor, unable to defend myself, while my classmates waited for the storm to pass, hoping only that they would not be its next victims. Grown men who had ducked snipers' bullets the year before, survived submarine attacks, airplane strafings, and hand-to-hand combat meekly accepted the destruction of conceits and lethargies because we knew that Meisner could free the talents that lay buried beneath them. In the privacy of our dressing rooms, we railed at him and ruefully nursed our battered egos; we were delighted to hear that the year before Dick Boone had stretched him flat on the floor during a classroom dispute. Boone merely smiled ambiguously when we approached him for confirmation of the rumor that gave us so much pleasure.

Louis Horst, still the image of the proverbial music master, sat at his piano, peering benignly through tiny spectacles, as we danced the solos, duets, and trios we composed for his approval. Resting his fingers lightly on the keyboard after yet another exhibition of perspiring arms and legs entangled in simulated intercourse, Horst would sigh, grin, and mutter, "It's far, far better to have failed your Wassermann than never to have loved at all."

In Van Machlin's speech-technique classes, we hummed and moaned, shouted, whispered, and sang to strengthen our voice projection, while that earnest woman halted before us, held her hand upon our stomachs to make sure we were breathing correctly, and peered into our open mouths to locate the source of our inadequacies. Across the hall, Carol Veazie, an imposing lady of uncertain years, abundant red hair, and overripe diction, coached us in speech interpretation; we read poetry and rehearsed scenes from Shakespeare between her rambling anecdotes about her great and good friends, Judith (Anderson) and Robbie (Jeffers).

Working hard under unrelenting taskmasters, we did the best we could, and some of us did much better than we ever thought we could. Few of us would ever be modern dancers, but we practiced leaps and falls, *entrechats* and *pliés* as if that was our total ambition; few of us would ever become Shakespearean actors, but we diligently repeated exercises to expand diaphragm support for voice projection and the tongue-twisting verses that trained us to speak clearly and audibly. Few of us, as a matter of fact, ever became actors at all, but we brought to our classes a strength of purpose and ability to work hard that I had not noticed in my earlier term in the school. We worked hard, but our instructors worked even harder: the singing teacher tried for a full year to teach me to stay on key before he resigned himself, as Donnolly and Doran had two years earlier, to the indisputable fact that some people really are tone deaf.

We tried, even the least talented of us, to be as good as they insisted we could be. We believed in ourselves, and in each other, and in the theatre we were being trained to enter. In the locker room, as we stripped off our leotards and changed into street clothes, we were still individual men within a band of men, as we had been for the past several years, united in a common purpose, accepting our differences with the tolerance of a patrol group. We paired off, as we had in barracks and on shipboard, to work on scenes together (Jan Merlin's Hamlet to my Claudius, Jack Howard's Othello to my Iago, Ben Malek's Richard II to my Bolingbroke), and grew to depend upon each other outside the school as well as within its walls. Jan Merlin, an impudent, slim Navy veteran, became my buddy. Like me, he came from a poor family; he was born in the basement of a church on the lower East Side of the city I had adopted at seventeen. Like me, too, he never mentioned his brothers and sisters, having jettisoned them, or been jettisoned by them, during his pursuit of the ambition

146

that must have been as alien to them as mine was to my family. Unlike me, however, he maneuvered his way through the corridors with a confident finesse, responding with an ingratiating grin to praise and with a sullen closed-off wariness to criticism. His hard-working mother, whose Polish accent and prominent gold front teeth set her apart from the occasionally glimpsed mothers of other students, included me in her unfaltering devotion to her mettlesome son, and fed me along with him several evenings a week on whatever his limited veteran's allowance permitted her to serve.

The girls, of course, did not share a common background of wartime service. Some of them were privileged daughters from sheltered homes, like pretty blond Mary Fickett, whose father was a radio producer; Charlotte Beckwith, a demure girl whose parents were genteel New Yorkers; extroverted Paula Morgan, whose father was a West Coast industrialist; and sardonic Patty Datz, who came from a wealthy suburb in Pennsylvania. Eager and amiable, these products of finishing schools and college campuses hesitated to plunge with us into the wider life we were told was essential if we were ever to become good actors. Other girls, on scholarship, had left homes behind them to live, as the boys did, from hand to mouth. They allied themselves quickly, if temporarily, with willing boys, but I cautiously resolved to let nothing stand in my way of becoming an actor: I would not allow myself the luxury of romantic attachment. I envied the few settled husbands among us—Ben Malek, whose wife was a costume designer; and Darren McGavin, who joined his wife, Melanie York, in our classes immediately upon his discharge from the service. But our individual backgrounds didn't matter much any more; memberships in country clubs or college sororities, valor on the field, or marksmanship on the rifle range was irrelevant: we were part of another army now, training to invade a different territory.

In early December, a new girl joined us straight from a university

147

campus. Tall, red-haired, and handsome in a vibrant outdoor-girl fashion, Priscilla concealed a desolate sadness beneath a somewhat self-contemptuous surface of ironic indifference. Attracted to her in spite of my resolutions, I bought her soup and coffee for lunch and took her to the movies and the theatre. In the late afternoons, I walked her home through the Park to the room she shared in a West Side residential hotel with a college classmate, before going back to my Fifth Avenue room to rehearse speech exercises. From time to time, I gathered up enough courage to take her hand in mine, which she tolerated with an uneasy smile. Sometimes, after classes when everyone else had left the practice room, I sat waiting for her while she escaped from inner confusion by playing Bach, Mozart, and Chopin on the piano. Her transparent vulnerability touched me as nothing ever had before. I wanted only to relieve the pain in her eyes. I built around her presence in my life a fantasy of being needed and wanted, of being an attentive ear for her unspoken thoughts, an anchor for her baffled gaze. She had just had, she confided, an "unhappy" time with a professor in the university she'd left to come to New York. She confided nothing beyond that and I did not press any further. I was content to walk by her side, to be allowed to look at her, and to include her in my plans for the future. By spring, we were inseparable—or, at least, I was her constant companion. We worked on scenes together and on voice exercises, and became, as actors tend to become when they work closely together, two parts of the same person. Or so I thought.

In despair after Meisner's assaults upon our classroom work, we comforted ourselves by watching scenes performed by second-year students. We hardly knew these determined youngsters who hurried past us in the corridors intent upon their own pursuits, but their work on the little platform stage in the rehearsal hall convinced us that we must endure, at whatever psychic damage, Meisner's onslaughts and Martha Graham's strict regimen. I remember best a long scene from Dorothy Baker's *Trio*. Marian

148

Seldes, moving like a figure from an ancient vase, played a Lesbian college professor with an assured technical command far beyond her seventeen years. In the dressing rooms, this tall dark-haired daughter of a literary family exhibited both a deadly seriousness and a zany humor, an adolescent naïveté and a brittle sophistication, as endearing as it was unsettling. Richard Boone and Barbara Baxley played the student lovers in the scene with her; his raucous laughter and longshoreman's physique were familiar to us from the locker rooms, but the tenderness they concealed was not; she, a diminutive wraith in the corridors outside, glowed with an incandescence we had never noticed in her before. Among the others, Anne Meacham, a legend to us even then, as she is today in theatre circles, riveted our admiration with a resilient energy and an originality of approach that have made her like no other actress of her generation. Those four, along with Kathleen Maguire, Peggy Feury, Fred Sadoff, and Charles White, were the stars of the class that preceded us and were to become stars of early television dramas and the off-Broadway theatre. Aspiring to their skills, we made them our models. Watching Richard Boone in films, Anne Meacham in *Suddenly Last Summer*, Marian Seldes in *A Delicate Balance* during the intervening years has merely confirmed the gifts we were the first to discern when they, barely out of their teens, played scenes from the dramas of Odets, O'Neill, and Lillian Hellman.

Still continuing as my guardian angel, Miss Potter insisted upon buying me theatre tickets I could not afford so I could keep up with what was going on in "my profession." She gave me a season ticket to a newly established repertory company in which Eli Wallach and Anne Jackson, both recent graduates of the Neighborhood Playhouse, played supporting roles to Eva Le Gallienne, Victor Jory, and Margaret Webster. With the arrogant partisanship of youth, we applauded the minor players and ridiculed the stars. There was scarcely a Broadway production in which we couldn't find one of ours to praise at the expense of a famous elder.

We snorted at Burgess Meredith in *The Playboy of the Western World* and cheered the brief appearances of ebullient Maureen Stapleton and fragile Julie Harris as two village girls. Over coffee cups in the Automat, we exchanged estimates of talented students in our classes and in similar ones conducted by Stella Adler, Lee Strasberg, Bobby Lewis, and Erwin Piscator. We knew that among them were those who would replace the names on the Broadway marquees. The most persistent legend attached itself to Marlon Brando, who had created a sensation in *Truckline Café* the season before, and then had played Marchbanks to Katharine Cornell's *Candida*. We were convinced that if he was cast in the right part in the right play, he'd be the star of our generation. Delighted when he was hired to play opposite Tallulah Bankhead in *The Eagle Has Two Heads*, we repeated gossip of rehearsal collisions between the darling of the Broadway theatre and the angel of the workshops who met, with the vocabulary of army sergeants, on the unlikely terrain of Jean Cocteau's never-never land of widowed queens and intellectual assassins. It came as no surprise to us when Brando was replaced by a film star. The old school had won that round, but not for long: we trooped to the opening night to gloat as the play limped to its rococo climax.

Much as we derided popular Broadway stars, nothing could have kept us from going to see them. Their deficiencies proved how much we were needed by the theatre. But it was really something more than that, and was being reflected in other areas outside the theatre as well. Army camps and battleship decks had made us contemptuous of the facility that disguised both the anguish and the ecstasy of life, at least on the Broadway stages. The Lunts purred seductively in *O Mistress Mine*, but we couldn't, even in the furthest flights of imagination, conceive of them naked in the urgency of sexual embrace. We may have admired the resourcefulness of José Ferrer's language and gesture as Cyrano de Bergerac, but we resented not being moved, as we knew we should be, by the humiliations and self-sacrifice the character was intended

150

to convey. In *The Fatal Weakness*, Ina Claire was an object lesson in stage diction and deportment, but we dismissed her as a chic relic from the high comedy of a decade earlier, which had no relevance to anything we had seen in life. Helen Hayes was truthful and believable, even recognizably human, but she wasted her gifts in a trivial play about a drunken librarian. Sandy Meisner spoke of Laurette Taylor and Pauline Lord as examples of intuitive acting geniuses who played, whether they knew it or not, within the method he had absorbed in the Group Theatre, which was the central reference point for our admirations and comparisons. We were being trained for combat against the old guard; already advance troops were appearing on Broadway. Judy Holliday's stubborn humor in *Born Yesterday* lightly challenged the world of corruption we knew surrounded us. In January, Arthur Miller's first successful play, *All My Sons*, voiced our rage at the greedy expediency of our elders; moreover, Elia Kazan directed Arthur Kennedy and Lois Wheeler in the same method Meisner taught us. In the spring, we gathered at the Biltmore Theatre to see Meisner himself in a Russian comedy with two actresses, Uta Hagen and Jo Van Fleet, who became, within the decade, stars of our own establishment. Convinced that the theatre needed us as much as we needed it, we threw ourselves into rehearsals of scenes Meisner assigned us from *Awake and Sing, Men in White, The Children's Hour*, and the one-act plays of Tennessee Williams.

Classes ended in June with public performances by the graduating students. In *Truckline Café*, Maxwell Anderson's melodrama of returning veterans and their girls, Anne Meacham, Fred Sadoff, Kathleen Maguire, Richard Boone, and Barbara Baxley filled the rented stage of the Hecksher Auditorium with violence and despair. A month later, Sadoff, Boone, and Miss Meacham were joined by Marian Seldes and Natacha Dorfman in the stately postures and archaic verse of the *Eumenides* of Aeschylus, breathtaking in costumes Martha Graham had sat up all night to fit onto the nearly naked bodies of the actors. There they were, up there

151

before us in theatrical make-up and costumes, bathed in the glare of stage lighting, finished products of two years of intensive drills in speech, dance, and acting techniques. Fully prepared for their professional life, they went forth into the theatre while we scattered for work in summer stock until we returned to our classes in September.

Jan Merlin and I were engaged as apprentices in a company in Fishkill, New York. We received no salary but were given one day a week off to hitchhike back to New York to sign for the unemployment check every veteran was entitled to for the first year out of service. The Fishkill company was directed by a lady of indeterminate age and fierce temperament named Elizabeth McCormick, who put her stock actors through fast-paced productions of popular farces and domestic comedies. She was my introduction to the professional theatre worker, and she was nothing like the intellectual, dedicated teachers at drama school. Impulsive, impatient, and endearing, she wasn't interested in our theories or our interpretations. Apprentices painted sets, gathered props, cleaned dressing rooms and the auditorium, and very occasionally played small parts. The performers' union, Actors' Equity Association, barred apprentices from playing more than three speaking parts in an Equity company unless they joined the union. My fourth role was that of a photographer in *Three Men on a Horse* who had more props to carry than words to speak. But with it I became a professional actor. Miss Potter advanced me the money to pay my initiation fee, and I waited eagerly for Miss McCormick to acknowledge my professional status with better parts. She, having probably evaluated my talents with a weary skepticism, seemed relieved when I announced that I was going to join Priscilla in another company, organized by classmates fifty miles away.

I arrived at the Maverick Theatre, in the rustic outskirts of Woodstock, one afternoon in late June. Paul Morrison, an instructor at the Playhouse who was directing the company, thrust a

152

hammer and a bag of nails into my hands and led me to a shed, where I spent the rest of the day constructing the set for the play which was to follow the one being performed. That night, my hammer was set aside while a small audience drifted in to see Lynn Riggs' folk comedy *Roadside,* in which Priscilla played with unrestrained vitality opposite a local boy named Lee Marvin, who was making his first appearance on the stage and whose animal magnetism more than compensated for his lack of training in speech and acting techniques.

The artists and writers who made up the summer colony in Woodstock seemed genuinely appreciative of the serious plays we staged, but occasionally there were more of us on stage than there were of them out front. If our productions of *They Knew What They Wanted, Our Town, Home of the Brave, Thunder Rock, Rope,* and *No Exit* were not the standard fare for summer-stock audiences, we were not, at least in our own evaluation, the usual summer-stock actors. We happily played difficult roles, built the sets, painted flats, sewed costumes, swept out the auditorium, sold tickets, cleaned the dressing rooms and the toilets, and split the meager receipts among ourselves after each Saturday night's performance. Some of us were acting before audiences for the first time, putting into practice theories that made more sense in the classrooms than on the stage of the Maverick Theatre. We played parts we would never have been cast in anywhere else, and if we were inadequate to them, we were much too pleased with ourselves to recognize it. The only good performance I gave was in Sartre's *No Exit.* I can't recall it very clearly because I was too drunk to know what I was doing. After a quarrel with Priscilla because another actor was paying too much attention to her, I was found passed out under a tree in the woods by one of the company. He slapped me awake, sobered me up on black coffee, held me under a cold shower, and then applied make-up to my clammy cheeks and shoved me out onto the stage, where Priscilla played out the long evening with me. Backstage later, visiting friends from New

York didn't conceal their surprise as they described my perform-ance in terms no one had ever used about my talents before. I never discovered how I had done it; perhaps the whiskey had unlocked an empathy for the tortured, corrupt man I played. Whatever it was, it eluded me whenever I tried to capture it again. But, having done it once, drunk or sober, I was certain I could do it again if I kept trying.

In spite of determination and diligence, I could not be at ease before an audience, as Lee Marvin, Fred Sadoff, and Jimmy Doo-han were. Ernest Cahn came up to see me in *No Exit* and said he was pleased by my performance. Walking with him through the woods, I blurted out that I missed the army, which at least had channeled energies and impulses I was not able to channel myself. He tactfully refrained from offering advice and went back to New York, leaving me to cope with the free communal life of the profession I had chosen. Withdrawing into daydreams of ovations for my triumphs as Hamlet and Peer Gynt, I evaded the casual promiscuity which is rampant in summer-stock theatres. Girls who cared less what they did with their bodies than how they used their talents changed bed partners as casually as they changed blue jeans, but I stood aside and circled warily the object of my obsessive love. Needing someone to love even more than someone to love me, I gradually made myself indispensable to Priscilla. The frantic haste of preparing a new part each week, the fragrance of the trees at night, the weaknesses within ourselves we could not or would not confront—all conspired to draw us closer. We laughed and drank and rehearsed together; slowly, with mute apprehension, she accepted my presence in her life. Little by little, perhaps alarmed by its intensity, she warmed to the love being offered from the confusions of a nature that had never allowed itself to love before.

In September, we resumed classes in a spacious building the school had bought and still occupies in the East Fifties. More

154

experienced, if not more accomplished actors, we were welcomed back by Meisner, Miss Graham, and the rest of the staff in a general meeting during which the first-year students gazed upon us with the same reverence we had lavished upon Dick Boone, Annie Meacham, and Marian Seldes the year before. At the close of the meeting, Mrs. Morgenthau, who ran the school with a shrewd intelligence disguised by her partridge-like exterior, called out the names of several girls, including Mary Fickett, Lita Dal Porto, Louise Dobbs, and Priscilla. She asked them to stand together against the wall so she could look at them, while we watched in bafflement. Perhaps they were to be told that they'd been dropped from the school, since only half of the first-year class was invited to return for the final year, or perhaps a producer had sent out a call for actresses. Mrs. Morgenthau asked each girl how tall she was; they were all over five feet eight inches. Beaming with maternal pride, she told them to return to their seats and then announced that Ingrid Bergman's success in *Joan of Lorraine* the season before had convinced her for the first time that being tall was no longer a disadvantage for an actress. Having disposed of that career obstacle, she sent us into our second year as student actors.

Meisner, glancing at me with habitual distaste, reported he'd been told that I'd done very good work during the summer, and asked why I thought that was. Chagrined, I replied it was probably because he was a hundred miles away from me. Smiling, he turned his attention to a more favored pupil. Sanford Meisner is recognized as a great acting teacher. His former students include popular stars (Gregory Peck; Efrem Zimbalist, Jr.; Eli Wallach; Joanne Woodward; Anne Jackson; Jo Van Fleet; Tammy Grimes; and Tony Randall), as well as hundreds of lesser-known actors (Lee Grant, James Broderick, Elizabeth Wilson, Leslie Nielson, Patrick O'Neal, Brenda Vacarro) whose successes constantly justify his reputation. Anyone who could be taught acting could be taught by him. Anyone except me. A great acting teacher is, per-

155

haps by necessity, something of a bully who rips aside defenses erected to maintain comfortable images. I had lived far too long among bullies, from father and brothers to belligerent vagrants and barracks tyrants; they had bred in me a defensive contempt for anyone who intimidates anyone else for whatever reason. Meisner demanded an unquestioning loyalty I had long since refused to give to anyone, including God. I judged him with the same harshness such men have always evoked from me. My response to his challenge was to withdraw; his response to mine was to give up trying to teach me at all.

Martha Graham's criticisms could be as devastating as Meisner's, but perhaps because she was a woman, I could accept them without rancor. Her steel-edged voice cut through a rehearsal of a dance duet with Jack Howard (my banished Romeo to his consoling Friar Lawrence) to point out that self-pity, however comforting to the individual, is destructive to the artist. Under her guidance, I gradually lost the self-consciousness which had dogged my bodily movements since childhood. She has taught thousands of us, some of whom have justified her efforts by becoming accomplished dancers and actors, but I wonder if even she realizes how often, and how deeply, she reached into the lives of the rest of us and reshaped our attitudes toward ourselves and the place we take in the world. Whatever I learned about acting at the Neighborhood Playhouse, and by extension about life itself, I learned from that indomitable genius whose knowledge of the savagery and anguish in the human condition does not permit her to dismiss any human being. Through her, I learned, and never forgot, that we have only one voice through which to convey the meaning of our lives and it is a violation of life to waste, distort, or degrade that voice.

Priscilla and I were married in the late fall. During an uncomfortable evening in her apartment, Miss Potter begged me tearfully to wait until I was established as an actor. Marriage and the inevitable babies would destroy my hopes for a career, she insisted, and dear Priscilla, whose importance to me she had never acknowledged, would surely understand, since she had her career to consider, too. I refused to postpone our wedding and she accused me hysterically of betraying her hopes as well as mine, but she was in the Saturday-morning congregation at the Little Church Around the Corner all the same. Among the classmates at the ceremony, my brother Ambrose appeared unexpectedly from my neglected past, with his wife. So did Aunt Maude, that glamorous echo from my childhood who no longer symbolized a world beyond my dreams. I had written home to tell Marianne that I was getting married, and she had seen to it that the Lemays were represented at the ceremony. Ambrose and Aunt Maude joined us at the reception Priscilla's parents had arranged at a midtown hotel. My new in-laws regarded my relatives with the same uneasiness with which they regarded their only daughter's choice of a husband. Maude seemed excessively proud of me, embracing me over and over as she drank more and more and laughed with uncontrollable shrillness. Ambrose watched me narrowly over our champagne glasses: we were both a long way from the farm and neither could span the bridge that separated us, in time and preoccupations, from our origins. He left to take his wife back to Queens after giving me their address and suggesting that it might be nice if I brought my bride to visit them.

My bride knew very little, if anything, about my family. Obviously intimidated by Ambrose's lean, mean good looks, she may have preferred to be kept ignorant of people I didn't consider worth discussing. When she inquired about my mother, I said she was mentally ill, and since her own mother suffered from a similar disorder, she hastily dropped the subject. In the tenement walk-up I'd found on the lower East Side, we enclosed ourselves within walls Jan Merlin helped paint lurid red, yellow, and black in a life that did not include her family or mine. Her parents sent on her piano from Washington; Miss Potter returned the books, old

157

Playbills, and manuscripts she'd kept for me during the army years. An impoverished classmate gave us a kitten we named Modjeska, and we placed the gifts of cut glass and silver trays from wealthier classmates on top of orange crates we nailed together for bookcases and coffee tables. On the streets, we found discarded tables, lamps, armchairs, and a sofa, which we hauled up five flights to our almost empty apartment.

A young husband of twenty-five, eight years after running away from home, I shared the first apartment I'd ever lived in and, with it, the constraints and conveniences of living with another person. Life within an enormous family, followed by years among vagrant boys and in army barracks, had created habits in me which were not easily broken. I read books during meals until sighs across the table prompted me to put them down reluctantly. I walked around the uncurtained rooms in my shorts or without them until a delegation of sniggering boys from the elementary school across the street arrived at the door to warn me that teacher was going to call the cops if I didn't put some clothes on. At the first sign of argument or tears, I withdrew to the bathroom with a book. But those were minor differences in the active life we shared. We rushed off each morning to school and returned at night to shut ourselves away from everything but classes and those who shared them with us. Painting cupboards and woodwork, we gestured extravagantly with dripping brushes as we memorized scenes from *Antigone* and *Idiot's Delight*, in preparation for the future when we would replace the Lunts as the leading acting couple on Broadway. Glancing up as she crouched in faded blue jeans and her brother's discarded sweatshirt, her long red hair caught up in the back with a ribbon, Priscilla returned my smiles from across the stepladder and rose to her toes to kiss me softly, while my breath stopped with wild and terrifying tenderness.

When we went back to school the Monday following our wedding, Mrs. Morgenthau summoned us into her office for congratulations and assured me, with birdlike nods of her head, that

158

marriage would make me "less self-conscious," a mystifying remark whose meaning was lost on both of us. Martha Graham told Priscilla in my presence that she had married an exceptional boy and to make sure that she helped him rather than hindered him. Her comment, gratifying as it was to me, was somewhat unsettling to my wife, and I had no explanation of it for her in the privacy of our apartment. In Meisner's classes, Priscilla's eyes sought out mine as he derided my efforts, just as, during our speech classes, mine sought out hers when she faltered in the intricacies of Juliet's eloquence. Leaving school hand in hand, we strolled over to late-afternoon film showings at the Museum of Modern Art to see John Barrymore, Marlene Dietrich, and Garbo in early movies before going home to sit in the lamplight after supper as Modjeska chased pieces of string in the living room and insects scurried along the walls of the kitchen.

My G.I. allowance was increased slightly to cover a new dependent; we lived on it as best we could, eating combinations of canned foods or cheap hamburger with noodles. On rare evenings, wealthy girls in class, who viewed us as courageous romantic figures, invited us to dinner in family apartments on Park Avenue, or took us out to expensive restaurants, but those occasions were infrequent interruptions in a frugal existence. One Friday afternoon, Priscilla cooked a large beef stew that was intended to last over the weekend. In the middle of the night, we got up, took it from the refrigerator and reheated it, and devoured it then and there in our pajamas, going back to bed having eaten more than enough for once.

In spite of its gaudy walls, bare furnishings, and inconvenient location, our apartment became a haven for students who lived in furnished rooms, residential hotels, or in a few cases, with bourgeois families in upper Manhattan or the Bronx. For several nights, the living-room sofa was occupied by the daughter of a manufacturer whose parents quite justifiably suspected her of having an affair with a classmate. We were awakened before dawn

159

one morning by pounding at the front door. Through the peep-hole, we observed her father, shouting a mixture of obscene protest and Victorian moral outrage. We denied knowledge of his daughter's whereabouts or activities and finally said we would call the police. He left, threatening reprisals, and his daughter crawled back into our bedroom from the fire escape. The next morning, he ambushed me in front of the school, striking me repeatedly about the head with his briefcase as tears of parental rage streamed down his face. Mrs. Morgenthau leaned from a second-story window and shouted, "Harding! Harding Lemay, you come in here at once, do you hear?" Only too willing to obey, I tried unsuccessfully to dodge past my assailant, whose tears aroused such pity in me that I couldn't bring myself to strike back at him. Finally, Mrs. Morgenthau ingeniously organized a troop of classmates, including the boy who loved his daughter, to rescue me from my weeping adversary. Later, in her office, as she applied iodine and Band-Aids to the scratches on my face, Mrs. Morgenthau investigated the exact nature of the romance, which had no more escaped her notice than it had ours. The couple announced their engagement in a week or two, but it was broken off soon afterward, and the boy turned his attentions to the daughter of a business tycoon who lived on the West Coast.

A hunger for theatrical excitement intensified our reactions to every situation. Meisner's brutal personal criticisms made men wince and sent girls flying into dressing rooms to bury their sobbing faces in pillows. The seemingly unbridgeable gap between intention and achievement built accumulated tensions that were released in casual matings, which usually resulted in dressing-room dramas of impending nervous breakdowns, abortions, and suicide attempts. Crucial phone numbers were exchanged, boys collected money from each other for hasty operations, and couples who had once left classes hand in hand now passed each other silently in the halls and interrupted work on scenes with vicious accusations of betrayals. Our apartment became the most accessible retreat; we listened, as we consumed the delicatessen sandwiches and wine

160

brought by distressed classmates, to tearful confessions and hysterical threats of self-destruction.

I read the notices of Judith Anderson's triumph in *Medea* to Priscilla over the breakfast table; she confided, with endearing self-mockery, that she always substituted her own name for the stars when she read reviews like that. I repeated this proudly to Miss Potter the next time she climbed the stairs with one of her little household gifts. She turned to Priscilla and murmured, "My dear, my dear, how sweet." Priscilla detested her, and Miss Potter did little to hide her disappointment that I had doomed my future by a hasty marriage. She blindly brought our conversations back to a discussion of my unappreciated talents, and then endured with a martyr's gravity the silence that ensued. When she insisted upon buying us theatre tickets, Priscilla insisted upon paying for them. When she gave me a single ticket, I shamefacedly handed it back to her. She refused to be rebuffed, but each unexpected appearance at our door on Saturday or Sunday mornings presaged a shorter visit and even shorter tempers.

The theatre tickets were missed more than the attentions I had taken for granted for seven years. We couldn't afford to go to the theatre often, and when we did, we went with classmates who joined in malicious condemnation of the old and unstinting praise for the new with all the conviction of self-established professionals. At the school benefit performance of *Antony and Cleopatra*, we dutifully applauded Katharine Cornell's sedate serpent of the Nile but shouted bravos for Eli Wallach, Maureen Stapleton, and David Stewart in minor parts. After a blizzard, Priscilla and I walked sixty blocks uptown to see *Crime and Punishment*, but it was not John Gielgud or Lillian Gish who drew us through the snowdrifts; it was Sanford Meisner in a supporting role and Marian Seldes in a bit part. Envy may explain our rejection of the genuine accomplishments of Katharine Cornell, John Gielgud, and Judith Anderson, but only egocentric cruelty explains the guffaws which greeted Eva Le Gallienne's glacial Hedda Gabler.

Contemptuous of the stylish pacing the critics praised in

Maurice Evans' *Man and Superman,* we were outraged when the same critics dismissed Michael Redgrave's raunchy, barbarous Macbeth. We filed backstage, casting admiring glances toward the stars, to tell Julie Harris and Martin Balsam, who played small parts, and Richard Boone, who carried a spear, that this, for once, was what Shakespeare had intended—blood, guts, guilt, and hallucination—not the remote poetry precisely enunciated by immaculately costumed mummies. In those airless dressing rooms, crowded by our own kind, we assured each other that Redgrave was ahead of his time but that his time would come, and so would ours.

And so it did, sooner than even we had anticipated. The realities we had confronted in bars and barracks, in spinster bedrooms and in the apprehension of death, stood before us when Marlon Brando whimpered for his Stella in *A Streetcar Named Desire.* That magnetic blending of tenderness and brutality was ourselves, and Brando quickly became the model against which we compared each other. He left the theatre to speed on his motorcycle, with his current girl hanging on behind him, to post-performance parties in our lofts and cellars and attics. His entrance into a room created a reverential hush; those of us who didn't know him well enough to speak to him tried not to stare as he flipped through the pages of a book from our shelves or gazed sullenly out our grime-streaked windows until his girl was ready to leave, having shown off her prize conquest. He was our answer to Gielgud and Olivier: he would play Hamlet, Othello, and Peer Gynt someday. Forgoing the temptation of easy movie money and celebrity, he would carry, until age or death forced him to relinquish it, our torch of theatrical truth, according to the gospel of Stanislavski as taught by disciples Meisner, Strasberg, and Stella Adler. That is what we thought. And so, perhaps, did he.

We made our public appearances as graduating students in Tennessee Williams' one-act play *The Purification,* a smoldering

162

mixture of murder, incest, and sexual aberrations set in the Southwest and, on the same bill, a Greek comedy, *The Arbitration*, in which I played a shepherd who found an abandoned baby in the hills. Once again, Martha Graham sat up all night, needles clamped between her lips, sewing us into our abbreviated costumes. She got no credit on the program for it, and she may have got very little credit from the excited youngsters she fitted into tunics and gowns, but when I've seen her, in the years that have passed, as Clytemnestra, Jocasta, Phèdre, or the Witch of Endor, I remember her biting off thread with the same concentration on a menial chore as she exhibited in her extraordinary dance dramas.

We were released from school in June on a cloud of optimism after a luncheon of squab and ice cream, and farewell speeches from Mrs. Morgenthau, Martha Graham, and Sandy Meisner, climaxed by a great lady of the stage who tearfully welcomed us into her profession. The next morning, we thickened the ranks of actors in search of employment. Priscilla was immediately engaged for summer stock. I carried her bags downstairs to the street, where she was picked up by a station wagon full of unfamiliar faces and carried off to play romantic leads. I climbed up to our apartment to face the first of many separations in our marriage and to try to find a job myself.

After several weeks of idleness, I was rescued by Elizabeth McCormick, who asked me to assist her in a season of popular nineteenth-century plays she was reviving in a tiny playhouse improvised in the grand ballroom of a mansion on lower Fifth Avenue. Having introduced me the year before to the realities of summer stock, she now plunged me into the even shabbier reality of the off-Broadway theatre of some twenty years ago, in which everyone worked for nothing. At the beginning of their careers, actors often waive salaries to be seen in good parts that will qualify them for better, and presumably more lucrative, engagements later. As an unpaid actor, I was grateful for the opportunity. Many years later, as a playwright whose work has been

163

performed almost exclusively under such conditions, I am more than merely grateful that actors prefer to work, even for nothing, than to sit home brooding about the waste of their talents.

No beginner could have had a better guide into the jungle he was entering than Elizabeth McCormick, whose colorful, outspoken candor was seldom tempered by patience or tact. Surrounding her young leading players—Darren McGavin, Mary Malone, Adeline Hiatt—with veteran stock actors who had worked with her before, she guided them all with cajolings, curses, and maniacal laughter through the outdated dialogue and antique plots of *The Contrast, East Lynne, Billy the Kid,* and *Peg o' My Heart.* Her many eccentricities did not extend to entrusting me with major parts, so I appeared onstage briefly as a butler, a mortgage forecloser, or a frontier deputy. Offstage, however, my functions were more essential ones of constructing sets, locating props, prompting actors during performances, and contributing anything that puts a play on the stage and keeps it running. Those ten weeks in a practical theatre situation removed me from the theories and techniques of drama school. I grew to understand and admire the obstinate dedication of Liz McCormick, squinting behind her tinted glasses through the smoke from a cigarette holder she removed only to shout instructions to her crew and to emit cries of rage, anguish, and frustration at her actors and at the world in general.

Actors and crew gathered after performances in her cluttered apartment on St. Mark's Place for fried chicken served by a sweet-natured black maid, Australia, while Liz hunched over her sewing machine, obscured by the piles of fabrics she'd purchased in odd lots on Orchard Street, and whipped up costumes for our next production, or occasional ensembles for penniless actresses auditioning for Broadway shows. How she earned a living was a well-kept secret from most of us. Years later, she revealed that she was the daughter of an old Virginia family who gave her an allowance to indulge her theatrical ambitions. Whatever the source

164

or amount of her income, she generously spread it out over a wide circle of actors, young and old, whom she fed, advised, and employed in summer stock and in plays she directed for high-school audiences. She lives today in a penthouse apartment with countless dogs, cats, pigeons, and plants above a disreputable welfare hotel for derelicts near Hell's Kitchen. At her annual Twelfth Night parties, I meet again actors with whom I began a career in the theatre, and my children listen, with admiration they seldom give their parents, to the uninhibited language which still issues from between teeth clamped firmly upon a cigarette holder.

Priscilla returned from stock in September with small-town newspaper clippings to prove she was a professional actress. Liz cast her in her final production and drew her, along with me, under her sheltering wing. Miss Potter was replaced in our lives. With unspoken accusations of betrayal, she turned to another protégé, unencumbered by a hostile wife. Priscilla and I began that singular process, known only to performers, of making the rounds. Every morning, we set off uptown, each carrying a list of offices compiled from published reports of plays being cast for production. We separated to go to producers' and agents' offices, met in drugstores for coffee, and assumed, when we ran into friends on the same mission, the jaunty bravado which is the trademark of the unemployed actor.

If there is a life more humiliating, especially to a man, than that of the job-hunting actor, I've never heard of it. Day after day, he smiles as indifferent voices repeat a litany of rejection: you're not right, dear—the wrong type, the wrong height, the wrong age, the wrong voice, the wrong man. Under that endless denial, whatever confidence he has slowly erodes, and he turns for comfort to too many drinks, destructive bedroom alliances, and compulsive, self-centered conversation. He assumes familiarity with celebrities, casually using nicknames for people he doesn't know well enough to call by their first names if he knows them at all— "Gadge" Kazan, "Buzz" Meredith, and "Kit" Cornell—exagger-

165

ating vague promises into signed contracts and casual acquaintances into close friendships. Like a carrier of disease, he hears and spreads the scandals that enmesh every name in the theatre as soon as it is prominent enough to merit discussion at all: this one drinks too much, and this one takes drugs, this one likes young boys, or young girls, or both, or keeps whips in his closet. He defends his failures by his virtues, and explains others' successes by their vices.

Not that the rumors didn't occasionally prove true. One husky young actor sent a producer's notorious assistant to the hospital with a broken jaw after an interview which he described, in hilarious detail, as the "Perils of Pansy" audition. Priscilla came home sometimes in surly depression after predatory advances from both men and women. I don't remember such incidents. I do recall appearing late in the afternoon at Guthrie McClintic's office hoping to be interviewed for a small part in a forthcoming Katharine Cornell production. Mr. McClintic was alone at his desk, looking through a script, and, glancing up, he invited me inside. A delicate, nervous man, he told me there was nothing for me in his wife's new play, but he softened my disappointment by chatting for half an hour about the Neighborhood Playhouse, Martha Graham, and his memories of Laurette Taylor and Pauline Lord in the stock companies of his youth. He seemed genuinely sorry that he had no job for me, and asked me to try again when his office announced a new production. His good manners persuaded me that I was part of the theatre; that generous sense of fellowship is rare among the producers I see today as an unproduced playwright rather than as an unemployed actor.

Beneath the routine of the aspiring actor's daily rounds runs a nagging question: What the hell am I doing here? Why don't I try to make something sensible out of my life while there's still time? At parties where the actor hopes to meet someone, anyone, who can help him get his "break," he joins others, like himself, drained of the buoyancy that carried them through the

166

day. Slumped dejectedly in a corner, he passes a bottle of cheap wine from hand to hand, looking up as Jan or Kim or Brooks or Natacha enters with the latest news—Annie Meacham's going off on tour with Ina Claire, Marian Seldes has just signed to play Cornell's daughter in her next play. Hope, the inextinguishable full of all our dreams, carries him high again. If Annie, and Marian, and Eli, and Jason can make it, so can he. Hang on. Wait. Believe in yourself.

While he waits, he earns money to support himself on whatever temporary work he can find, leaving it at a moment's notice to go off to audition for his big break. He dozes behind a night clerk's desk in a shabby hotel, runs an elevator, stands behind a Christmas counter in a department store, types scripts he'll never be called to read for, solicits magazine subscriptions by phone, and earns a couple of dollars by reading cue lines for a friend, no more or less talented than he is, who has landed a lead in a Broadway play. Month after month, he uneasily ignores the twinges in his teeth, patches his shoes with masking tape, and turns the frayed collars on his shirts, convinced that his talents will be recognized tomorrow in some producer's office, or the day after. However he earns the money to pay his rent, he lists himself as an actor when applying for a library card. The theatre is his profession; all other means of support are transitory.

My odd jobs included all the usual ones, and some odd assignments organizing dramatic clubs and reading groups in settlement houses, and stamping books and filing cards in the branches of the public library. Through them all, I stole an hour or two to keep appointments for my real vocation, until my employers could no longer tolerate the halfhearted attention they received in return for the salary I desperately needed to keep us afloat. Among other jobs, Priscilla and I posed in the nude for artists, almost as broke as we were, who somehow managed to scrape together the few dollars we took home. We gave up posing for artists after an unsavory session with a lady sculptor in a private studio, where it gradually became clear that the unusually high fee was for a performance rather than for a pose. Liz McCormick, a veteran of defeats and disappointments herself, invited us in for Australia's chicken-and-rice, created dresses for Priscilla on her Singer, nursed our aspirations, and pampered our bruised egos. She once sent us by limousine with other out-of-work actors to a Long Island estate, where, costumed as Tyrolean villagers, we waited on tables at an outdoor dinner party. Annie Lincoln, a mischievous ingénue whose romances with Brando and Montgomery Clift tended to overshadow her considerable acting gifts, sneaked a roast beef from a serving platter into the hatbox she carried for such opportunities, and the boys filched bottles of whiskey from the pantry. We feasted on the beef for days and substituted quality Scotch and bourbon for the cheap red wine we usually drank.

The winter passed us by. Priscilla returned home from occasional auditions and played the piano with sullen concentration because she'd been told she was too tall for a part, or too young, too old, too American, or too English, too fair, or not fair enough. After reading for the Lunts for a maid's role, she reported that Lynn Fontanne had pleasantly but firmly informed her that she was much too tall. Several days later, we read that our classmate Mary Fickett, who was even taller, had been cast in the role. But Priscilla at least got past the outer barriers into inner offices, which is the first step toward getting onto a stage. A well-known agent sent me to read for one of the sailors in the long-running *Mister Roberts*. I hurried optimistically to the stage door, where I joined fifty others, most of them summoned by the same agent, and many of whom were my friends. In groups of ten, we were herded inside to stand under glaring lights and be inspected by unseen faces out front. Later, Jan Merlin, grinning, appeared at the Astor Pharmacy, having got the part. My envy of his good luck was diluted only by the conviction that if it could happen to him today, it could happen to me tomorrow.

That winter, we began to get work in television dramas. In vast

168

rehearsal halls, surrounded by unfamiliar, formidable equipment, we would be introduced to Veronica Lake, starring in a Maugham story, or to Uta Hagen, playing Lady Macbeth. Stars and extras alike, we plunged into several frantic days before we were thrown before the cameras and our friends gathered in corner bars to watch us on the sets they couldn't afford to own. Live television, with its miles of cables and hordes of technicians, was, in the rumored words of Shirley Booth, "like summer stock, except September never comes." Under-rehearsed actors forgot lines, bumped into the cameras, and stumbled through doors that wouldn't open, or, if they did, usually wouldn't close. Edith Atwater tugged me from the balcony set to another one in the middle of my single scene in a smart comedy, and explained with weary professionalism when the scene was over that our camera had "blown," and she was following signals from a floor assistant I was too nearsighted to see. Television parts didn't pay very much, but it was work. Through them, other actors recommended us for jobs, directors recognized our faces, if not our names, and casting offices called us to read for forthcoming shows.

After a winter of hardly working at all, we spent the summers in stock companies where we worked without pause. From our summer salaries, we banked security for the winter. Coming back from ten-week seasons in Cape May or Allentown, we would meet with other actors to compare experiences and compose résumés listing the parts we'd played, or should have played, to accompany the composite photographs we left with casting secretaries. Friends preparing auditions for musical comedies dropped in to take advantage of Priscilla's piano. She would put aside her Bach and Mozart to accompany them over and over again in songs from *Finian's Rainbow* or *Brigadoon*. Maintaining the habits started in drama school, we rehearsed scenes together not only for auditions for parts in plays but as material that might qualify us for the charmed circle of the Actors' Studio. It was harder to get into that select group than it was to get a part in a show. I must have

169

appeared in their dingy audition room ten times, playing scenes from *The Sea Gull*, or *The Glass Menagerie*, opposite girls who collapsed afterward in tears against the walls outside, realizing that Elia Kazan or Lee Strasberg had not been sufficiently impressed to admit them into the company of Kim Stanley, Jo Van Fleet, Lee Grant, Eli Wallach, and Brando himself. They dried their tears over coffee at the Astor Pharmacy and, a few weeks later, applied for another audition preceded by the same optimism, and followed, usually, by the same despair.

The essential vagabondage of theatre life nourishes a generosity and loyalty to one's own kind. Stray actors slept for weeks on our living-room sofa, and then departed to move in with someone else, to go off on tour, or to disappear without a trace, perhaps back to the lives they had left to become actors in the first place. We accepted all variations of personal problems—comic, scandalous, and tragic—as part of our lives. Before dawn one morning, a phone call took us to a police station where a young actor who had become friends with Priscilla in stock was booked for murdering his father, an actor himself who had deserted his family long before and recently returned to share his son's apartment. The boy, who had always seemed rather mild-mannered when he shared meals with us, sobbed out a confession that he had hammered his father's head to a pulp after submitting to sexual advances in the middle of the night. We spent the day arranging for bail, locating a lawyer, and soliciting money from friends and relatives. He was released eventually, but we never saw him again. Another friend was arrested on charges of stealing jewelry from a friend's apartment, and another was found beaten to death in a Greenwich Village alley. Distraught girls requiring abortions showed up in hysterics at the apartment door, and we calmed them down before initiating the series of underground phone calls that got them to doctors in Pennsylvania or New Jersey. Romantic crises, burglaries, suicide attempts, and assaults on homosexuals sent us to hospital wards, police stations, and, in several cases,

170

funeral parlors. But some of our friends were luckier. A few, coming into sudden fortune with a Broadway hit or a film contract, called us over to go through discarded wardrobes to see what we could use. Priscilla took armloads of skirts, blouses, suits, dresses, and coats to Liz McCormick's apartment to adjust hems and repair the ravages of wear while other men's jackets hung loose across my shoulders and their trouser cuffs flapped against my shoes. The petty economies of poverty forced us to postpone buying underclothing, to turn up frayed shirt cuffs, mend seams, and borrow clothes that would give us the air of prosperity when we stepped into casting offices. Summer-stock actors supplied their own wardrobes. Every June brought a frenzied exchange of fur pieces, evening gowns, ill-fitting tuxedos and double-breasted pin-stripe suits. When our shoes wore out, we picked up a note from Actors' Equity entitling us to a new pair from a chain shoe store, a legacy from a one-time actor whose will had remembered the footsore companions of his youth. We inspected the displays in the window to make selections before we entered, hoping to avoid the condescending stares of shoe clerks, some of whom were actors themselves, and the embarrassment of meeting friends on the same mission. It was necessity itself, not a new freedom in personal style, that made T shirts and blue jeans the uniform of the struggling actor. Hundreds of us wore the casual garb that Brando popularized; the unexpected vision of the newly prosperous actor in his well-fitted suit and new suède shoes sent us back to our shabby tenements convinced that our prosperity, too, was within reach.

Since actors work together with an intimacy unknown to most people outside the bedroom, it's not surprising that their onstage lives dominate those offstage. The actor exists within a feverish immediacy of emotional response and physical sensuality. Friendships blossom quickly, sometimes passionately, to end abruptly when companies disband in a flurry of promised phone calls, weekly reunions, and continued fellowship. Tomorrow is the cru-

171

cial word to the actor, not today, and certainly not yesterday. Tomorrow brings another engagement; another engagement brings new friends; new friends supply the narcotic intimacies through which past disappointments are buried and the forebodings of the future ignored. Watching actors embrace each other today in theatre lobbies and in restaurants, I am touched as I never used to be by the naked vulnerability beneath the casual gestures and language of love. I am more in sympathy with the tenacious protection of one's dreams, even at the cost of carelessly used bodies and emotions, now that I no longer try to maintain that particular dream myself.

Marriage between young actors is a series of separations interrupted by domesticity. Loneliness adds yet another stress to lives already strained by too little money and too many thwarted hopes. As summer stock put distances between Priscilla and me, we began to rely upon others to accommodate personal weaknesses and to bolster our professional ambitions. I can only speak of my own deceits. I don't know, and no longer care, if hers were as numerous or as degrading as mine. We had been married almost three years when we overheard in the next restaurant booth our best friend gleefully cataloguing the betrayals we inflicted upon each other in our marriage. We rose to face him in the best Noel Coward manner, and swept out. Later he pretended he'd been talking about another couple, and we pretended to believe him.

While Priscilla was in stock, I became that sought-after social asset, the extra man, at dinner parties and in theatregoing groups. The time I spent with older women was no threat to my marriage but a fawning, self-serving use of the loneliness and terrors that old age brought to once-beautiful, once-famous actresses. One of them was Jane Cowl, who had been a favorite of my first Manhattan playgoing season ten years earlier. No longer the popular star she'd been for thirty years, she woke young acquaintances from their sleep insisting that they take her to late-movie showings or come up to her apartment to play two-handed bridge or Monop-

172

oly. A woman of extravagant gestures and compulsive conversation, she was good company for a short time. She bored easily, and so did I, and she dropped me for other midnight companions and escorts. Late in the summer, I made my way toward her in a theatre lobby, but turned away when I realized that she couldn't place me among the parade of young men who had provided similar social services for her over the years.

I had my own loneliness to assuage. I continued a hobby, started in boyhood, of copying the casts of films from fan magazines. I used to hide them in boxes and tin cans within silos and sheds so my brothers wouldn't find them and destroy them. One of the few possessions I brought to the city with me was a cardboard box of index cards linking my rural life to the celluloid wonderland of Ramon Novarro and Marion Davies. At the Brace home, I began another file, this one of Broadway plays. After Miss Potter returned it to me when I married, it was brought up to date through the years I'd been away in the army. When Priscilla and I were thrust from acting school into the profession itself, afternoons that should have been spent making the rounds were wasted in the public library until I had recorded every major Broadway and London production since the end of the First World War. It kept me busy; perhaps it merely kept me from being busy. In any case, it occupied most of my spare time, in spite of Priscilla's obvious irritation at the attention I gave to it. At parties, she would look away embarrassed as I recited the players in movies from the thirties, beginning with the minor actors—C. Aubrey Smith, David Niven, Mary Astor, Raymond Massey, Douglas Fairbanks, Jr., Madeleine Carroll, Ronald Colman—until someone called out the name of the film itself. Priscilla considered my hobby neurotic. I sometimes have visions of her telling friends today, "I was once married to this creep who had a box full of cards, listing every . . ." Whatever she thought about it, though, other actresses called upon my index cards for assistance in inventing lists of parts they'd played in summer stock to impress

173

casting directors. I began to work on them privately to avoid Priscilla's cool, reflective eyes resting on me as I typed happily away at the kitchen table.

When she returned from her second season of stock, we met Torin Thatcher, an English actor making his first Broadway appearance in *Edward, My Son*. With avuncular kindness, he frequently invited us to his hotel suite to meet other English actors, who treated us with a courtesy implying an equal footing in their profession. Torin's invalid wife sat with a blanket over her knees and talked to me of their early days with the Old Vic and in the English provinces, openly pleased that I recognized the names she mentioned. Torin's conversation tended to be more about himself, and the rumored discord between Robert Morley and Peggy Ashcroft, the stars of his play. We had seen the play, but had never met the stars, who were noted actors in completely opposite methods. Miss Ashcroft's gentle naturalism was counterpoised against Morley's flamboyant theatricality, and we listened to stories about them, and about Edith Evans, Ralph Richardson, and Laurence Olivier, feeling that we were inching closer to the area inhabited by the great stars.

Although Thatcher was a supporting actor in his play, he was a star to us, and we soon became satellites around his sun. Priscilla cued him for his frequent television appearances, and I read to his wife, typed letters, and answered the telephone, making, postponing, and canceling his appointments. We were not paid for these services, but our rewards were considerable. Whenever possible, he insisted that one or both of us be given small parts in his television plays, and he sent us to agents, producers, and directors we had never been able to see before his intercession. Priscilla began to work quite regularly in television. Although she still came home dejected after auditions for Broadway plays, she was becoming known in that small inner circle where theatre reputations are built and careers start.

Mrs. Thatcher was too ill to leave their hotel suite, so Torin

174

occasionally came down to have a quiet Sunday supper with us. Over coffee one evening, Priscilla mockingly mentioned the hobby that kept me from making the rounds. Torin got up to examine the file drawers on top of a bookcase, murmuring "remarkable," and "well, well," until Priscilla joined him to explain various notations. Torin took out card after card, commenting on this Lady Teazle and that Claudio in London productions he hadn't thought of for years. He found his own name, and that of his wife, and from then on we often spent evenings with the cards scattered on the coffee table before us, listening to his recollections. Priscilla never scoffed at my hobby again.

Restless during the long run of *Edward, My Son*, Torin persuaded us to join him in working on scenes from Shakespeare. During his earlier years as an actor, he had played many of the secondary parts and now he longed to play the great roles through which every serious English actor hopes to test his gifts. Over and over again, in our living room or in his hotel suite, we read scenes between Othello, Iago, and Desdemona; Hamlet, Claudius, and Gertrude; King Lear, the Fool, and Cordelia. We thought him, privately, rather hammy and affected. He attacked our colorless vocal delivery and pleaded for more of what he called "panache." We uneasily hid our discomfiture when he contradicted the principles of acting Sandy Meisner had taught us. Beneath our quiet discussions of what we were trying to achieve within each scene was a guarded truce between us. We were too flattered by his attention and overawed by his stature to challenge his views, and if he sensed our resistance, his courtesy restrained him from forcing our disagreement out into the open.

At the same time Thatcher coached us in classical roles, Liz McCormick drew us into her dream of reviving the sentimental valentines and melodramas of the nineteenth century. I spent weeks on end reading once-popular plays, writing synopses for her fund-raising brochures, and making copious notes on how to adapt *The Heart of Maryland* or *Meg Merrilies* for contemporary audi-

175

ences and modern actors. I typed out scenes from dramas about shipwrecks, hunchbacks, ante-bellum heroines, and European courtesans, and mimeographed them in Liz's apartment, then distributed them among prospective backers in the sitting rooms of society matrons who knew "Elizabeth's" family. Annie Lincoln, Priscilla, and I served drinks and plates of tiny sandwiches to small groups who suffered through our mercifully brief performances of scenes from *East Lynne, Billy the Kid,* and *Diplomacy* with which Liz demonstrated the enduring appeal of bygone theatre. To aid her somewhat fanatical pursuit of backing, she enlisted whatever Broadway stars she could persuade: Ruth Gordon, Mady Christians, Basil Rathbone, and, our contribution, Torin Thatcher. When the potential angels reached for their hats and minks rather than for checkbooks, Priscilla and I devoured the leftover sandwiches and gulped down coffee before the sardonic gaze of the neatly uniformed maids in the pantry waiting for us to bring the cups and saucers in to them.

Undaunted by constant rebuffs, Liz had me duplicate the glowing reviews of our summer season of revivals and make them up in handsome brochures. Then, dressed with unusual care in her best furs and with the cigarette holder clamped confidently between her jaws, she carried them and us along with her on forays into the offices of executives "interested" in the theatre and into the dressing rooms of Broadway stars she hoped to enlist as sponsors of the project. On one of these expeditions, she took us to see Ruth Gordon in a just-opened, soon-to-close mild variation on the Candida theme. Backstage, Miss Gordon's quick dark eyes glowed from a mask of greasepaint as she chattered shrilly like a sparrow on the brink of a breakdown: ". . . The critics . . . spiteful, malicious. . . . It's a lovely play . . . isn't it, darlings? . . . Treated like an amateur . . . after thirty years of stardom . . . by nitwits who laughed at Ibsen, too . . . and Chekhov . . . and Duse. . . ." We tiptoed from her dressing room, leaving her to

176

humiliation as galling even to one of the great stars of the theatre as ours was to us.

Liz McCormick's dream came to nothing. The past would not rescue us; we had to turn to the future. Taking advantage of the G.I. Bill of Rights once again, I enrolled in courses at the American Theatre Wing. Under Herbert Berghof's sweet-tempered guidance, my acting improved immeasurably, but my focus began to shift elsewhere. In directing classes, Lee Strasberg elaborated on theories evolved from his years with the Group Theatre with a combination of rabbinical dedication and pushcart abrasiveness. Strasberg was the leading, and certainly the most articulate, exponent of the Stanislavski approach to the theatre, but I had already survived another in Sandy Meisner. I could no more pay obeisance to this fierce disciple than I had been able to do to his equally demanding predecessor. My mind wandered during Strasberg's interminable monologues, but through him, and other instructors in film techniques and play analysis, we got passes to Broadway hits nearing the end of their run, or to failures closing almost as soon as they opened. I learned more by watching performances than I did from teachers. I analyzed the differences between actors in the same roles: Uta Hagen's Blanche Du Bois in *A Streetcar Named Desire*, which I saw at least ten times, shifted from performance to performance in a never satisfied search for the truth of behavior, demonstrating the superiority of the replacement to the competent star who had opened in the part. Each time a new actor played Willy Loman, I returned to see *Death of a Salesman*, and studied the different approaches brought by Thomas Mitchell, Gene Lockhart, and Albert Dekker to a part and a play wide enough to accommodate a multitude of approaches. Torin Thatcher could insist that Shakespeare provided the ultimate test of the actor's ability, but Broadway provided the plays of Tennessee Williams and Arthur Miller and the musical talents of Rodgers and Hammerstein. "Gadge" Kazan

177

and "Josh" Logan were the powers behind the throne, and the Actors' Studio was grooming the crown princes and princesses who would inherit the positions held by Alfred Lunt and Katharine Cornell.

Late in the spring, a group of unproduced playwrights, who couldn't afford to pay a real director, asked me to direct two new plays in workshop presentations in a Greenwich Village dance studio. I persuaded Jan Merlin, Lita Dal Porto, and Jason Robards, among other unemployed friends, to play the leads, and relied upon their talents rather than my own to pull me through. I plunged from scene to scene, deluding myself that I was learning by doing; the review in *Variety* left little doubt that I had it all to learn even yet. However, someone who saw the performances was impressed enough, or desperate enough, to give me a job in a season of summer stock. In June, we boarded Modjeska with a friend, packed our bags, and separated—Priscilla going off to perform *The Philadelphia Story, Dear Ruth,* and *The Voice of the Turtle* in the Catskills, and I to direct a season of "package" productions starring Ruth Chatterton, Kay Francis, and Nancy Carroll, treasured figures from adolescent daydreams, in the fertile hills of Pennsylvania.

Package productions were replacing the traditional resident summer-theatre companies. Film stars, well past their popularity, like Gloria Swanson, Sylvia Sidney, Ann Harding, and Miriam Hopkins, combined with one or two other actors, usually husbands or "companions" serving the same function, to tour a circuit of theatres in plays the resident director rehearsed with his company according to promptbooks sent on to him by the booking agents. Underpaid, overworked actors in the regular company rehearsed the roles stars would play before the audiences, stepping aside when the glamorous ladies arrived, accompanied by specially designed gowns, sometimes maids, and almost always dogs, to saunter through the final rehearsal, which they interrupted to criticize the sets, the lighting, and the acting and costumes of the other actors. A varied lot, they treated me and my actors with contempt, indifference, or disarming graciousness, depending upon their natures. One early talkie favorite, whose reputation was made by playing flower-faced victims of social injustice, paused in her languid run-through of a trivial comedy to inquire with ominous sweetness why a supporting actress was wearing a mink stole during their one scene together. The intimidated ingénue, who had probably borrowed the stole from a new friend in town, replied that it seemed right for the character she played. Our star reached out with feline quickness, ripped the fur piece from the other's shoulders, and flung it straight across the footlights to me, hissing: "Nobody wears furs in my plays, honey, except me!" Another, as gentle in person as she had seemed years before on the screen, moved through the week in an alcoholic daze, silently pleading for forgiveness. When she left, she was the only one who remembered the cast and crew with presents. After a predawn adjustment of the lighting to pacify a once-sultry beauty, I returned to the local inn to find her sitting soddenly at the bar. She insisted I have a "little drinkie" with her, and, hunched over her glass, she poured out convulsive sorrows of lost stardom, broken marriages, and a wasted life. The bartender finally assisted me in getting her upstairs, and we left her sobbing in the doorway of her room, where her "co-star" was snoring naked on the sheets. The next evening before the performance, she looked away frostily from my friendly greeting, and didn't speak to me again for the rest of the week.

In spite of high percentages of the gross receipts and inflated estimates of their audience appeal, our stars could not fill the theatre and we ended our season early. Liz McCormick, learning that my directorial début was over, wired me to join her as stage manager in an arena theatre not far from New York. There actors my own age were performing in the then new arena style, surrounded on all sides by a responsive audience drawn from the mushrooming exurbia of veterans and young executives. Back among my own kind again, I helped Liz present energetic productions of *Anna Christie, Arms and the Man, Dangerous Corner,* and *The Animal Kingdom,* in which Ann Lincoln, Tom Poston, Adeline Hiatt, and Nolia Trammel played with a grace of style and a sincerity of approach long abandoned, if ever known, by the goddesses of my youth.

In the fall, I was engaged for my first good acting job, playing Jack Worthing in a school tour of *The Importance of Being Earnest.* Since the company was a non-union one, I assumed another name to avoid penalty by Actors' Equity for playing with actors who were not my professional equals. The salary for this deception was double what I probably would have earned in an Equity company, but I no longer tried to understand why the union formed to protect actors so often bars them from gaining essential acting experience. Oscar Wilde's comedy was condensed to an hour's running time to fit high-school assembly programs, and the cast of nine was whittled down to only the two romantic pairs and the Gorgon dowager. We also played before men's clubs and women's groups, but for these occasions we presented a full-length Hungarian romance called *By Candlelight.* In addition to acting the leads in both plays, I managed the company, made hotel and motel reservations, and maintained our liaison with the producer in New York and the various school and club officials who booked us.

We left New York in a converted airport limousine, costumes and sets stored snugly beneath the seats, and drove from engagement to engagement through New England, New York, New Jersey, Pennsylvania, and Ohio. My fellow actors, graduates of the same Ohio college, were younger than I and even more inexperienced. The other boy did most of the driving, since I don't know how and only one of the girls was willing to hazard the winter roads. As the girls chattered or dozed, I read in the back of the limousine with the fading light blurring the pages of Flaubert, Proust, and Tolstoy. We parked outside high schools and village halls and hurriedly slapped on greasepaint in locker rooms, stepped into trousers too tight in the wrong places or slipped into gowns too dirty to be worn anywhere but on the stage, and shouted Wilde's flawless epigrams into echoing gymnasiums packed with snickering school children. The laughter came at all the expected places, and we moved through that charade of bloodless courtship like the trained monkeys we were. But just beneath the surface of the dialogue and the embraces, my mind sifted over the complex lives of Emma Bovary, the Baron de Charlus, and Natasha and Pierre. I rose early in darkened boarding-house rooms to wander through villages exactly like the one I'd wandered through the morning before. In all-night diners, men like my truck-driver and construction-worker brothers eyed me contemptuously and waitresses resembling my sisters winked over my head to them as they poured my breakfast coffee.

After a Friday morning performance in a school near the Canadian border, two giggling girls came backstage to introduce themselves as my first cousins. They took me home with them to see their mother. We were not due in another town until late Sunday night, and Aunt Cécile persuaded me to drive with her the next day to visit my parents. Over three years had passed since I'd last been home. My mother, mumbling fragments of prayers and curses in her rocker, didn't know or care which son this was who unexpectedly bent down to kiss her cheek. My father motioned me outside and took me to the corner bar, where we talked alone for several hours for the first time in my life. Mother was now hopelessly insane: he dressed and undressed her, cooked meals for the children, and maintained the household as well as his badly paying job in the village creamery allowed. Gabrielle had escaped into marriage with a local boy at seventeen. The boys had left home as soon as they could, and only three children still lived in the house. Taking my checkbook from my pocket, I wrote a check for three hundred dollars (already inventing explanations for Priscilla) and pushed it into his hand. He looked at it for a moment and then wordlessly tore it into pieces and let them fall to the floor. We stared at each other: a rancid defeat, mingled with defiance, gazed back at me from eyes I'd never looked into closely before. "I can't take money from you," he mumbled finally. "Why not?" I asked. "Of all my boys," he told me tonelessly, "you're the only one I've never liked." He pushed away the five-dollar bill I offered to the woman at the bar and paid for the beers himself. We walked silently through the ruts back to the kitchen, and a few minutes later Aunt Cécile drove me to my hotel a hundred miles away.

Three weeks later, I found a telegram under the door of my hotel room when I returned from a performance. Forwarded from Priscilla in New York, it was from my brother Ambrose, and read simply: "Dad found dead. Come home if you can." An unusually subdued Rudolph met me in Crescent and drove me to the house. The kitchen, deserted a few weeks earlier, was crowded with brothers and their wives, sisters and their husbands. From a neighbor's house, I telephoned Priscilla in New York and asked her to come to the funeral. She refused: she had an important audition the next day. Standing outside the kitchen door in the falling snow, I could justify her refusal (she had never met my parents, she had seldom even heard me mention them; it was my life, not hers), but I could not think of an explanation for my brothers and sisters. I left them to the family gossip, the card games, and the shots of whiskey through which they numbed their reactions to our common loss, and made my way to the funeral parlor to what remained of the man I had never allowed to be my father. I removed my glasses so I couldn't see that rouged and powdered face and the discoloration where the rope he had knotted around his neck had bruised his skin and ended his life. I cried that night as I had never cried before and have never since, leaving his company only when others came to sit with his body, driving me outside where impotent tears froze on my cheeks as I walked the desolate, ice-crusted roads I had always detested.

182

After the funeral, we gathered in the kitchen to decide what to do with the mother who muttered curses at us from her chair and hummed French lullabies with which she had once rocked each of us, in turn, to sleep in her lap. Our fruitless discussion opened hidden wounds. I escaped, as I always had, by not listening, or speaking, or seeing any of them. When it was over, Evangeline's husband drove me back to the railroad station so I could go on entertaining Ohio school children and Kiwanis clubs.

The touring company disbanded in the late spring. I returned to New York, after playing for thirty weeks one of the best roles ever written, and I had learned only that I did not like acting. I didn't like audiences or other actors, and I most particularly did not like myself, as an actor or as anything else. I knew that I was a mediocre actor and, realizing that, I understood why friends who had come to see us when we played near New York talked about everything but my performance when they paid their duty calls to the lunchrooms where we changed costumes. Among them were any number of actors who could have played Jack Worthing much better than I, and who needed the money and the work just as badly. Priscilla, who had seen it early in the tour, never mentioned it. When we talked about my career, which wasn't often, she hinted that perhaps I'd find "more satisfaction" in directing than in acting. We didn't pursue the subject: I could not demand respect from others for something that no longer aroused respect in me.

There was nothing else I knew how to do. Looking backward, I saw the family I had discarded for a life I not only didn't like but wasn't any good at. Looking forward, I saw the bleak prospect of unemployment and incompetence as an actor, and no alternative, in my late twenties, through which I could satisfy what had always been a strong desire to excel. It became clear that I had always known I was pursuing the wrong profession. My resistance to brilliant teachers, evasion of making rounds, burying myself in recording theatrical performances rather than seeking opportunities to perform—all these had been unconscious acknowl-edgments that my desire to be an actor was not rooted in talent or in genuine ambition. During months spent in futile attempts to escape what I could no longer escape, I read book after book, picking one up as I let the one I'd finished drop to the floor. But the writers I read—Capote, Mailer, Carson McCullers—intensified the despair I sought to numb by reading them. I scrubbed the floors and the bathroom, made war against the cockroaches in the kitchen cabinets, shined the windows, painted the woodwork, but no matter how I occupied my energy, my mind remained a vacuum, emptied of fantasies of ovations and rave reviews that had filled it from childhood. Like several of my brothers, I turned to whiskey, but my stomach, unlike theirs, closed that family route. Concealing her growing distress, Priscilla left each morning to make the rounds before I got up and brought friends home to divert me with games of bridge and Monopoly until we stum-bled, exhausted, into bed. I'd wake forlornly in the dark to find my wife in her pajamas at the window, crying softly, an eerie ghost of my mother silently sobbing by the farmhouse door in her flannel nightgown as her adolescent sons returned from mid-night visits to the girls down the road. Unable to comfort my wife as I'd been unable to comfort my mother, I pretended to be asleep until she came back to bed.

I gave up all pretense of looking for an acting job and buried myself instead in my card file, leaving the apartment only to walk uptown to the public library and gather information about pro-ductions from the beginning of the century to the end of the First World War. Priscilla came home, irritated, from late-afternoon rounds, smiled tensely on her way past me seated at the kitchen table surrounded by notes and cards, and played Bach on the piano in the living room. All winter long, I typed out names of actors long dead and titles of plays long forgotten. Priscilla went out to dinner and to parties without me, came home late at night, and avoided my eyes over breakfast. One night, I was awakened by a mutual friend telephoning with tactless urgency, reporting that my wife was about to make a fool of herself with an older, somewhat notorious character actor. I slammed the receiver down in his ear and went out into the kitchen to type index cards until she came home.

One of her close friends, married to one of mine, stopped by to borrow a book, and provided an unexpected occasion for revenge upon both our mates. In her husband's bed, or in my wife's, we continued our shabby couplings. If Priscilla knew or suspected, she was too proud to admit it. When we were with others, we assumed the roles of a devoted, affectionate pair. We had solved, like the civilized people we were, the essential problem of our marriage. Priscilla seemed less concerned about her marriage, actually, than she was about a career that had not moved beyond summer-stock engagements. At least, that is what I believed then. Now I am not certain of anything about our life together. She withdrew often into long silences, some of which lasted for a week at a time. When we did speak, it was usually in disagreement over actors. Taken by friends to see Edith Evans during the brief Broadway run of her London triumph *Daphne Laureola*, we disagreed politely in front of others about the performance. Alone in our apartment, the disagreement terminated when she threw her highball glass at me and stalked into the bedroom. I spent the night in the living room with my card file and a bottle of whiskey. We made up sheepishly the next morning, but soon Uta Hagen in *The Country Girl* or John Gielgud in *The Lady's Not for Burning* triggered off yet another round of insults, suspicions, and disparagement hidden behind our praise and condemnation of the talents and ambitions of others.

Oddly enough, there were interludes between explosions of accumulated ugliness when we reached a tenderness with each other we had never known before. She made it clear that she didn't care how I compensated for the discontinuance of our own intimacies, if it was done discreetly, and if it made me happier.

185

She sometimes sat by the living-room sofa, which was now my bed, and softly sang me to sleep. Our lives began to feed upon our weaknesses, not our strengths, and we did not plan to live apart. She was proud, talented, and vulnerable; I could not allow her to become one of those disgruntled actresses we both knew who worked behind counters or in offices during odd hours, slowly eroding into bitter echoes of their former selves. I might not be a good actor, but she was. If we put aside our individual weaknesses, we could find a mutual strength through which she, at least, could fulfill her ambitions. There were numerous examples in theatre marriages of the success of such relationships. We would try.

Summer separated us again. She went to Chicago to play leading roles. I stayed behind in the apartment with Modjeska, reading popular novelists who revealed, if little else, that other lives were more unbearable than my own. Walking through the streets, by the East River, past warehouse and bridges and docks, I traced and retraced the maze of my childhood which, no matter how I tried to reorder it, led me into the maze of my maturity. Admitting my marriage was a failure meant admitting my life was a failure, and that would throw me back upon the nature I had evaded since seeing my first movie and reading my first book. For as long as I could remember, anything on the screen or on a stage had always been more believable than what I saw around me in my own life; but now everything on a stage flung the inescapable facts of my life back into my face. Maureen Stapleton as an alcoholic wife drove me weeping from the theatre with the vision of my mother drunkenly slumped across our kitchen table. The sophisticated prattle of *The Cocktail Party* rubbed my nose in the sterility of my own marriage. Nothing in that world that had led me from my family so long ago could now free me from an obsessive preoccupation with a suicide father, an insane mother, a baby-talking adolescent brother, and a marriage consuming itself in mutual narcissism.

186

After lengthy family consultations by letter and telephone, my mother was admitted into a state asylum, and her two youngest sons placed with older sisters. Marianne, the youngest of the girls, who had cared for my mother after my father's death, married in her teens and moved to Queens, where Ambrose and his wife were living. Gabrielle and her husband lived in Connecticut, where they worked as attendants in a state mental hospital. The family which had always been conveniently distant from me was gathering in my immediate vicinity. We began to see each other, tentatively at first and then regularly. Each of us locked within himself his response to a father who'd escaped life by hanging himself and a mother who'd escaped it through insanity. I do not know, nor have I ever asked, how they coped with it, but asleep or awake, I could not shake the specter of my father's body swinging from a beam in the cellar, or shut out the echoes of my mother screaming in an asylum ward. I lived, unable to talk about them even with those who shared them with me, among shadows stretching back to the night I'd run away from home, and even before.

My friends must have been aware that I was rapidly heading for some kind of breakdown, but Liz McCormick was the only one who did something about it. She recommended me to Margaret Anglin, who was looking for someone to help her in a theatrical project, and bullied me into making an appointment with the once-famous actress. I sat in the soft afternoon light of Miss Anglin's living room while her grotesquely mascaraed eyes roamed over me, as if in search of something she had lost, and moistly painted lips explained the project to me. Then in her mid-seventies, she planned to return to the stage after an absence of nearly ten years, and she wanted me to help her adapt Pinero's Victorian farce, *Dandy Dick*, as a vehicle for her comeback. Could I sacrifice my afternoons to help an old woman, she pleaded girlishly, adding she would pay me fifty dollars a week. I allowed myself to be persuaded.

187

The work that occupied us those summer afternoons was little more than making changes we agreed upon in the promptbook of the play. "Memory goes so fast," she explained sadly. "What we have to do is rewrite certain speeches; oh, not mine, but those of other characters, so that we scatter within them words that will help me remember my own." It soon was evident that all she really wanted was to be onstage again, no matter who spoke the lines. When I objected that a line was much too effective to be given to another character, she said it didn't matter. She no longer cared if her speeches were long or short, or if she had any speeches at all. If she was on the stage again in the company of other actors, visible to an audience once more, her life would not, could not, be over yet.

Until she was before that audience she longed for, she settled for my attention. After several hours of work on *Dandy Dick*, she became, within the protective shadows of that pleasant room, the great lady of the stage once more. She had known Mrs. Pat, and Duse, and Bernhardt, Coquelin, Henry Irving, and Ellen Terry; names that crowded my card file filled her memories. Fingering the amber beads that swung against the crêpe of her lavender tea gown, she repeated gossip and recalled ovations of fifty years earlier: Ellen Terry was charming, but she could never remember her lines; Duse was extraordinary, but only if she was audible, which wasn't often; and Bernhardt was a perfectly dreadful Roxanne in *Cyrano de Bergerac*, the role Miss Anglin had created in New York before "the Divine Sarah" came over in Coquelin's French production. Exhausted by her recollections, she fell asleep on the sofa, her painted cheeks sagging against hands speckled with huge liver spots and glittering with jewelry. With nothing to do, I'd glance through her scrapbooks, matching the yellowing photographs of Medea in tiger skins, Joan of Arc chained to the stake, and Rosalind in doublet and hose to the snoring relic across the room. Looking up, I'd find her puzzled eyes staring at me. She had forgotten I was there but with a childlike trust she permitted me to lead her back into life, until another recollection of

Mr. Frohman animated her gestures, or the scarlet mouth tightened with scorn at a long-dead rival still threatening Margaret Anglin's place in the profession.

At the close of each afternoon, her maid brought us Manhattans. Settling back against her pillows, Miss Anglin reminisced about old restaurants in New York, London, and Paris, riding in the Park with her husband before the turn of the century, Calvé and Emma Eames at the Metropolitan, Owen Wister, Richard Harding Davis, and William Vaughn Moody, playwrights, politicians, and poets. With the actor's exaggerated respect for literal accuracy, she complimented me when I mildly corrected a name or a title for her. "A most unusual asset in the theatre, that memory of yours," she told me. "You should be proud of it."

I told her that it didn't do me much good in the theatre.

"There's a world outside the theatre, you know," she retorted with unusual asperity. Then she patted my hand and murmured, "An old woman, my dear, forgive me."

Several nights a week, she treated me to dinner in a French restaurant around the corner from her apartment. During one of those placid meals, when she drank three Manhattans and ordered, but did not eat, a bowl of soup, she glanced at me and asked, without preliminary comment, why I was unhappy. Through theatre friends, she had obviously been gathering information about me, my wife, and our marriage. I refused to discuss myself. With a studied indifference to my embarrassment, she leaned across the table and asked, "Is she a good actress, that wife of yours?"

"She's much better than I am," I replied, adding that she made a living from acting, which was more than I did.

She demanded to see a photograph of Priscilla, which I handed across the table to her. She inspected it carefully while I dawdled through one of the many courses she always ordered for me. She waited until I looked up at her, and then said with a curiously dry inflection, "Give her up!"

I started to rise but her featherweight hand restrained me.

189

"Give her up," she repeated. "She's an actress. Good or bad, she's an actress. She has no need for you, except as a porter, or a book-keeper, or a nurse. Actresses don't have husbands, they have attendants." Taking my hand in hers, she gazed at my fingers as if she'd forgotten what she wanted to say, and then smiled with a tremulous self-mockery, not unlike Priscilla's, and released my hand. "No one knows that better than I," she said, collecting her furs and purse, "for I married a man very much like you."

She didn't mention my marriage again. When the new script of *Dandy Dick* was neatly typed and inserted into its folder, she took me out to a celebration dinner and slipped a bonus check into my pocket.

Alone again in the apartment day after day, I made a number of firm resolutions. I broke off with my wife's friend and had no interest in replacing her. I determined to be an honest husband, if not a good one, and to resist dwelling upon the failures in our marriage. I decided to forget what could not be changed: my father's suicide, my mother's insanity, my incompetence as an actor. I would do the best I could. Ironically, now that it didn't matter so much any more, I was offered work. I signed to go out on another school tour, playing the comic lead in the nineteenth-century farce *Our American Cousin*. I adjusted the dreams of a lifetime to the necessities of earning a living, nothing more.

Priscilla came back after Labor Day, subdued as if she, too, had made resolutions. She tolerated my overtures at night and smiled at me with genuine friendliness in the morning. Some inner resistance to our situation had dissolved in her as it had in me; she talked more candidly about her fears and anxieties, about her childhood and its effects upon her. Pleased that I had a job for the fall, she said—and seemed to mean it—that she would miss my company. She cheerfully made her rounds each day, and we met in the evenings for supper with friends and to go to the theatre. If our life together was less exciting than it might have been, it was also more peaceful; we substituted caution for pas-

190

sion, courtesy for compassion, and seemed to find some satisfaction in each other.

Miss Anglin telephoned me in late September to ask me to go with her to a producer's office to discuss "our" play. We rode from the upper East Side to midtown Broadway, and she chatted about how New York had changed since her arrival over fifty years earlier. Her husband, she told me, had walked her home every night from the old Empire Theatre, holding her hand in his like the country boy he really was. He, too, had been an actor, though not a very good one. She paused and then blurted out, "He was too good a man to be a good actor!"

Without warning, she buried her painted face against my only good suit, sobbing out remorse at sacrificing a kind, good man to scrapbooks and newspaper clippings. She had robbed him of a normal life, and of the children he had always wanted and should have had. He died alone in a hotel room, she whispered, while she was acting some foolish part on the stage. She quieted gradually and I held her in my arms until the taxi drew up before an office building. She wiped her eyes, arranged her veils and furs, took the manila envelope from my hands, and we got out. When I turned from paying the driver, she had vanished through the revolving doors.

I walked slowly home through eighty noisy city blocks, oblivious to the sound of human activities all around me, examining for the first time without romantic fantasies the dream of stardom in the theatre that had led her to a lonely, embittered old age. She had come to the end of the dream fulfilled, as poor Jane Cowl had —telephoning young men to take her out to midnight movies. Was that the end that the dream I'd dreamed for twenty years would lead me to? That sterile conclusion to life faced not only me but almost everyone I knew, and the girl who was my wife. In our empty apartment, I tried to find diversion in the card file on top of the bookcase. Standing with a typed index card of useless information before my eyes, I saw myself as I was: a silly, vacant man, avoiding life by self-created dreams. Before Priscilla came home, the garbage cans downstairs in front of the building were stuffed with paper bags filled with ripped index cards.

We moved a few weeks later into a more expensive apartment uptown. There we entertained people who could help Priscilla get better parts in more important productions. At dinner parties, I fought boredom by starting quarrels with our guests. Mannerisms and attitudes which had amused me before became intolerable to me. And I became a man I detested: arrogant, touchy, promiscuous, unloving, and unlovable. All the resolutions I had made a few months earlier were forgotten. Between my wife and me, I erected a dead space rooted in my distaste for myself and supported by the dishonesties with which I tried to hide it. She very sensibly withdrew from me. My rage and frustration desperately sought an object: the sound of her voice speaking to a friend on the telephone prompted an almost uncontrollable urge in me to get up and beat her to death with a chair. Love had turned, within five years, into implacable hatred.

I solved the problem of my married life as I had solved the problem of my family life twelve years before. I ran away. I didn't come home one night for a dinner party she was giving for a director who was casting an off-Broadway production. I stayed in a hotel overnight, and the next day found a cheap apartment uptown. The following morning, I watched from across the street until Priscilla left our apartment house before noon, then went in, packed a suitcase, put my keys on the table in the foyer, and let the door close itself upon me. I didn't appear, either, for the first rehearsal of the play I'd contracted to tour in. Without regret and without pain, I deserted the theatre that had been the single focus of my life since childhood and the marriage that had been my strongest link to it.

...among books... 1952–1967

M_y thirtieth year repeated the pattern of my twentieth. Once again, an older-woman acquaintance got me a job in the public library, this time in a small branch just around the corner from the cold-water flat I had moved into. My working hours were from noon to nine in the evening each weekday, and beyond the undemanding chores that filled the days and the books that deadened the nights, I moved within a limbo of self-pity, broken from time to time by lapses into numbing encounters that ended almost as soon as they began. I can't remember the transient partners in these interludes as well as I remember the books I took from the library shelves each night. Huddled beneath the blankets one November night, I read straight through Faulkner's *Light in August* as I had sat in toilet stalls at Brace years earlier with copies of *Look Homeward, Angel* and *Sons and Lovers*. With no Miss Bromhall to discuss what I read with, I put down on paper my extensive, often incoherent impressions of Sholokhov, Sartre, Camus, Mauriac, and Graham Greene. I retreated again into the vast resources of a library. The only difference between

195

my life in that unheated three-room flat and the life I'd lived at Brace was that I seldom went to the movies, and never to the theatre. I had turned my back on all that.

I turned my back, too, on the daydreams of stardom. Without their protection, I woke in terror and went out into the dark to walk away obsessions with insanity and suicide, retracing the route that had led from pasture paths to cement walks along the East River. Eventually, I acknowledged that the tense girl who was still my wife was a younger version of my mother, that traits I detested in myself were those I'd detested in my father, and that the brothers I had always disdained were not inferior to me but merely different. I had deserted a wife and a career, just as I had abandoned parents and family, because they could not be contained within the fantasies I had constructed. Priscilla, however unresponsive in certain aspects of our marriage, had been far more honest than I; she had never pretended to be other than what she was; I had never accepted her as other than what I wanted her to be. Moving through a blur of work, reading, and self-incrimination, I waited for someone or something to rescue me from myself. If Priscilla had asked me to return to her during those early months, I would have done so gratefully, and accepted any terms she imposed. But, luckily for both of us, she never did.

Just before Christmas, I ran into her in a department store with one of her more fastidious male friends. Face to face with her, I longed to apologize for the pain I had caused but blurted out some brutal, inane joke instead. She backed away in tears while her escort hissed insults after me. I telephoned her later to apologize, but she wouldn't speak to me. We never saw each other alone after that. When I stopped at her apartment by appointment to pick up a book I wanted, she always made certain a friend was with her. She quite rightly shut me out of her life. That the friends we had shared for five years were hers, not mine, was brought home forcefully one morning when the actor who'd been my best man turned furtively into a side street when he saw me approach. I was hurt, but only momentarily.

My sister Evangeline and her husband tracked me to the library somehow. One evening, they drove me through the rainy streets for hours trying to persuade me to return to my wife. My oldest sister, who had always been proud of the interests and ambitions that set me apart from her other brothers, pried into problems I would not uncover in an effort to salvage something I didn't want to save. I listened silently as they both confided that all marriages, even theirs, go through bad times, that perhaps children would bind Priscilla and me together. I could not tell that earnest couple that if there was anything my wife wanted less than me in her bed it would be the children that might result from it. They finally released me on the corner and drove back to their domestic happiness as I turned to make my way to the apartment I kept secret from everyone.

The library was closed on weekends. Left with too many hours to fill, I sought out Marianne and her husband, Lou, in Queens. My youngest sister, a pretty, placid, openhearted girl who was expecting her first child, drew me into her household for Sunday dinners. I gradually grew closer to brothers and sisters I had hardly known. Eighteen-year-old Vincent was living with Marianne and Lou since Mother's admission to the hospital. Introverted, quick-witted, he was an appealing boy whose long silences alternated with impetuous angers out of proportion to any discernible provocation. Once those tensions were released, however, he grinned sheepishly and became again the docile youngster who reminded me of myself at his age. Gabrielle and her husband occasionally joined us from Connecticut, bringing along Floyd, the baby of the family, who lived with them. Gaby, a striking, clownish girl, had married a morose Air Force veteran in Clairepont as soon as she had graduated from high school. That marriage, which later ended in divorce, was obviously full of dissension

197

but Gaby didn't bore us with explanations, or apologize for the quarrels that sometimes ricocheted around the dining-room table where I tried to establish friendships with attractive youngsters I had known only as toddlers. Floyd was a sullen, obstinate boy still trapped in the grunts and stammers of baby talk. His childhood in Clairepont had somehow deprived him of several fingers on one hand. He kept to himself, glancing at the rest of us with assumed indifference, only occasionally allowing himself the trustful smile that identified him to me as the baby whose diapers I had changed years earlier.

Ambrose ran a restaurant nearby. He appeared at Marianne's from time to time but his wife seldom accompanied him. His lean good looks made him a natural object of other women's attentions, and his wife's tight-lipped resentment cast a pall over our reunions. In the living room, where Lou kept the television set turned on loud, we settled down with tumblers of whiskey and rummaged cheerfully through memories of childhood. Of all my brothers, Ambrose has always mystified me the most. His gleaming teeth and dark eyes remind me of our part-Indian uncles; a caustic tongue reminds me, too, that the Mohawk strain is mixed with another from my father. If his wife wasn't with him, he would drive me back to Manhattan. Sitting behind the wheel of the automobile that cost more than my yearly salary, wearing a shirt more expensive than the shabby suit I wore, he sang in his off-key baritone the cowboy laments of our boyhood. He would pull up before his restaurant, escort me inside, and introduce me to slatternly waitresses and slovenly habitués at the bar. As he pressed drinks upon me, he talked of baseball scores and conquests of women, assuming a role of public virility as alien to me as it was somehow necessary to him. Sometimes he made a quick, sharp gibe at my expense, usually at the theatricality of my speech, but seeing my immediate humiliation, he eased his fraternal malice by pouring more whiskey into my glass. Every now and then, he hinted that his marriage was intolerable, but he confided in me no more than I did in him. If I presumed to pry, he would answer with a quick grin, replace the change on the bar with several dollar bills, and drive me across the bridge to my apartment.

Except for my brothers and sisters, the only people I visited were Ernest and Evelyn Cahn. When I showed up uninvited at their Greenwich Village apartment, they ushered me in, poured me drinks, and listened to whatever I allowed myself to tell them. Because they did not pass judgment on me, or on Priscilla, I tried to tell them the truth, but my efforts usually petered out into self-justifying evasions or compulsively irrelevant monologues. No matter how tiresome I was or how exhausted they were, they cheerfully listened to me until I left them to the serenity of their own lives.

On Christmas Eve, I tried to revive the solace of my ancestors by attending Midnight Mass at the French church near my apartment. The familiar choir music, the immaculate altar boys, the sweetness of incense, the mysterious Latin phrases, and the depictions of Christ carrying the cross comforted me until the priest started to harangue his parishioners on their neglect of religious duties. I left him and his uneasy flock and went to stare at the lighted Christmas tree on Rockefeller Plaza and into shopwindows along Fifth Avenue until boredom sent me back to bed to the comfort of a more familiar ritual of boyhood.

By the New Year, I decided to stop brooding about what could not be changed. The Cahns had tactfully suggested psychoanalysis, but even if it had been within my financial means, I doubt that I would tell the truth to an analyst any more than I had to a village priest. Whatever method was to free me from myself would have to be devised by myself. In the freezing January temperatures, I rose early, heated water for instant coffee and for shaving, and began to include among my typed opinions of Edith Wharton and Alberto Moravia recollections of my childhood. Piecing together vague memories of my brothers and sisters, I regarded them for

199

the first time without rancor, even with the affection I had always withheld from them. Thoughts of my mother were free from shame, and those of my father free from bitterness. Without conscious intention, my recollections began to shape themselves into a novel.

I was a very rapid reader who had never stopped to consider how a writer achieves his effects. Before long, the problems of syntax, paragraphing, sentence structure, and punctuation seemed insurmountable but I refused to let mere ignorance impede me. I concentrated solely on typing each morning a dozen pages of incidents, attitudes, and relationships I had never allowed to surface in my mind before. Whether I wrote them well or badly, those pages were the route through which I would accept what could not be changed.

By April, I had finished the rough draft of the novel. I celebrated by splurging on a ticket to a Martha Graham dance recital. I have never fully comprehended what choreography is all about: I don't attend Graham recitals to see a dancer, but to see a human being wresting order from the chaos of human experience. I had seen *Hérodiade* at least half a dozen times before that spring performance, but watching Martha Graham defying anonymous dreads that haunt us all prompted me to revise the pages which put my own dreads into an order I could accept. I had confessed on paper what I had never told another person: that my father hanged himself, that my mother was insane, and that an inescapable contribution to their unhappiness had been mine.

One morning, I woke up realizing I was free of Priscilla. I no longer loved her; I didn't care if I never saw her again. I wasn't interested in replacing her in my life, even temporarily. I was content to remain as I was. Sitting at the typewriter, I stared in wonder at my hands: life was bursting through my skin and hair and fingernails. At noon, walking around the corner to work, I smiled broadly at the staring passers-by. From that day on, I teased the mildly eccentric elderly women in the library who showered me with innocent maternal affection. Baptizing them with nicknames, I ex-

200

changed anecdotes about them with the rest of the staff during our afternoon-tea breaks. We repeated the outlandish tales told by "Congo Annie," an apple-cheeked little dumpling who wore a woolen toque in all seasons, and recounted imaginary journeys to Africa and Australia while she waited, with overflowing shopping bags on either side of her, for me to check out the two books we limited her to because she sometimes lost them. "Mrs. Babble" was a bleary-eyed female version of W. C. Fields, whose whiskey-roughened voice had croaked "My God, at last, a rooster in this barnyard of hens" the first time she'd seen me at the charging desk. Costumed in a fur coat whose bare patches testified to buttons moved during her losing battle against an expanding girth, she peered at me with the insouciant eyes of the happy inebriate, complimenting me shamelessly on my haircut, shirts, and ties. Another matron, whose voice sounded like a foghorn, stood by the double entry doors, her white poodle on a leash, to bray: "Mr. Lemay, take poochie outside so he can uuuu-ri-nate!" In the casual company of these endearing women, and among others less bizarre, I began to look at them rather than at myself, and found them, and myself, far better company.

The branch librarian was a gentle, gracious woman named Emily Davis, who knew my personal history but never commented on it. I told her I was writing a novel, and she encouraged me with the same confidence in my talent that Miss Potter had displayed when I dreamed of becoming an actor. I see now that I was exchanging one dream for another: reading Faulkner for the first time and Hawthorne for the third, I preferred to fail trying to match their gifts than matching Alfred Lunt's or Paul Muni's. When the novel was finished, I took it immediately to a publishing house, leaving it at the receptionist's desk. I was prepared by the rejection that had dogged my efforts to be an actor, and was not too distressed when the manuscript was returned within a month; I left it with the receptionist at another publisher's office, and began to make notes for a second novel. A writer without readers, like an actor

201

without audiences, tends to paranoia; I left a carbon copy of the manuscript with Ernest and Evelyn Cahn. Their comments, while not extravagant, were judicious; Ernest admitted surprise at my honesty in it, which was perhaps the highest praise from him. Probably to demonstrate that I had survived, I called Priscilla and asked her to read it, too. We had a drink together in a crowded bar when she returned the manuscript to me, as noncommittal about my writing ability as she had been about my acting talents. I attributed her response to leftover spitefulness, leaving her to rehearsals of a stock-company production of *Desire Under the Elms* to go back to my daydreams in which Pulitzer Prizes were already replacing Academy Awards.

Now in the habit of writing every morning, I began a second novel, this one based very loosely upon my theatre experiences, an unhappy marriage to an actress, and an old lady resembling Margaret Anglin. I asked Miss Davis for a leave of absence for the summer which she granted without hesitation. Renting a small cabin in the mountains of New Hampshire, I spent the next three months there. Since the cabin in the woods was five miles from the nearest town, I walked back and forth into the village for provisions. The local public library was seldom patronized; I borrowed books that hadn't circulated for over thirty years. During the cool summer mornings, I wrote from eight o'clock until noon, or later. In the afternoons, I lay nearly naked in the sun reading writers I had never read before—Jane Austen, Thomas Hardy, and over thirty of Trollope's "Barsetshire Chronicles." I no longer read for escape but in a thirst to discover how other people had lived, and how they solved their personal problems. Stretched out on a blanket, with the book shading my face from the sun, I read *As You Like It* for the fifth or sixth time out loud and enjoyed it for the first time. I graduated from dutiful reading of Shakespeare to an unqualified delight in his language and characters. Ripe for something that summer, but unaware of what it could be, I made my way through the days, singing happily as I carried my shovel

202

and roll of toilet paper into the woods every morning after breakfast, and staring at the stars through the window just before I fell asleep at night.

On my hikes into town, local farmers picked me up in their half-ton trucks, regarding me with quizzical Yankee forbearance. In my evening walks through the fields, I'd encounter them and we'd sit on rail fences talking, as my father and uncles had, of crops and stock. One afternoon, I helped a farmer named Eager pitch hay against the threat of a summer downpour. He took me back to his kitchen where his wife fed me the first home-cooked meal I'd eaten in months. Later, we sat rocking on their front porch as the sunset moved across the White Mountains like a gigantic paintbrush. Glancing at his wife, farmer Eager offered me room and board for the winter if I'd replace their son who had gone off to the city after finishing school. I mumbled that I was a writer, not a farmer. He allowed as how I could write in the mornings if I'd work in the barns and fields with him in the afternoons. More than mildly tempted, I looked away at the mountains, saying I had to clear up some personal matters in New York. He promised to hold the offer open until I wrote him a definite reply from the city, and went back inside his house. I strolled past the haystacks we'd put up together that afternoon, wondering what my father would have said if he'd seen me ungrudgingly doing a chore for a stranger I had always resisted doing for him.

I finished my second novel and returned to New York. Miss Davis, who had written occasionally during the summer with news of the staff, welcomed me back and so did the elderly lady patrons. I settled again into the routine of stamping out books and filing catalogue cards. One weekend, inspecting Marianne's infant daughter born during my absence, I felt a piercing desire for children of my own, for a life like that of other people. I met with the lawyer husband of a library colleague who agreed to handle the termination of my marriage, and I began the additional economies in food and clothing which would eventually pay his fee. In a week or so,

I wrote to Mr. Eager in New Hampshire, asking if his offer was still open. I got a postcard from him saying, "Sure is."

Buried in the harmless chatter Miss Davis had written to me during the summer had been the announcement of her new assistant branch librarian, a Miss Shaw; her description made me anticipate an efficient but somewhat dowdy young woman not unusual among librarians. One morning in late September, Miss Shaw returned from a holiday in the Caribbean. Mrs. Franzl, my favorite on the staff—a frail white-haired woman with few remaining teeth, who supported an artist husband—smiled broadly as she introduced us. Dorothy Shaw was not what I had anticipated. A trim, exquisite girl with a quick smile and quiet speech, she wore no make-up except lipstick, and regarded the world, as she regarded me, with an uncomplicated directness of manner and independence of outlook. It was clear as we shook hands, under Mrs. Franzl's benign approval, that I was not what she had anticipated either. She later confessed that, from my effusive letters which Miss Davis read at staff meetings, she had expected another library male of uncertain gender just as I had expected another, somewhat mannish library female. Whatever our expectations, we could not conceal an immediate, mutual attraction. For several days, every time she caught me staring at her I blushed and turned quickly away, and so did she.

One afternoon, I ended a telephone conversation with my lawyer by slamming the door to the closet which served as a private phone booth for the library staff. Miss Shaw looked up inquiringly from charging out books at the front desk. I blurted out, in explanation, that my wife was suing me for legal separation and support, which, in view of my salary, was preposterous. Miss Shaw looked at me for a long moment and, leaning over her desk, spoke with firm conviction: "Don't let her get away with it," she advised me. "I was married once myself, in Ohio. . . ." She seemed not to notice that my jaw had fallen, and continued, "My lawyer told me to take my husband for everything he had, but I refused. Fight

204

her, even if you lose." Having given me personal information I never would have dared solicit from her, she went back to stamping out books and I returned thoughtfully to filing cards in the catalogue. A moment later, I approached her and, trembling visibly as she looked up, asked her to join me at the neighborhood restaurant during our supper break. She arrived with an older, considerably less appealing librarian, and we embarked upon several days of wary circling of each other until she agreed to a date with me. Our previous marriages had left scars. Hers, from five years earlier, may have been somewhat more healed than mine, but neither of us was eager to risk being hurt again.

Dorothy shared a railroad apartment in Greenwich Village with a college roommate named Barbara King, who was a social worker. They invited me to supper one evening and we were joined by two other girls, both Oberlin classmates, who were obviously inspecting me. I must have passed whatever tests girl friends require of prospective suitors, for subsequent weekends were spent in Dorothy's apartment instead of Marianne's living room in Queens. Suddenly incredibly alive in the autumn sun, I walked from my apartment down to Perry Street to take Dorothy out for a walk or to the movies. Barbara disappeared, leaving us in their living room, where Dorothy sat on the couch and, accompanying herself on her guitar, sang with perfect pitch and muted irony imitations of Dietrich's "Falling in Love Again," or an uninhibited ballad about the sexual exploits of an extraordinarily potent sailor. Another Oberlin classmate lived nearby with her infant son, waiting for her husband to return from duty in Korea, and other friends shared inexpensive apartments in the vicinity. Dorothy drew me with her into a life that resembled nothing I had ever known before, with people unlike any I had ever seen outside of the movies of my childhood in which Jean Arthur and Margaret Sullavan shared easy companionship with boys like Joel McCrea and James Stewart. Attractive, articulate girls and the boys they dated raced in and out of each other's apartments for cocktails, suppers of chili or

205

meat loaf with cheap red wine, folk songs about workers and lovers, and spirited conversations which mingled politics and social concerns with college reminiscences and arguments about books and movies. My theatre background was seldom mentioned. If they went to plays at all, it was for amusement; certainly no one they knew would ever try to make the theatre a way of life, not when real life was so much more interesting. The soldier husband returned from Korea to his wife and baby, and to graduate study at Columbia. Dorothy and I baby-sat while they went out dancing or to the movies. We'd wistfully leave their toddler in his crib, hold hands on their living-room sofa, and listen to Edith Piaf and T-Texas Tyler on their record player.

Dorothy read the manuscripts of my two novels warning me she couldn't possibly evaluate them, but she accepted those painfully personal revelations about my family and my marriage without judging me or them. We worked together every weekday. Each morning, I left my typewriter to hurry, early, to the library for her company. Behind the bookshelves, out of sight of others, we touched hands as if by accident, and my eyes searched her out as she arranged books in the far corners of the reading room. In her trusting, untroubled gaze, I saw the faces of my children, and I knew that we would marry. She knew it, too, although I don't think we openly discussed it. She co-signed for a bank loan which would pay for my release from Priscilla; at the same time, by the inviolable force of her own integrity, she released me from the lies with which I had always evaded reality. I told the truth for the first time; not all at once, and certainly not all the truth—not at first. In her company, I no longer needed inventions and evasions. She was the first person I'd ever known, and remains the only one, to whom I am willing to expose what I really am. When she asked what went wrong with my marriage, or why I was so embarrassed when she mentioned my family, she was neither repelled nor distressed by truthful answers. Her acceptance of Lemay shames and sorrows (a brother in a penitentiary, several alcoholics, insanity, suicide) brought me closer to them at the same time that it drew me closer to her. In Marianne's house for Sunday dinners, she responded to my brothers and sisters, whose tastes and viewpoints were alien to everything she had known, with the same ease with which she accepted her friends, her fellow workers, and the more bizarre patrons of the library. Her inbred tolerance is foreign to me. Content to be herself, she is impatient only with pretense of any kind. After the actresses with whom I had spent most of my adult life, she was the original and they were commonplace.

Before Thanksgiving, Marianne brought Mother from the state hospital up north and settled her in a double bed in her dining room. Evading a direct confrontation between the past and the future, I left Dorothy in Manhattan and visited Queens one Sunday afternoon. I hadn't seen my mother since my father's funeral three years earlier. Although her complexion was ashen and the well-shaped mouth now hung slackly, her high Indian cheekbones and liquid dark eyes had not changed. I sat by her bedside while Marianne attended to chores in the basement and Vincent escaped with Lou to a bowling alley. She was more coherent than I expected, but her memory was vague. When I mentioned my father, her eyes went dull as she retreated behind the senility, or insanity, which protected her from pain. I left her muttering protests, tears streaming silently down her resentful face, as Marianne stolidly spooned food between her lips, as she did with her infant daughter.

That evening, I met the woman who is my mother-in-law. In Marianne's dining room, I had left a ruin whose body had carried mine and twelve others, whose face had seldom worn lipstick and rouge, and whose only piece of jewelry was the gold wedding band which had bound her to a man she had come to hate. In Dorothy's living room, I was introduced to a pretty woman in an expensive suit, her hair attractively groomed, who smiled at me with the same direct, accepting graciousness that I loved in her daughter. I drank my cocktails, ill-at-ease in my shabby sports jacket, nagged throughout our friendly conversation by the memory of the woman I had left behind and by apprehensions that I did not lose for years. I was unaccustomed to love, not only love for a girl but the kind of love which expressed itself easily in banter between Dorothy and her mother. Mrs. Shaw seemed to like me, but she is not a woman who reveals her dislikes; I saw her, however charming, as a likely obstacle to the happiness I wanted.

During the Christmas holidays, Dorothy planned to visit her parents in Swarthmore. She brushed aside my attempts to cajole her into staying with me, and resisted, as she always has, my ill-tempered attempts to bully her. She told me she loved her parents and that she wanted to see them; there would be other weekends for us. Beneath my irritation at being placed second in her affections, I was oddly pleased. Walking back to my apartment after putting her on the train, I realized she was the first girl I'd ever met who genuinely loved both her parents. Priscilla had hated her mother and pitied her father, as I had hated my father and pitied my mother. It seemed to me that if Dorothy did not use love to turn one parent against the other, as I had and as Priscilla had, then she wouldn't turn father against children, as our mothers had done, either.

I spent Christmas Day with Vincent and Mother, so Marianne and Lou could have dinner with his parents. When I arrived, Marianne was seated by her mother's bedside, stroking her hands and smiling, more mother than daughter. After Marianne left with her husband and baby, I prepared a light lunch which Vincent and I ate around Mother's bed. Then he escaped, first to wash the dishes and then to some unrevealed diversion, and I sat by my mother's bed, alone with her for the first time since I had run away from home thirteen years earlier. Propped up against her pillows in a bedjacket one of her children had sent her, she seemed unusually lucid and oddly girlish. She whispered that she knew I would take care of her; I was the favorite of all her children and

I wouldn't let Marianne go on mistreating her. Her customary lethargy gave way to flirtatiousness and quick, energetic gestures. Grasping her hot hands in mine, I looked into eyes I had evaded for many years and told her that I would not, and could not, rescue her from Marianne. She stared at me in utter disbelief, nodding her head at everything I said, hearing nothing. I told her I was getting divorced (she had never seen my wife), and she nodded her head in approval. I told her I was going to marry again (she had never met Dorothy), and again she nodded approvingly. She forgot, I think, the promise she had tried to extract from me, and rested quietly for most of the afternoon. Once, turning to me, she asked with a childlike clarity of speech, "How old are you, Harding?" "Thirty," I replied, and she fumbled for my hand. "You're in the prime of life," she comforted me, patting my hand as she had often done when I was a boy.

Lying back, she muttered something I couldn't understand until her urgent movements made me realize she required the bedpan. I raised her flaccid body to perform that function, which embarrassed me far more than it did her. When I came back from emptying the pan in the bathroom, she was asleep, her face peaceful against the pillow, her breath coming in sharp little grunts. I watched her as I was to watch, in later years, our young children asleep in their cribs, merriment and tantrums wiped from their faces, leaving only blank slates upon which a father (a son?) can write what he pleases. She was still sleeping quietly when Marianne and Lou returned, and I made my way back to Manhattan.

The following Sunday, I asked Dorothy to meet my mother. But just before we were to leave for the subway, I withdrew my invitation. I could not reveal to that girl, fresh from the affection of her parents, that testament to my miserable childhood, so I visited my mother alone. She was thrashing about in bed, ill-tempered, noisy, and blatantly antagonistic toward everyone. Marianne told me she refused to ask for the bedpan until it was too late. They could no longer tolerate the disorder she brought into their household and were making arrangements to commit her to another hospital. I took Marianne's place by the bedside and tried to talk quietly to Mother. It was no use. She had given up. She seemed, for the first time, openly hostile toward me. I had betrayed her, I realize now. I was not going to rescue her, after all. She cried softly, inconsolably all through the long afternoon, staring at me from the chasm of the years. The lost son to a lost mother, I avoided her eyes. We had each reached the end of secret daydreams which had never allowed us to see ourselves as we were. I could not comfort her, and I could no more assume a filial devotion to that bereft woman than she could assume a maternal affection toward any of her children.

She suffered a stroke the following week and died in a Long Island hospital. I drove in a carful of Lemays through a January blizzard toward Clairepont, where she was to be buried between the graves of her husband and her thirteenth child. Midway in the journey, the car hit something in the road which punctured the gas tank, and we sat for hours in a chilly garage placing phone calls to brothers in Schenectady, Niagara Falls, and Lake George, until one of them appeared to drive us the rest of the way. We arrived in Clairepont at four in the morning, and since there was no longer a family house to contain us, Ambrose and Vincent shared a room with me at the local inn. The next morning, we drove twelve miles to Crescent to meet the train carrying my mother's body, transferred the casket to the undertaker, and delivered parcels containing the black silk dress, new shoes, and undergarments my sisters had purchased in Albany the evening before. My mother's five sisters and two brothers were present when the body was "laid out" that night in the funeral parlor, and so were all but one of her surviving eleven children. Frenchie had been killed in Korea some months earlier, and Annabelle was unable to leave an ailing child in California. The rest of us embraced aging aunts and still-vigorous uncles, accepted the whiskey thrust into our

210

hands, and talked quietly through the night, interrupted occasionally by townspeople who shook our hands solemnly and murmured regrets for our "troubles."

I had not seen some of my brothers since our father's funeral. One of them, escorted by a prison guard, was almost a total stranger. He sidled up to me to inquire in a whisper if I knew "W. W." I not only didn't know W.W., I didn't even know what the initials stood for. "Winchell, you damn fool," he hissed at me. I took a pencil from my pocket to copy down instructions he muttered furtively, but his guard approached and good-naturedly advised me to put my pencil away. My brother was led back to the corner to stare silently at his mother's body in the open casket, just as he had stared, under the surveillance of an earlier guard, at his father's. In the small room off the display parlor, I joined my other brothers and various cousins and uncles passing a whiskey bottle from hand to hand. Half listening to the swaggering exchanges between them, I pretended to ignore the jars of chemicals on the shelves behind us and the stains from mysterious fluids on the enamel preparation table against which they leaned to tell their stories.

My old antagonist, the village priest, appeared unannounced from time to time to lead the mourners in the rosary. If I saw him coming, I slipped away unobtrusively to the inn, but Aunt Cécile often led the prayers without him. My brothers either knelt and mumbled the half-remembered phrases with the others or left without excuses, but I sat stony-faced on the sidelines while aunts and uncles stared at Jeanne's unbeliever son who refused to pray for his mother's soul. Between those murmured recitations, we renewed acquaintances long since abandoned. Cousin Jean-Pierre, my taciturn playmate of twenty years before, drew me down to him and, like a baffled child, stared into my eyes. "Your momma and papa were the happiest people I ever knew," he told me, holding me in his lumberjack grip. "I used to wish they was my folks, not yours." He released me and turned away, grief-stricken, still en-

211

vious of the boy who had envied him his glamorous city mother. Later, Aunt Leila herself, now an overripe parody of the goddess of my boyhood, told me her son locked himself away in the county asylum periodically to protect his wife and small children from his recurrent bouts of melancholia. His wife, who sat dry-eyed across the room from him, was our first cousin, the daughter of Uncle Charlie, killed bootlegging when we were boys. Later, in the all-night diner, Jean-Pierre flung a careless arm around my shoulder as he sang "Way Down Yonder in the Indian Nation," to irritate our college-professor uncle, Gaston, who deserted us to get more coffee from the counter. Jean-Pierre punched me lightly in the stomach, and winked broadly, saying Gaston pretended he wasn't part Mohawk now that he could read books.

Ancient creatures in black shook our hands, mumbling they hadn't seen Jeanne since she was a girl teaching school up Bangor way, or at a funeral thirty years earlier in Valleyfield or Three Rivers. They hobbled off supported by younger versions of themselves, and memories of them once glimpsed in similar settings and half-recollected names—Thérèse, Mathilde, Gérard, Etienne, Juliette—flickered briefly in my mind and then were lost again. More than mere time separated us, in our well-cut suits, neat ties, and gold cuff links, from those bent figures in wrinkled "best" clothes. None of my parents' many children lived as their forebears had lived since the middle of the seventeenth century: not one of us was a farmer, none of us spoke French, and only two of us had married within the faith that had been theirs. My mother's dream of the farm as an ideal place to rear her boys had brought her finally to this, along with us. A first cousin lived on the old Beaupré farm on the Indian reservation twenty miles away, but if he was among those mourning the aunt who had spent her girlhood in his pastures, he did not identify himself to us. Twenty years had scattered us from the geography of our kin to New York City and California, to Florida and Cleveland. We had deserted the barns and fields that had nurtured countless

212

generations for offices, truck cabs, construction sites, and lending libraries. That body, resting in a hastily chosen casket in a black silk dress she had never seen, was our last link to our heritage. None of these drab strangers, with faces smooth as leather and eyes quick as birds' in the woods, would appear at our wakes if we had them when our time came. Our children will not be lifted to kiss the cheeks of departed aunts, as we were, and then sent upstairs away from the screams of grieving relatives. What they know of death comes from discovering canaries lying at the bottom of cages, or cats killed on the highway, or, like much of what they know of life, from the television screen. Too late, they will sit, as we did, mute survivors, not knowing the proper responses to bereavement.

After the funeral service, during which a storm blacked out the lights and interrupted the electric organ, my mother's casket was placed within a vault in the graveyard to await spring burial. Ambrose and Vincent went back with me to the inn, where we had slept in a double bed (echoes of distant nights of puberty), to pack our bags. On our way, we were accosted by two border patrolmen tracing illegal immigrants from Canada. Angrily, we protested that we were Americans, home for our mother's funeral. They apologized profusely and went on their way as we stared after them. It was a reasonable, if unsettling, error on their part; we were strangers in that region where Lemays had lived and died for over three hundred years.

I buried my past with my mother and returned to what I hoped would be my future. During her Christmas visit home, Dorothy had told her parents she planned to marry me, hiding nothing about my personal or professional background. She reported that her father was violently opposed to our marriage. He doubted my capacity to support a family, she said, a doubt amply justified by my library salary and my history of employment. She did not elaborate further upon his objections, and my only defense against them were my intentions, but I knew better than he or anyone else how frail my intentions had proved in the past. My salary was less than two thousand dollars a year; Dorothy, who had taken a degree in library science, as her father and a brother had, earned much more. Without a degree, there was no hope of advancement in the library. Trained for nothing but the theatre, I had no intention of returning to that. Dorothy offered to support me during the years it would take to get a degree, but I refused. Going to college did not attract me; even less appealing was the prospect of being supported by a wife at the age of thirty. I demanded only her unqualified faith in me, knowing that without it I am a useless man. My ambitions to become a writer could very well prove as foolish as had my ambitions to become an actor, but I asked her to take a chance on me to match the chance I was taking on myself. Only now do I fully realize the enormity of the demand I was making upon a girl who had been protected from such risks all her life; only now do I fully comprehend, and appreciate, the generous nature which accepted the challenge without complaint or visible apprehension.

My divorce was granted in late January; during the months before it became final, Dorothy and I courted discreetly side by side among the bookshelves during the day, and out of sight of our fellow librarians after work hours. I found a cheap apartment a few blocks west of hers. After work, we went to movies, occasionally to plays, danced in a neighborhood bar, and talked endlessly about ourselves, our hopes and preoccupations. We even earnestly discussed politics and social problems, subjects I had never seriously considered since my army friendship with Mainville ten years before. I began to read the daily newspapers thoroughly, and books by Rachel Carson, C. W. Ceram, and Margaret Mead alternated with the novels that had always been my exclusive reading. At parties crowded by well-tailored, well-barbered graduates of the best colleges, I became restive under evaluating eyes. The inevitable question after introductions was "Where did you go to school?" My first reply was an ill-tempered "Clinton County Reform School." Dorothy whispered that I'd better find another alma mater, since that institution served only girls. I played a game from then on, saying simply "Brace," and watched cynically as some placed that home for vagrant boys as a college in Ohio, others nodded vaguely in recognition, and still others pretended to know other alumni. Dorothy, shepherding me through this alien territory, smiled in acknowledgment of my automatic hostility to the sort of men she might have married. She accepted the gaps in my education much more lightly than I did. After a vehement party argument about Asian politics, she sent me an atlas that clearly indicated the separate states of Pakistan which had been unknown to me the night before. If she corrected my errors, it was usually in private, where she also tolerated my occasional ridicule of her friends as she escorted me from the limitations of my world into the casual freedom of hers.

Before she risked introducing me to her father, she took me to meet Eduard Lindeman, the man who had been her "second father" since birth. Mr. Lindeman was a distinguished teacher, a man of imposing presence and sympathetic intelligence, who had been rescued from an early life as a farm hand by an employer who recognized his extraordinary intellectual capacity and put him through long years of schooling. The first night we met, we played bridge with him and his wife in their Manhattan apartment. He expended a great deal of charm and tact to put me at my ease in a setting which was not only unfamiliar but vaguely threatening to me. I suspected the Lindemans were spies for Dorothy's father, alerted to the dangerous liaison she was planning, but in spite of my suspicions I found them both friendly, comfortable people I wanted to like—and wanted, even more, to like me. The next day, Mr. Lindeman called Dorothy to ask if I had not worn a tie to dinner because I couldn't afford one. I was unreasonably offended at the query, but Dorothy mollified me by saying it was his way of telling her that they approved of me.

215

I showed Dorothy off to the only friends I still had, Ernest and Evelyn Cahn. They accepted her with the same courtesy with which they had always accepted me. An actor who had been a close friend ran into me on the street and invited me to bring my new girl to dinner. Along with the after-dinner liqueurs, his actress wife brought out a group of photographs and handed them to Dorothy. The face smiling from the glossy prints bore so little resemblance to the face waiting for compliments that Dorothy innocently remarked, "How beautiful she is. Who is she?" unaware that no actress is likely to display the photograph of another woman. Dorothy did not know theatre people and had no reason to seek out the company of actresses. Although we seldom discussed my marriage, she held the theatre profession, as well as the actress I had married, responsible for much of my previous unhappiness and had evolved an image of my wife as a glamorous creature with whom she could not possibly compete. To rid her of that feeling, I took her to a basement performance of *As You Like It* in which Priscilla played a minor part. Impressed by neither her performance nor her appearance, Dorothy refused to go backstage to meet her, so I determined to bring them face to face to free the girl I planned to marry from the shadow of her predecessor. I finally persuaded Priscilla to allow me to pick up some of my books and bullied Dorothy into going with me. Standing in the doorway of the apartment we had shared, my ex-wife stared balefully at us. Embarrassed now that I had arranged their confrontation, I stumbled hurriedly through introductions, realizing too late that I had called Priscilla "Patricia." That, perhaps more than anything else, convinced Dorothy she had nothing to fear from a residual attraction in my first marriage.

Certain now that we would marry, we fell into petty, unexpected arguments, most of which arose from my habit of saying things without thinking, or of hiding what I did think behind trivial badinage. Unaccustomed to facetiousness about love or self-pity about oneself, Dorothy took me much more seriously than she

216

should have, certainly much more seriously than I took myself. She would confide a desire to go to Spain after we were married (her husband had been a Spanish professor in college), and I'd launch into a tirade about bullfighting, a subject that had never interested me before. In her wistful reveries about the babies we both wanted, I'd hear my voice coldly announce that if my impoverished mother never had a baby carriage for any of her thirteen children, I saw no reason why my wife should have one. Whatever the subjects through which we aired our mutual apprehensions, we slowly uncovered those areas in which our marriage would either succeed or fail. She gradually accepted the prospect of poverty with me, and I accepted the prospect of family life at the cost of my ego and my ambitions. Unpleasant and unpredictable as our quarrels were, we endured them, parting with tears in her eyes and sullen anger in mine, to call each other later, laughing at our childishness.

That winter, Dorothy accomplished what no one else had ever done: she brought me to telling the truth, even when the truth proved me silly, stupid, weak, and vicious. I regretted what my life had been, mostly for the pain it obviously caused her, but the risk of losing her was preferable to winning her on false, or incomplete, grounds. There came a time when there was nothing I knew about myself that she did not know as well. After the worst of these many revelations, she went home alone shaken, and I spent the entire night sitting in the dark by the telephone. She called me the next morning, and from that moment on neither of us saw any obstacle to our spending the rest of our lives together. In spite of her father's objections, which he had not withdrawn, she would do what she believed she should. Her determination was evidence of a faith not merely in me but in life itself which was apparent in everything she said and did. I gave up analyzing the differences between us and using them to provoke arguments: we had arrived at a common life from opposite ends of experience.

When my second novel was finished, I took the manuscript from one uninterested publisher to another. Among Dorothy's friends

217

was a young literary agent named John Cushman, who read the manuscripts and agreed to handle them, more as a favor to her, I suspect, than because of any merit he found in them. Over the years, John Cushman tirelessly tried to place my unpublishable novels; more important, he eased the depression of rejection with solid good humor and once sat me down during his busy day and gave me a much needed lesson in syntax. His friendly interest kept me writing, which was probably more important at that point than being published. Dorothy refrained from criticisms that would discourage me, but when I suggested that we delay our wedding until John found me a publisher, she tactfully replied that one had nothing to do with the other. Luckily, she persuaded me or we wouldn't be married yet. We had taken Miss Davis into our confidence, and she kept our secret in the library (one of us would have been transferred to another branch if she hadn't) and set about trying to find more interesting work for me. On her recommendation, I was asked to write and broadcast occasional book talks for the library's public-relations office. At first, I kept within familiar theatre subjects: Chekhov's plays, Shakespeare's heroines, biographies of Edwin Booth and Henry Irving, and the correspondence between Bernard Shaw and Mrs. Campbell. As people, within the library and outside of it, praised my broadcasts, I was encouraged to move into fiction and general subjects. Without my knowing it, my future work was evolving.

At Easter, Eduard Lindeman lay dying in Harkness Pavilion. Dorothy's parents, his closest friends since long before her birth, came up to see him. They invited me to join them and Dorothy's roommate for lunch at a Gramercy Park hotel: my audition for the role of son-in-law was upon me. In a quiet dining room occupied by discreet people like themselves, the Shaws greeted Dorothy affectionately, Barbara warmly, and me with gracious, if studied, politeness. Mrs. Shaw, whom I had met only once, smiled encouragingly at me but, like Dorothy and Barbara, remained in the background while Charles Shaw and I talked for the first time.

218

What I saw, and liked, was a man with his daughter's direct gaze and delicately boned features, as well as her quiet, ironic self-assurance. What he saw in me must have been a mystery which he was determined to explore before it damaged the daughter he obviously adored. He had been librarian of Swarthmore College since Dorothy was a year old; his preoccupations, outside of a private printing press in his cellar and gardening, were the poets and obscure diarists of the eighteenth and nineteenth centuries. Early in our conversation, Charles began reciting a line of poetry to Dorothy and then, pausing as if he couldn't remember the rest of it, asked her what the next line was. She didn't know, but I did. We went from poem to poem, by Wordsworth, Keats, Thomas Hood, and, for one uneasy moment, John Milton, until he turned with a satisfied smile to his radiant daughter. Later that week, at the hospital, Eduard Lindeman whispered to Dorothy that Charles had liked me very much.

We were married the following September in a quiet ceremony by a minister who, at our request, did not mention God during the service. Afterward, we attended a small reception, at the Gramercy Park hotel where I had met Charles Shaw, with Dorothy's parents, two brothers and their wives, Eduard Lindeman's widow and daughter, Barbara King, and several of Dorothy's college friends. No one in that group of twenty or thirty people was anyone I had known a year before. We spent our wedding night at the Algonquin, where I awoke next morning with one of the worst colds of my life, a present from my sneezing bride. We went back to my apartment in the Village, somewhat relieved since we couldn't really afford the hotel room. The following day, we both reported back to work, Dorothy to the branch she'd been transferred to twenty blocks north of the one we had met and courted in.

Unable to choose among them and unwilling to invite them all, I had not asked any of my family to our wedding. The following Saturday, however, we attended Vincent's in a Catholic church in

Brooklyn, holding hands during the High Mass which united him in his new army uniform to his pretty bride in traditional white satin and veiling. Later, at a lavish reception in a big hotel, my bride met more of her new in-laws. Ambrose approached us with a lupine smile. "So, you're Harding's new wife," he said, looking Dorothy over with practiced eyes. "You're kind of skinny, ain't you?" She smiled, and he continued: "I hear you been married before." "Yes, I have," Dorothy replied, "seven times." With a guffaw, he left to badger someone else. Gabrielle's husband danced with my wife, holding a half-empty whiskey bottle in one hand. He sullenly informed her that she had married "bad blood," information she viewed, as she viewed the drunken man who conveyed it, with complete serenity. Evangeline, peeved because she had not been invited to our wedding, thawed to the point of offering marital advice, predicting that we would become religious (she had embraced her husband's Jewish faith with overwhelming earnestness) once we had children. Eventually, we escaped from well-meant advice and ill-meant innuendos alike to the peace of our three drab rooms near the Hudson River docks.

One Saturday, several weeks after Dorothy and I were married, Charles Shaw left my wife with his in the pleasant house he'd built on the Swarthmore campus and drove me in to lunch at his club in Philadelphia. Settling across from me, he told me he owed me an apology. At Christmas, when Dorothy had told him she was going to marry me, they had argued the entire night through for the first time in their lives. He would not listen to her, or to her mother, who kept repeating, "But, Charles, you haven't even met him!" "I told them both that I didn't want to meet you, I didn't have to." He met my puzzled gaze with the candor I was just becoming accustomed to in his daughter. "Your wife will never tell you why I objected to you," he told me, "but I'm going to."

"It's not because you'd been divorced. After all, so has Dorothy. It was not because you'd never been to college; I've spent too many years on campuses to attach much importance to that. It's not because you'd been an actor, although that's hardly a reassuring background. It was not your Catholic upbringing; you're probably as devout a Catholic as Dorothy is a Quaker. No, it was none of those objections she'd anticipated and was prepared for." He paused and looked at me with a faint pink blush beginning in his cheeks. "Can't you guess what it was?" he asked. I turned away. He reached across the table and touched my jacket sleeve lightly, continuing to speak only when my eyes met his. "You're right," he said. "It's because you're French Canadian." I started to interrupt but he wouldn't let me stop him until he had explained that he had grown up in Worcester, Massachusetts, where French Canadians were domestics and mill hands. As he spoke, I recalled the handsome, freshly painted Protestant homes in Longview that we Lemays were never invited into. "I'm afraid I told her that she'd have a baby every year," Charles said ruefully, "and that you'd be out drinking every night." His honesty, like Dorothy's, extracted honesty from me. "Some of my sisters are having babies every year," I told him, "and my brothers are out drinking every night." "Dorothy hasn't married your brothers," he said, closing the subject. "She's married you, and I'm delighted she has."

In my thirties, I had the parents I'd dreamed of as a child: a well-groomed, vivacious mother, who encouraged every ambition and praised every achievement, and a witty, cultivated, candid father. On frequent visits to New York, they took us out to dinner and the theatre, but never entered our shabby first apartment, waiting patiently until we invited them into the more presentable one that followed it. They did not intrude upon our lives, never criticized the neighborhoods we lived in, or commented upon the economic hardships we encountered. They were exemplary in-laws as they had always been exemplary parents. Charles complimented me on the work I did on radio and later on television, sending me articles to read, and exchanging parodies of nineteenth-century poems with me; more important, he took my opinions and attitudes seriously, as my own father had never done. Mrs. Shaw knitted

221

sweaters and socks, mothered me as I had never been mothered, and tolerated my teasing. We spent many weekends in Swarthmore with them, where I met articulate college professors and their wives whom Dorothy had grown up with. We played cards and word games before the fire, ate beautifully cooked and served meals by candlelight, talking of books and elections, poets and professors. I stared in astonishment the first time I saw them, then in their late fifties, awkwardly break from an embrace like embarrassed teen-agers as we came into the living room from an afternoon walk outside. Within their presence, I slowly became a son, as in the company of their daughter I became a man. When Charles died nine years later, it occurred to me that he had been closer to me in some ways than he may have been to the two grown men who are his sons. I suspect even they could not have loved him as I did; perhaps it is easier to love a father if one hasn't spent one's childhood with him.

It is as impossible to describe a happy marriage as it is to describe the woman who makes it so. In observing the marriages around us, I have concluded that a man is seldom better than the woman he marries. My wife is the only human being, outside of our children, who reaches beyond my defenses into areas that are unknown even to me, or perhaps especially to me. Her presence in the next room, while I read or write or merely brood, is essential to me; the only genuine discontent I have known during our marriage has been during unavoidable separations. During the first months in that apartment we furnished with discarded furniture we found in the streets, she kissed me each day, as I sat before the typewriter on the kitchen table, and hurried off to her job uptown. We met for hasty dinners during my hour break somewhere between her branch in the East Nineties and mine in the Seventies. In our free time, I read books, worked on my manuscripts, and typed out radio broadcasts for the library while she cooked, sewed, cleaned the apartment, or washed her hair in the kitchen sink. In the tiny, overheated living room, we danced in our underclothes to music from the radio, or sang popular songs ourselves, my tuneless monotone drowning out her melodious pitch. We seldom argued any more: the compulsion to convert each other had exhausted itself during our courtship. The mind I had arduously built contained a lot of concrete in it which would not give way. Her mind, as agile and adaptable as her body, did not challenge mine as much as accommodate it, gradually diluting my natural obstinacy and anchoring me in sanity rather than in fantasy.

She earned twice the salary I did, and insisted upon spending money on matters I had always neglected. I had seldom gone to a doctor or a dentist during the years since I'd been discharged from the army. Dental neglect was paid for now, both in money and in loss of teeth. Dorothy saw to it that my trousers were pressed, my shoes shined, my suits cleaned—matters of personal grooming I had never considered worth the money they cost, a stubborn attitude ingrained in me by the economies of the unemployed actor. Unlike me, Dorothy enjoyed handling checkbooks and household accounts. She kept lists of things to be done and, surprisingly, she did them. I learned more in a few months about the management of daily life than three decades of previous living had taught me.

What I taught her was much more trivial. She had been subjected to the restrictions of a Quaker upbringing and had never seen the movie favorites of my boyhood, so I took her to see Garbo in *Camille* and Carole Lombard in *My Man Godfrey*. She had never seen Katharine Cornell on the stage, and when I pointed her out at a Martha Graham recital, she remarked that the famous actress reminded her of the matrons she had grown up with. She didn't care for Graham's dance dramas, but accepted my enthusiasm for them as just another indication of my strange preoccupation with the abstract.

When Frenchie was killed in Korea, his insurance was left to my mother. After her death, it was distributed in small monthly payments to her eleven surviving children. We used those payments to buy theatre tickets. After performances viewed from the second balcony, Dorothy diffidently followed me backstage, where Eli Wallach, Jo Van Fleet, or Darren McGavin chatted absent-mindedly with us until they were diverted—or rescued—by people they knew better. Dorothy's interest in actors was mild, to say the least. She found their narcissistic self-absorption as offensive as coarse language or personal dishonesty; she tolerated them, as she did the plays they appeared in, because I wanted to see them.

In the evenings, I read aloud to her as she ironed my shirts or did the supper dishes. Once, while she was in the tub, I invaded the bathroom to read from a Faulkner novel. With the sponge in her hand, she listened to the more than usually obscure passage and then, with a full-throated laugh, said, "You're crazy, do you know that? Crazy!" She was right: I was crazy, crazy in love, crazy with delight in her literal-minded common sense which reined my impulsive imagination. She read the scripts I wrote for the library radio program with praise for the ideas and the originality with which I wrote them, and with penciled corrections of my grammar and syntax. "You *take* something there, and *bring* something here," she repeated until I'd anticipate the comment. "The possessive with the gerund," she'd interrupt me in midsentence, until I finally confessed that, while I certainly knew what possessive meant, I didn't have the foggiest idea what the hell a gerund was. Reading, with a pencil in her hand, sections of the novel I was writing, she'd look up to demand what I really meant by what she read back to me. Unimpressed by my belligerent defenses, she'd tell me to write it the way I said it instead of imitating someone else.

In the spring, we found a larger apartment on the upper West Side; my typewriter graduated from a kitchen table to a desk in the extra room we hoped to convert to a nursery as soon as possible. Although the rooms were large and sunny, and the closets spacious, the apartment was handicapped in other ways. On the top floor of a brownstone, it was accessible from the floors below, and since each room opened into a common hallway, we were obliged to lock three doors when we left. The bathroom was in the hall; during our first night, the toilet flushed mysteriously and continuously by itself while we lay in bed too frightened to get up and investigate. We grew accustomed to the sound in the months that followed. There were no kitchen facilities, which prompted Charles Shaw to remark that Dorothy had finally found the apartment she always wanted. The dishes we used were washed in a sink in a closet, and the landlord supplied us with a roto-broiler and promises of a stove that never came. We didn't really mind the inadequacies, since the apartment was attractive enough so we could invite friends and Dorothy's parents in without being ashamed. The only thing we really wanted was a baby, but no amount of calculation of month and moon brought us closer to that. As the months passed, I began to wonder if a malignant fate was punishing us for the stupidities and sins of my earlier life.

We came back one night from seeing *Cat on a Hot Tin Roof* to a burglarized apartment. It was the third time it had happened, and we stood in the hall, with the toilet flushing repeatedly beside us, to survey the damage inflicted by intruders who had found nothing but books to steal after prying off all three locks. Dorothy, whose face was taut with tensions I'd been too content to notice before, muttered that we'd already been robbed once that night by Tennessee Williams. We moved back to Greenwich Village the following week. Within a month, we were expecting our first child.

Rapturous at the news, Miss Davis determined to find me more suitable and better-paying work within the library. Through her that summer, I was hired, at double my salary, by John Cory, the chief of the circulation department downtown in the main building, to devise programs about books for an educational television channel being developed by the city's cultural institutions. An amiable, energetic man of exceptional executive ability, John Cory put the entire resources of the greatest public library in the world at my disposal. Planning and writing sample scripts, I spent each morning at a typewriter just outside his door, and each afternoon isolated downstairs in a cubicle where elderly librarians who had known me as a page fifteen years earlier stared through the glass partition at me hunched over a table of open books, making penciled notes. A lifetime of serious reading, first begun from the books on the shelves that surrounded me, was put to practical, profitable use.

That we didn't even own a television set seemed irrelevant to me, since my concern was the literary content of the programs not the technical aspects of their production. To test out ideas, I broadcast revised scripts over the municipal radio station. I wrote a total of thirty or forty scripts, educating myself as I went along, not only in television writing but by reading memoirs, biographies, diaries, and correspondence with the abandon of an addict, which in a sense I was. I walked downtown every afternoon to my pregnant wife in constant euphoria, astonished at being paid for doing what I would gladly have done for nothing. My infatuation with books, the dreadful secret of my childhood, no longer had to be hidden; my wife and her family shared it, and my work demanded it. By the time an educational television channel materialized in New York City, I had moved on to other work, but the scripts I wrote for John Cory now rest in a closet with unpublished novels, infrequently produced plays, book reviews, professional articles, and scraps of poetry—mementos of an occupation which provides intense personal gratification, if limited public recognition. I keep those scripts, amateurish as they might prove if I read them today, because they were the bridge I crossed from the daydreams of my youth to the work of my adult life. If I could have supported a family on the salary I earned writing them, I would still be doing it for a public library somewhere.

Stephen was born in January, 1956, to incredulous parents who, after the admiring grandparents, uncles and aunts, and friends departed, crept into the little room he shared with my typewriter to stare at the sleeping infant. In our early thirties, beyond the age when most couples have their first child, we had everything we wanted—except money, and we didn't worry too much about that.

John Cory realized that my salary was hardly sufficient to support a wife and child, and unobtrusively paved the way for my advancement into work that would pay more. He sent me in his place to serve on committees with book publishers, educators, and broadcasters. As his deputy, I organized the annual Book Festival over the municipal radio station, programing readings by well-known actors, discussions with critics, and interviews with authors, many of which I conducted myself. At lunch and over cocktails with celebrities as disparate as Claire Bloom and Margaret Mead, Tyrone Power and Moses Hadas, I entered expense-account restaurants directly from the self-service counter of the library's cafeteria. The next year, John Cory recommended me as a radio and television consultant to the American Book Publishers Council, the industry's trade association, at a much higher salary than I could ever hope to receive at the library. I left him, and the librarians I had worked with for four and a half years, with genuine regret which I have never lost, to take my first office job.

From that point on, every professional decision I made was based upon two necessities: the support of my family, and the freedom to write what I pleased. During the previous year, I had finished my third novel and delivered it to my agent. He showed me a friendly letter from an editor rejecting my previous book, which suggested that my proper field might very well be playwriting rather than fiction. As I approached my new job, with associations and activities that did not basically appeal to me, I took stock of what I had accomplished in the five years since I had given up acting. I had written three unpublished novels: I had read widely enough to acknowledge that they were probably unpublishable, even in those years of easily published, easily

227

forgotten fiction. However, I had not chosen to write in the first place because I longed for publication, or even because I was desperate for other people's approval of what I wrote. I began writing to maintain my sanity by releasing the anguish and angers which flooded my memory of experiences too distressing to be viewed any other way. I had discovered, if nothing else, that I did have material to write about. I had also discovered that I lacked essential knowledge of science, history, sociology, and economics, all of which are inherent in the good novelist's trade. Worse than that, I wasn't interested enough to learn what I didn't know. People were what interested me—not ideas or politics or factual knowledge, but people who reflected those I had known in my early life, and they interested me primarily in direct conflict with each other. The sympathetic editor was right. At least, if I didn't know how to bring a chapter to an effective close, years of reading, studying, and acting in plays had taught me what a curtain line is.

In the spring of 1956, I began two new careers, one out in the open, the other in secret. For the next eleven years, I rose every working day before my family was awake and walked uptown to my office, where I wrote in solitude for two hours until the secretaries arrived at their desks. This was interpreted, I realized later, as unusual dedication to my job, but that was not the only misinterpretation business colleagues drew from my activities, although it may have been the most serious. During those morning hours, I rewrote my first play at least twenty times, and wrote five others. Since plays deal nakedly with human behavior, they proved much more gratifying than writing fiction. In what is, it seems to me, really a compulsive process, one play engenders the next, and since the professional theatre operates in a selective system no one can anticipate or explain, the playwright soon writes almost exclusively for his own pleasure. I evolved a triparted pattern: writing in the early morning, executive work during the day, and domestic life in the evenings and weekends. That pattern provided us with comforts I had never expected, but also with

228

anxieties and expediencies it took me many years to acknowledge.

In the fall of 1956, Virgilia Peterson, a prominent book reviewer and lecturer who had worked with me on various committees, invited me to alternate with her on "Books in Profile," a weekly radio series. Every other week, she interviewed the author of a new book, Kathryn Hulme, Frank O'Connor, B. J. Chute; the following week, I broadcast a commentary on the book itself, with readings by actors I persuaded to donate their services. The next fall, Miss Peterson and I began a four-year partnership on a book-discussion program heard in various cities over noncommercial stations, which meant we did not receive fees. Being what she called "book drunks," we didn't really mind, since we enjoyed talking about books more than we required the money we would have been paid by a commercial station that would have restricted the freedom we exercised in unorthodox and uninhibited exchanges about the books we read. Virgilia Peterson was an articulate, opinionated, handsome woman some fifteen years my senior, who could often be exasperating, but no more than I. A woman of humorous forthrightness and strongly held, pungently expressed views, she liked arguments, and our programs quickly became public dissensions about God, man, morals, sex, politics, and any other topic prompted by sometimes as many as four books a week. Provoking each other into overvehement defenses of carelessly stated positions, we became loyal, affectionate friends, even though listeners wrote partisan postcards in the belief that we were bitter enemies. Virgilia Peterson forced me to say what I think without fear of making a fool of myself, to match the opinions she expressed with the acid disdain for the shoddy that marked her entire life. Since her death several years ago, I seldom finish a new book without wishing I could pick up the telephone and begin an argument with her about it. Beyond our deepening friendship, however, she was instrumental in leading me from the tedious work of a trade-association executive into the heart of the publishing industry itself.

When Stephen was thirteen months old, his sister Susan was born. Before Stephen's birth, we had been reconciled to having a daughter because we wanted a boy; when his sister was born, we considered ourselves luckier than we had any right to be. We moved from our little apartment in Greenwich Village into the larger one we've occupied ever since. Gilly Peterson, as her intimates called her, recommended me for lecture engagements and book reviewing to supplement my income. She persuaded Lyman Bryson to use me on his "Invitation to Learning" literary radio discussions, which, she gleefully alerted me, paid a hundred dollars a broadcast, and she forced me upon the producers of her own occasional television discussion programs. As my name became familiar to publishers, they offered me positions in their editorial departments which I automatically declined. I had been close enough to the publishing industry to realize that men who wanted to write their own books became buried for years behind stacks of unread manuscripts by others. Nor did I want to align myself to one publishing house when I could choose from all of them for books to discuss in lectures and on the radio.

My resistance vanished in March, 1958, when Pat Knopf offered me the post of publicity manager for his father's firm. When a friend who had tried to hire me at Doubleday reminded me that I had rejected her offer because I didn't want to work for a publisher, I tactlessly replied that it had never occurred to me there would be an opening at Knopf. Every profession has its glamorous legends: in the theatre it was the Lunts; in publishing it was Alfred and Blanche Knopf. Although it was generally acknowledged by others that they were the leading book publishers in the country, their superiority was most energetically promoted by themselves, especially Alfred A. Knopf, whose name frequently appeared more prominently in his advertising than those of the authors he published. In forty years, the Borzoi imprint had introduced great European writers—Spengler, Mann, Gide, Undset, Kafka, Sartré, and Camus—to American readers, as well as publishing a variety

230

of Americans such as Willa Cather, H. L. Mencken, Dashiell Hammett, and John Hersey. Young writers like me usually received their first rejection letters from Knopf before collecting them from less celebrated publishers.

Once I had been hired, acquaintances who had worked for them, usually briefly and unhappily, warned me against the Knopfs. Everyone spoke of the publishing house as "the Knopfs." Their professional activities and personal eccentricities prompted much the same kind of gossip I had heard about the stars of my earlier profession. I had never spoken to either of them. Indeed, I had never even seen her, but he had been highly visible in his brightly colored shirts and ties, with dark piratical eyes darting above a Franz Josef mustache, at various publishing functions. My boss at the Book Publishers Council offered to match the salary they promised me and, when I refused, told me they would fire me within six months. I laughed off his warning, determined to work only for the imprint I had always admired, not for personalities whose virtues and failings were magnified by rumor and envy.

I was mistaken. The imprint did not exist apart from the two egocentrics who had founded it forty years before. By the time I joined their firm, Alfred and Blanche Knopf were in their sixties, veterans of decades of flattery from those who worked closely with them and victimized by the inflated vanities such flattery breeds. The atmosphere I entered was hardly that of a business corporation. If anything, it resembled a small intimate royal court of eighteenth-century Germany, with its tyrannical Emperor, devious Empress, and ebullient, if somewhat apprehensive, Crown Prince. Pat Knopf, several years older than I, is a likable man of disarming candor and impulsive generosity. His contempt for the fawning courtiers who surrounded his highly competitive parents was repaid by their playing his parents off against him. During my early weeks, I separated the courtiers into toadies and lackeys: there was the Gray Eminence (a somewhat blurred imitation of the Emperor himself, who wore the same mustache, drank the same wines, and

231

even owned the same breed of dog), the Lord High Chancellor (a bustling, rather engaging grandfather from Queens), and the Court Jester, who served as a sort of private secretary-confidant to both Emperor and Empress. They composed, with Pat, the executive committee of the best publishing house in America; lesser posts were filled by various spies, sycophants, and minions in the guise of editors, publicity and advertising managers, and salesmen who placated the royal couple and ingratiated themselves as best they could with those closer to the throne. It became very clear at weekly meetings I attended that the Crown Prince himself was hardly a favorite with his parents, which neither bothered to hide during the rages that erupted at the head of the table and the counterfire of weary sarcasm from his consort at the other end.

I decided then and there that if I ever took those people seriously, I should be fired. I had watched in my own family the destruction caused by unrestrained rages and quick sarcasm, and refused to be drawn into a similar performance even if the principals wore London shirts and Chanel suits instead of overalls and housedresses. I had no desire to know the Knopfs personally; I was interested only in the books they published. I continued broadcasting radio programs with Virgilia Peterson for the next two years, got up early to work on my own writing, released the tensions of my working day by loving my wife and playing with our babies. When Pat Knopf came to me to say that his father was going to offer me a position as editor, to replace the most recent victim of conference-room politics, I sent him back to his father with the message that I didn't want to be an editor.

I liked my work as publicity manager. I was obliged to read those books already being published, many of which were among those Gilly Peterson and I discussed on the radio, instead of the manuscripts the editors read and rejected as unfit for publication. A publicity manager tries to get as much free attention as possible for the books he represents, which means distributing review copies to newspapers and to radio and television commentators. He lunches with reviewers, attempting to persuade them to devote their limited space to his books rather than others; he accompanies authors to lunch at Sardi's and cocktails at the Algonquin for interviews with book reporters and to television stations for appearances on early-morning or on late-night talk shows. In short, he performs any chore that will draw attention to the author and the book, hoping to stimulate sales in the bookstores. Since many of the authors published by Knopf were either dead or foreign, promotion in my office focused less on the author than on the publisher. The Gray Eminence (whose duties clearly included carrying messages) frequently stopped me in the halls to inquire what I was "doing" for Alfred and Blanche. In time, I learned to do what I could and, sometimes, even what I couldn't. If I inadvertently omitted his name from a press release or referred to her as "Mrs. Alfred A. Knopf" instead of "Blanche W. Knopf," it was brought to my attention, either by phone or in person, by their soft-voiced emissary, almost always before Pat could reach me with his customary good-natured reproof.

I kept my distance from Alfred Knopf for the first few months, and Blanche Knopf kept her distance from me. One day, Alfred summoned me into his office and launched into a ferocious denunciation of a release I had sent out to newspapers on a forthcoming book. He instructed me to submit all future releases to him before mailing them. I refused, explaining that while I had no objection to being reprimanded for errors, I could not work effectively if— He cut me short, roaring at me to get out of his office. A few minutes later, Pat Knopf, distressed, appeared at my desk to say he would deal with his parents for me from then on. That afternoon, the Gray Eminence halted me in the corridor and informed me that I was "on very shaky ground" and glided suavely past. At our subsequent weekly meetings, everyone ignored me except Pat; Mr. Knopf didn't acknowledge my greetings and Mrs. Knopf turned cryptic smiles in my direction but did not speak. Pat seemed more harassed than usual, and I continued to send out newspaper releases without clearing them first. After two months in their employ, I had reached what seemed like an impasse until, one lunch hour, Alfred stepped into the elevator which was carrying me down. Glancing at the magazine that was obviously going to be my sole lunch companion, he casually invited me to join him at a luncheon he was giving at his club for distinguished historians. From that day on, he treated me with an Old World courtesy, as if there had never been a disagreement between us. Working directly with him on books he was particularly interested in, I realized that the rudeness which repelled me at meetings covered a desperate need for other people's approval. A tyrannical exterior harbored a surprisingly gentle man whose frequent gestures of sympathy touched and startled me.

Blanche Knopf was quite different. It was some weeks before I could refrain from staring at what had once been a beautiful woman but was now a frail creature, ravaged by age and illness. She weighed about ninety pounds, and ten of those must have been jewelry she wore. I assumed the abundant and flamboyant hair was a wig, but I could find no suitable explanation for the fingernails, lacquered a deep purple, which curled at the tips like the claws of a jungle bird. On the surface, she reminded me of ancient actresses I had known, but the woman beneath the surface had nothing in common with those sad relics. Intuitive and shrewd, reticent and witty, she was a proud, wary, unapproachable lady who had survived in a man's world, and who kept her distance from strangers, especially those hired by her husband and her son.

An interior signal system connected my desk directly to those of the Knopfs. One day, my buzzer rang and I picked up the telephone. A cultivated voice announced, "This is Blanche Knopf. Would you like to meet Elizabeth Bowen?" I replied that I would, very much indeed. "Why?" she asked. Falteringly, I explained that I admired Miss Bowen's novels. "I'm sure you do," she said, and waited for a better reason. Finally, wondering if she was slightly deranged, I suggested we postpone the introduction until

Miss Bowen's next book, which would give us an official reason for meeting. "As you wish," Mrs. Knopf told me brusquely, and hung up. It was several days before I concluded that Miss Bowen had probably asked to meet the new publicity man, and Mrs. Knopf, not certain how long I would be with them, had adroitly managed to make it sound, from her end, as if I weren't really very interested.

My predecessor at Knopf, who had survived twelve difficult years, was what the Gray Eminence called one of "Pat's boys." He had made close friendships with important authors, which aroused the suspicions of the management. Authors are sometimes more loyal to the editors and friends they work with on a publisher's staff than they are to the publisher himself. In fact, it was reported that Alfred had started his own firm by persuading a popular novelist to desert the publisher who had employed young Knopf. Whether or not that was true, the Knopfs discouraged friendships between their authors and their employees. Editors strong-minded enough to withstand the constant undermining of their confidence in their own taste and judgment tolerated Alfred's sabotage and Blanche's more refined maneuvers. An unknown author, published against the active opposition of the Knopfs, was suddenly enthusiastically adopted by them if his book became either a critical or a commercial success. The editor who had fought, not only the Knopfs but those associates who echoed their hostility, to publish an author in the first place seldom appreciated the attention his discovery later received, however flattered the author might be at his inclusion among the celebrities at Blanche's dinner parties in her Manhattan apartment or at Alfred's Sunday luncheons in the country.

The publicity office was the final refuge for authors whose books were not successful. Otherwise sensible men petulantly demanded attention no one could achieve for them. One, with a bad stammer, insisted upon being booked on radio discussion programs; others, whose novels were ignored or dismissed in the Sunday book

235

supplements, demanded that I telephone the newspapers to complain, in their presence, of unfair treatment. Editors, smarting under Alfred's brutal reminders of lapses in judgment and sensing imminent dismissal in the furtive glances of the palace guard, blamed publicity and advertising for bad reviews and disappointing sales. The publicity manager, who sees the editors at their worst, is often caught between them and those who hire them. When heads of a firm consider themselves primarily as editors, as the Knopfs did, the publicity man is enmeshed in a trap that can destroy him. I found no way out of the trap except utter honesty.

When an editor asked me to spend a weekend that I preferred to spend with my family reading a long manuscript instead, he received the candid opinion I believed he was soliciting. Not unreasonably, editors confused my opinions of their projects with opinions of themselves, and my candor made me few friends among them. When Alfred asked me to read one of his South American favorites or a novel about the American West, I reported my responses as candidly to him as I did to any other editor. The first time I told him one of his enthusiasms was unreadable, his jaw dropped while he glared at me unable to say anything, and the courtiers at the conference table studiously examined their fingernails. A moment later, he exploded at the advertising man, who had been much milder in his criticism of another book, saying that those who don't agree with the boss should look for other jobs. He may have hotly disputed my opinions in the years I worked for him, but he never asked me to disguise them or retract them.

Completely ignorant of the economics of book publishing, I was surprised to find that literary merit had little to do with commercial success. Novels which were prominently reviewed and won literary prizes often sold fewer copies than those I had never heard of: Harold Robbins sold five times what Conrad Richter did; a poet I had never heard of, Kahlil Gibran, was the all-time best-seller on the Knopf list, while Camus, Kafka, and Sartre were

236

outsold by writers whose names were forgotten within a year. Knopf had fewer mediocrities on its list than most publishing houses. While Doubleday and Simon & Schuster, among others, issued several titles a year that sold over a hundred thousand copies, forty years of Borzoi books included no more than twelve that had reached that figure; among the others were hundreds that sold solidly year after year, creating the economic soundness for a publishing house known as a "back list." The Knopfs had built their success on the continuing sale of good books, not on the transitory sale of bad ones. What their imprint represented, and why it was worth the aggravation of working for it, was quality in literature. Ashamed of inferior books that sold well, Alfred often personally rejected as unworthy to bear his name novels that became sensational successes on other publishers' lists. His insistence upon quality did not mean that each book should not pay its own way. Publishers cannot survive on Nobel Prize winners alone, and it took conscientious, time-consuming work to turn a questionable prospect into a profitable venture.

When Pat Knopf left for his summer vacation, he asked me to read the galleys of a book his mother had bought in Paris, but advised me not to waste too much effort on it, because it was hopeless from a sales point of view. That weekend, I read the book: *Tanguy*, the personal history of a young Spaniard who had grown to manhood in concentration camps. Its anguished artlessness awakened in me a long-dormant rage suppressed since my experiences in wartime Germany. Monday morning, I asked Alfred to postpone publication for several months; the book was scheduled to appear in August, when most reviewers would ignore it and most readers would hardly buy it for seashore diversion. Alfred echoed Pat's caution about wasting my time on a hopeless project, but I answered that my office would devise special promotion for it. He gave me a skeptical glance and said, "Go ahead. The book doesn't stand a chance, but see what you can do."

The title was changed to *Child of Our Time*, and a campaign started to counter the sales department's resistance to the depressing story. At the public library, I searched through old indexes to periodical literature and copied names of distinguished writers, ministers, psychologists, and other public figures who had written articles ten years earlier about the effects of the Nazi horrors upon children and, more precisely, upon the capacity to love. We sent out over fifty carefully worded letters, each beginning with a recollection of an article read years before, asking for advance comments to be used in advertising and promoting the book. Thirty people wrote back agreeing to read it. Twenty of those, including Karl Menninger, Adlai Stevenson, Kathryn Hulme, Kay Boyle, and Eleanor Roosevelt, gave us comments we circulated on postcards to ensure wide and favorable review coverage. The book, advertised almost exclusively by the quotations we had gathered, did not become a runaway best-seller but it sold very well and continues to sell year after year. That publicity campaign brought me immediately into Blanche Knopf's unwavering favor. Alfred praised me before his nodding executive committee, and even the Gray Eminence greeted me affably in the corridors. One day, he took me to lunch.

On a visit to the Shaws in Swarthmore the following Easter weekend, Stevie and I walked through the campus to buy the Sunday papers. On the front page of the *New York Times*, I read that Pat Knopf had left his parents' firm to establish his own publishing house, Atheneum Press. On Monday morning, the Knopf offices were in complete confusion; Pat's decision was as much a surprise to everyone else, including his parents, as it had been to me. Blanche was, fortunately, in Europe. Alfred called his executive committee together to begin plugging up holes left by Pat's desertion. He had been the company's sales manager, and had taken the advertising manager and several key salesmen along with him. The executive committee, suspecting that others originally hired by Pat would soon follow him, asked me point-blank if I intended to join Atheneum Press when it required the services of a publicity

238

director. I told them what I told Pat later that week when he called to offer me the position when it became available: I had come to work for Knopf, not for individuals within the firm. In a few months, I was swallowed up in the vacuum created by Pat's departure, given responsibilities and authority which would have been unthinkable if he had stayed within the firm. I maintained a friendship with all three Knopfs during the early years of Pat's new firm, which, considering the gossip and resentments caused by his abdication, was not an easy accomplishment. When the Gray Eminence spied us lunching together, he summoned me to his office for an unmistakable warning that it would be wiser not to be seen in Pat's company if I wanted to continue working for his father. I left him to go directly to Alfred, whom I told, before anyone else told him, that I was his son's friend. Alfred stared at me from across his desk, then said impatiently, "Why do you bother me with this?" After listening to my reasons, he ushered me to his door, saying with a slightly aggrieved dignity, "Your friends are your business; they don't concern anyone else here."

For the next seven years, I worked very closely with Alfred and Blanche Knopf. Officially, my position was merely that of publicity manager at the beginning, but they drew me quickly, as an ally and an assistant, into those areas of publishing they dominated. They fiercely competed for my time: if I read a manuscript for Alfred overnight, the next evening I carried a manuscript from Blanche home in my briefcase. If I compiled a list of people to whom he would send complimentary copies of a new book, I compiled another the next day for her. I suggested guests for luncheons Alfred gave at his club and for cocktail parties Blanche gave in her apartment. I met with authors, agents, and foreign publishers they couldn't or didn't want to see themselves, wrote letters for their signatures, blurbs for the dust jackets of books they had contracted for, and endlessly rewrote advertising copy they seldom found acceptable because they seldom knew what they wanted said. My childhood had taught me the hazards of carrying messages

239

from one warring family faction to another. When Alfred complained about something Blanche had done, I suggested he go next door and talk to her about it. When Blanche asked me to relay an opinion to Alfred, I offered to send him in so she could tell him herself. Within a few months, they abandoned the practice that had destroyed others who had tried to work harmoniously with both of them. I may have avoided being drawn into warfare between the Knopfs, but I was propelled into the crossfire between them and their editors. I prided myself on being neither Alfred's boy nor Blanche's, but I unknowingly became management's boy. Alfred asked me to write confidential reports on manuscripts submitted by the editors, and then, without my knowledge, used them as ammunition in his editorial competition with his own staff. At the semiannual sales conference, at which forthcoming books are presented to the salesmen brought in from throughout the country for the occasion, Alfred and Blanche asked me to make the presentations for those books they were involved in. Editors, who are often quiet, reflective men, are not always articulate performers, and I was drafted, at their request, to either present books of theirs I admired or give supplementary talks to kindle the enthusiasm of the men who had to sell the books to the bookstores. In the large ballroom of a midtown hotel, I shared the platform with the Knopfs and members of the executive committee as overworked, underpaid, and underpraised editors described the books they had worked on for many months. Impatient when anyone else was speaking, Alfred would take out a pocket watch to time their talks. Distinguished men who brought profitable and admirable books to his imprint were cut down in midsentence with demeaning gibes that made the collected salesmen squirm in their chairs, but Alfred seemed blissfully unaware of the effect he was creating. I realized early why excellent editors so often resigned from Knopf; what I could not understand is why so many of them stayed. Watching men fifteen years my senior submit to degrading insults from the man who should have supported them instead of undermining them, I came to believe that since he never made me his target, there was some inherent weakness in those who allowed themselves to be treated in that fashion. In later years, when I conducted the conferences myself, I tried to interpose myself between Alfred and his editors, but I never found an effective way of doing so. The audience Alfred desperately needed nourished a streak of cruelty in him. The good, kind men who edited his books were safe only during his absence, but the conferences were always less exciting without him.

The dictated memo, that weapon of those who talk into machines because they can't talk to people, reflected the arrogance which originated in Alfred's office and spread throughout the firm, although his were by no means the rudest. The Gray Eminence could be relied upon for several each morning, and his were the most accurate barometer of who was on the way out and who was on the way up. One position at Knopf could only be described as a revolving editorial chair. Year after year, young editors of brilliant reputation were hired, with glowing promises of future authority in the company, and then, within the year, fired, usually after unpleasant scenes in the conference room, but sometimes more discreetly. One of them received notice of his dismissal while he and his wife were on vacation in Europe. Another returned from too many Martinis at lunch with me, over which he had boasted of his security as Alfred's favorite, to find the Gray Eminence waiting in his office with the bad news. The more independent of them did not wait to be fired; one challenged Alfred with a stevedore's vocabulary and walked out; he was the only editor I ever heard Alfred regret losing. In spite of a chronic state of crisis, there was a cadre of editors who, season after season, produced the books that commanded prominent reviews and won literary prizes, as well as making considerable profits for the firm. The three-man executive committee which, with Alfred and Blanche, approved or vetoed all publication proposals, seldom read the manuscripts whose fates they decided; when they did, I

241

considered their judgment limited at best and capricious at worst. Without quite intending to, I invaded the domain of editorial decision, first when Alfred asked me to read manuscripts submitted by the editors, and then when the editors themselves, recognizing my influence with him, asked me to read what they hoped to publish. My unofficial, and genuinely unwanted, authority was made abundantly clear when a young editor resigned complaining that the publicity man had usurped powers that did not belong to his office. Alfred, gleefully repeating the conversation to me, seemed completely unaware of my discomfiture.

Walking from our office to the hotel for the sales conference one brisk November morning, Alfred turned to me and demanded why I wasn't wearing a warmer topcoat. I shrugged it off as carelessness, but when he asked again the next morning, I replied, with some irritation, that I didn't own one. The salaries at Knopf were low, even by publishing standards, and Dorothy and I have seldom wasted money on what we can do without. Late that afternoon, the treasurer called me into his office to tell me Mr. Knopf had insisted upon my receiving a rather substantial raise, retroactive to September. Until close to the end of my years in his firm, such acts of generosity diluted my irritation at the bad manners which sent a genteel woman editor from his office in tears or plunged an entire floor of secretaries into a panic because they couldn't find the carbon copy of a letter he had written ten years before.

In spite of their privileges and sophistication, the Knopfs sometimes reminded me of my parents. Like them, they were transparently unhappy with each other, and like them, too, they provoked and defied each other, especially in the presence of others. I realized, too late, that Alfred played off employee against employee, in open meetings and in the privacy of his office, as my father had set son against son in the barn. Blanche, for all her style and intuition, was nearly as irrational as my mother. Distrusting almost everyone, but especially her husband and her son, she told me stories about them that I put out of my head

242

as soon as they reached my ears. I didn't want to know those secret family betrayals reaching back to the First World War, but she had a compulsion to tell them to justify some mysterious existence I was not interested in. I could not then, of course, acknowledge the resemblance between the two Jewish cosmopolites who employed me and the backwoods French-Canadian Catholics who had brought me into the world; if I had, I probably would have run away from them, too, recognizing, if nothing more, the futility of establishing a reliable relationship between us.

They left me little time for anyone else in their organization. Planning business trips to Europe, Blanche took up entire afternoons with me, going over her itinerary and making up, and then revising over and over again, releases to send out to newspapers and wire services alerting the world to the famous figures in London and Paris she was going to see. Recalling the attention she had received on such occasions a generation earlier, she complained bitterly when nothing appeared in print except in the trade journals, and departed nursing her resentment that no one knew, or cared any longer, who she was. I was learning that discontent knows no barrier of class or income.

Alfred shared her hunger for publicity, but his was focused on everything that marked him as a gentleman of leisure, not a mere tradesman: a wine cellar, amateur photography, honorary degrees, and his intense interest in music and conservation. A prolific, if not particularly talented, photographer, he demanded that his photographs appear on book jackets instead of those authors preferred but were too timid to insist upon. As if to dispel a fear that it might disappear if it wasn't always in sight, his full name was printed prominently wherever it could be placed, from the spines of the books he published to the advertisements that promoted them. His vanity surpassed even that of the actors he held in lofty contempt and was the only possible explanation for the frequent, and often fatuous, letters he fired off to the editors of the *New York Times* which he read out loud to the rest of us at weekly meetings. After lengthy negotiations, a national magazine finally ran a two-page spread of his photographs of Mencken, Thomas Mann, Willa Cather, Elizabeth Bowen, Camus, Sartre, and other famous authors he published. He called me into his office to complain about the layout and the reproduction of the photographs, but I assumed that he was grateful for the reassurance that he was somebody in a world of nobodies.

On my way from his office that afternoon, Blanche called me into hers across the hall. She informed me, in icy rage, that half the writers attributed to Alfred in the magazine text were not "his" but "hers," and that I had no right to allow the photographs of her authors to be used without consulting her. From behind her enormous desk, the frail old woman flung the magazine across the room against the wall as I turned to leave. She had made her point: from then on, I maintained as best I could a balance between them as if they were two publishers, each of whom had to be approached, and certainly publicized, independently of the other.

During my second summer vacation at Knopf, Dorothy and I stayed in the city, leaving the children with sitters, to go to the theatre, movies, and art exhibits. During one of our expeditions, I saw Blanche Knopf staring forlornly into a shopwindow, and asked Dorothy if she'd like to meet her. Having heard little about her outside of constant and bitter complaints, Dorothy said, "God, no!" But there was no way of avoiding it. In the afternoon sunlight which exposed the punishment time had left on her face, Blanche rested her eyes upon my wife with the fixed stare of the myopic. "I'm delighted to meet you," she said. "Elizabeth Bowen, who ordinarily detests children, tells me you have the most enchanting boy and girl she's ever seen." With one sentence, she endeared herself forever to my wife, not because she liked children, which she didn't, but because she had remembered what was important not to herself but to another.

After that, we were often invited to her small dinner parties.

Proud, indiscreet, incapable of demonstrating affection for anything but the Yorkshire terrier which, she confided to Dorothy,
she loved more than anyone she had ever known, Blanche Knopf
aroused a protective loyalty in those of us who liked her. There
were many who did not. Her dinner guests included composers,
newspaper and television reporters, critics, writers, lady agents with
clusters of jewels on their fingers, visiting English and European
publishers, and numerous French dignitaries, translators, and
sometimes bankers and perfumers, whose wives suffered through
table conversation with my French-Canadian monosyllables, as
well as the stray males of uncertain age and gender who customarily round out Manhattan dinner parties. The food was excellent and the conversation generally pleasant and relaxing, in
spite of the yapping of the pampered dog and the surliness of the
French maid who served the meals under instructions from a
Negro cook obviously tippling in the kitchen. Whoever the guests,
and whatever the commotions outside the living room, Blanche
reigned with serene composure, never allowing differences in the
office to follow her home.

Alfred, as obtuse a host as she was considerate a hostess, summoned us to his country house for Sunday lunch from time to
time, usually when more desirable guests were obliged to cancel at
the last moment. Settling the babies with a sitter, we'd taxi to
the station for a train to White Plains, and then taxi to his house
to join four others for the light wines he served instead of cocktails
before consuming a heavy lunch. Alfred's guests were similar to
Blanche's; sometimes they were the same people, with the addition
of wealthy country friends or members of the Jewish élite we
had never encountered before. Whoever they were, Alfred, at
home as in the office, seldom permitted conversation to stray far
from himself. Interrupting others more distinguished and often
more interesting than himself, he would read fawning letters from
obscure South American novelists he published, or compliments
on the widely circulated *Quarterly* he pieced together from news-

paper clippings, the opinions of others, and jacket copy written by editors for the books the firm published. If she was present, Blanche sometimes supplied an antiseptic counterpoint to his self-obsession, but even she followed him willingly into certain areas we could neither enter nor particularly wished to. Once, we listened in silence as they lovingly examined, with the detail usually reserved for the Stuarts or the Plantagenets, the family relationships and financial standing of a clan named Warburg, whom we had never heard of. We began to dread those gatherings, in which we were out of place, preferring to remain at home on Sundays with our children. In time, Dorothy refused to accompany me, for although she is a sympathetic audience for anyone in genuine distress, she is ill-at-ease with bad-mannered men. Alfred, in spite of his repeated boasts that his father had brought him up to be a gentleman, was the rudest man she had ever met. It irritated her to watch me nod my head at opinions she knew I didn't share, but she was too well bred to defy her host. Making excuses for her, I was relieved that only one of us was forced to pay the social price for working at Knopf. If Alfred recognized the transparency of the excuses I made for my wife, he never commented upon them. He may have been as relieved as she was, for wives were little more to him than encumbrances unless they were important enough in their own right to justify, if not his courtesy, at least his attention.

The man one was alone with had very little in common with the tyrant in the office or the host in his dining room. Leaving the other guests to amuse themselves on his patio, he'd take me up to his study to show me yellowing photographs of himself forty years earlier with John Galsworthy or Joseph Conrad. That sad old man, whose fingers trembled as he opened albums or bent over voluminous correspondence files, should have been displaying his mementos to grandchildren, not to me. Even in the company of others, he began to direct his comments to me, fixing his restless dark eyes upon mine as he rambled on about Sigrid Undset and Joe Hergesheimer. He had been rather a young man when he had published some of the greatest writers of the twentieth century, but time had made him a senior to his authors instead of the brilliant youth who had impressed Henry Mencken, Thomas Mann, and Willa Cather. As he talked of Mencken's final, pain-filled days in Baltimore, Alfred's eyes would fill with tears which he didn't bother to wipe away. Once, going through a folder of letters from Willa Cather, he started to read one aloud to me and then discovered it contained cautionary, somewhat maternal, advice about his teen-aged son, and he put the letter away slowly, momentarily lost in a secret sorrow which his rudeness to others almost always denied. I had become, in some way, a substitute for Pat, I suppose, since the younger Knopf's desertion of his parents' firm had made friendly relationship between them difficult. If I had never received such attention from a man old enough to be my father, perhaps he had never received it from his son, either. Forgetting my intention of never taking the Knopfs seriously, I grew fond of him in spite of his manners and opinions that would have appalled me in anyone else, and I grew to love Blanche Knopf in spite of the quixotic and sometimes ridiculous defenses she erected against humiliation and the pain that constantly assailed her.

In the spring of 1960, the Knopfs sold their publishing firm to Random House. Once again, I read the news on the front page of the *New York Times* as I walked from the Swarthmore drug-store to my in-laws' home. Once again, I was offered positions in other firms but they held no temptation for me. I still worked for the Knopfs, no matter who owned the company's stock. I had no intention of switching loyalty to the brash, energetic organization headed by the brash, energetic Bennett Cerf. If my first impression of Knopf had been of an eighteenth-century court, Random House resembled a movie studio of the nineteen-thirties, and I preferred the intimacy of the old court, however riddled with intrigue, to the garish show-biz atmosphere of the new. However much I may have faltered in my once-determined resolution not to take the Knopfs seriously, I knew there was no danger of my ever taking anyone at Random House seriously. The ambitious, alert executives who now attended some of our meetings were exact prototypes of the kind of man I had sworn not to become twenty years earlier when Miss Potter arranged an interview for me with an oil-company executive.

One of them took me out to a "get-acquainted" lunch. He told me I was the fair-haired boy at Knopf and that my future at Random House was assured. He proceeded immediately into what seemed like a cross-examination: How old are you? (We were exactly the same age); married? (Twice. One up, or down, on him); children? (Two, a boy and a girl. He scored one up on me there); what college? (Finally convinced that I really had never gone to college, he revealed an Ivy League citadel as his, and won the match hands down). In a commanding position, he turned to more casual conversation: the stock market, golf, his new automobile, and life in the affluent suburbs. I wearily dismissed each subject: we don't own stock, I don't play golf or know how to drive, and we live in one of the shabbier sections of lower Manhattan. He paused, searching for something we could talk about for the following hour, and I waited for him to mention books: after all, Random House did publish Isak Dinesen, William Faulkner, and William Styron. He gave no indication of having read anything other than profit-and-loss statements, and our game of playing executives was a sham. Too astute not to recognize an enemy, he could not yet identify it. He glanced at me and said, without preparation, "Have you ever sat across the table from someone and realized he was anti-Semitic?" It occurred to me that he was trying to find out if my name concealed another, and, irritated, I replied that being French-Canadian deprived me of that particular crutch: if someone dislikes me, I am forced to conclude it is me they dislike, not my ethnic origins. Just before picking up the check, he assured me once again, with buoyant

248

cameraderie, that big things were being planned for me at Random House, if I played my cards right.

A year later, I was put in charge of the entire publicity operation for Random House, Knopf, and Pantheon Books, which had been added to the conglomerate in the meantime. The Knopfs didn't release me from my duties to them; they allowed me to add many more, and to acquire, as well, three other bosses from the Random House offices. My life changed. The days were spent discussing forthcoming books I didn't have time to read, accompanying best-selling authors to television studios to appear on talk shows in which they were sandwiched between Hollywood starlets and authorities on sex, juvenile delinquency, and marital problems. The prestige of the Knopfs and the seriousness of the books they published had shielded me from the tawdry aspects of publicity which were everyday affairs to the Random House staff. I quickly disliked success-driven authors of careless books about important subjects and drone-like editors who passed them along to me before going out to solicit others like them for the following season.

Since nothing I did at work nourished my self-respect or held my attention, I retreated into my own writing. I continued rising early and walking uptown to my office to work on my plays before starting business days that often seemed much more unreal than what I put down on paper. Days begun in the solitude of writing ended usually with cocktail parties for authors and agents which Dorothy, much more interested in her own friends and our children, declined to attend. I came home irritable, depressed, with manuscripts to look over, not read, publicity campaigns to plan, and advertising copy to revise. I stole time from my family to write plays. Dorothy watched, concealing the pain it must have caused her, as my weight shot up fifty pounds from too many drinks and too much French cuisine, and I took out my frustrations on the children or on her.

I hardly knew my children. Susan, a sunny-natured four-year-old, tumbled out of bed at six in the morning to eat her cornflakes across the breakfast table from the father who left her, and her sleeping mother and brother, to walk up to his office. On weekends, I'd take Stevie to the office, where he patiently amused himself with paper clips, stapling machines, and pencil sharpeners while I caught up on writing reports or the memos that have replaced conversation in big business. In Swarthmore on other weekends, I lay on the living-room floor reading galleys while they sat on either side of their ninety-year-old great-grandmother, who amused them by playing "Oh, Dem Golden Slippers" on the piano until someone touched her on the shoulder to turn her attention to another song. I was a morose stranger who came home with a briefcase full of work, before whom they trembled when I raised my voice, or scampered back to their own rooms when I stared at them thoughtfully from a galley page held up to the light.

When Steve was five years old, I took him away by himself to a seashore hotel while Dorothy and Susan stayed home. A good-natured if slightly tense little boy, he hardly knew what to make of the father he was suddenly alone with. He obediently ate what was placed before him in the hotel dining room, carried his bucket and shovel out onto the sand to dig clams, and slept in the same bed with me, perfectly willing to make friends with the preoccupied man who helped him dress and undress. Rising early in the morning to stare first at the ocean through the window and then at the sleeping boy, whose handsome features reminded me of his mother, I considered whether I was losing everything I had gained in work that supported my family so I could write.

Back in the office, I resigned from my position at Random House and returned full-time to Knopf, where I was named assistant to the chairman of the board (Alfred) and to the president (Blanche), which officially confirmed the role I had been playing for three years. My alter ego of the stock market, golf course, and suburbs took me to lunch again, this time to tell me humorlessly that I had ruined my prospects at Random House: I was secure at Knopf only as long as Mr. and Mrs. Knopf were still in control of the firm. Then, switching with obvious relish from the professional to the personal, he asked if it was true that I was getting divorced. My lighthearted office account of spending a holiday alone with my son had reached him in a somewhat exaggerated form. Having met his own discontented wife, and listened to her stories of his neglect of his children, I explained that most decisions in my life were based on regard for my family, nothing else. Strangers in ambition and in viewpoint, we eyed each other warily as we parted, he to future promotions and I to a slow retreat from business opportunities held enticingly before me.

Charles Shaw died in 1962. He refused an operation that would have saved his life but made him an invalid burden to his family, and returned home from the hospital without telling his wife or his daughter of his decision. A week or two later, he rose in the middle of the night so he wouldn't disturb his sleeping wife and went into the living room, where he collapsed and died. During the ten years I had known him, he had silenced forever the painful echo of my father. His death deprived my children of a good-humored grandfather, my wife of the father she could talk to about anything at any time, and me of the man whose company during quiet weekends in Swarthmore made tolerable the man who dominated my working days.

Several years later, Alfred concluded the announcement of my appointment as vice-president by saying, in the presence of his entire editorial and executive staff, "You may be the most ambitious fellow to come down the pike for all I know. I hope I'm doing the right thing." I had watched others appointed to high positions in the firm on the assumption that someday they would take over the authority the Knopfs would have to relinquish. I had watched, too, their humiliating dismissal after months of thwarted ambition

251

on their part and ruthless undermining by those who had hired them. Alfred's apprehensions about me were justified, but there was no way I could have made it clear to him, since my ambitions were not within a sphere he could have understood. What was important to me, and to my wife, would have been as meaningless to him as his Rolls-Royce, London shirts, and proper wines were absurd to us.

What did mean the most to me, beyond my family, were the plays I wrote. The first one, begun in 1956, was finished in 1962, after at least twenty drafts. In those years, only my wife and a few friends read what I was writing. The agents to whom they were submitted sent them back, usually without comment (although one accidentally enclosed two readers' reports, the first embarrassing in its unqualified praise, the second embarrassing in its unqualified rejection), but I kept on writing anyway. Writing plays for a theatre which puts every possible obstacle in the path of production is a foolish, if harmless, pastime, but I was not writing to be produced. The gratification received from creating situations and characters was an antidote to the hostility I accumulated toward those I worked with. As long as invented characters could be posed against each other in personal conflict, I could observe the Knopfs and my colleagues at Random House with some degree of detachment.

However, even self-directed therapy proved useless against antagonisms that surfaced more frequently and violently than I wished. Everything I most dislike about men, from coarse sexual evaluation of women passing restaurant tables to crude ethnic jokes in conference rooms, drove me from those who worked with me to those who populated my imagination. I avoided lunching with men whose approval could lead to promotion, preferring to spend my time with writers and reviewers who discussed the contents of books rather than their sales potential. Every three or four months, I lunched with a laconic reviewer friend to go over the list of books we were publishing. One day, in an expensive

French restaurant, he grinned at me over our drinks. "Lemay, what the hell are we doing here? You the son of a Canuck manure spreader, and me the son of a Maine lobsterman. We should be waiting on tables, not sitting at them." Within a year, he resigned from his job on a national magazine and disappeared into the anonymity he preferred.

An unsettling nostalgia for what I had deserted swept over me unexpectedly at odd moments. Seated at Blanche's dinner table, I'd find myself staring blankly at jewels on the fingers of the stylish matron reaching for her wineglass next to me and see instead my mother's broken nails and chapped hands. When Alfred made his customary jokes about French Canadians in my presence, as he joked about the Irish in the presence of the Irishman who headed his college department, I refrained from matching his bad manners with the jokes about his people that had been the staple of my bigoted childhood. At his home in Purchase, he made a derogatory remark about the Canucks in front of people we didn't know. Dorothy, who didn't like him, and never would, said quietly, "Pete is French Canadian, you know." Alfred looked at me with a smile before replying, "Yes, of course I know. He'd still be up there with them if he didn't agree with me, wouldn't you, Pete?"

I buried my resentments and guilts in plays that pitted fears of failure against expediency, that matched my impoverished past with the comfortable present. Few areas of my life were left uncovered in what I wrote, and I might have been content to go on writing secretly forever if I hadn't met Marian Seldes again. During a theatre intermission, she greeted me with the effusive friendliness I remembered from fifteen years before at the Neighborhood Playhouse. We chatted about her brother, an editor at another publishing house, and about the Broadway career she was resuming after five years in Hollywood with her producer husband, before she asked if I had really given up the theatre completely. When I confessed to having finished a play, she demanded that I let her read it. Such demands are not unusual among actors, and are seldom genuinely intended, so I did not send her the manuscript. Several weeks later, she called to remind me of my promise. I left the script at her apartment with a note, expecting a long wait before I heard from her about it, if I ever did. She called that night as soon as she finished reading it, with the first encouragement from anyone remotely connected with the profession I was writing for. Going beyond mere encouragement, she sent the script to Uta Hagen, who called me with breathless criticisms, and to other actors, as well as to directors and producers she had worked with. She quickened hopes of my becoming a professional writer rather than a publisher.

She was making arrangements for actors to read the play aloud in her apartment, so I could hear what it sounded like, when I was accepted into the New Dramatists Committee, where my plays have been read, evaluated, rehearsed, and presented in workshop productions ever since. Founded twenty years ago by Howard Lindsay and Moss Hart, and supported by donations from foundations and theatre people, the New Dramatists is composed of about forty playwrights who elect each other to membership after reading scripts submitted to them. Most successful contemporary dramatists (Robert Anderson, Paddy Chayevsky, James Goldman, and William Gibson) and hundreds of lesser-known ones have received early encouragement and practical assistance within the group. My first play was read by five fellow members who met with me to suggest ways of improving it. From that three-hour session, I learned more about writing a play than seven years of isolated application had taught me. After I revised the play, the New Dramatists presented a staged reading directed by Paul Shyre, with Marian playing the lead. We rehearsed for a week, in the evenings, and performed it three times before invited audiences, who filled out cards with often devastating criticisms. Collating the comments, I revised the play again, and in the fall of 1963 the Neighborhood Playhouse presented it for eight benefit

254

performances for their scholarship fund. Since that production received wide publicity before it opened, my secret life was now exposed. I included Alfred and Blanche among those at Knopf invited to the performances, leaving announcements on their desks. Blanche, who could not attend because she was leaving immediately for Europe, called me into her office to congratulate me, and asked to read the manuscript when she returned. Alfred ignored the invitation completely until the performances were safely over; then he told me he was sorry to have missed the play, because he had heard very good things about it. The subject of my writing did not come up between us again for several years.

Robert Anderson has been quoted as saying that a playwright can make a "killing" in the theatre, but can seldom make a living. For the next four years, Knopf supplied my living as I became a playwright. My four-week summer vacation in the Fire Island house we'd bought in 1963 was spent writing the first draft of a new play. During the winters, I spent the early mornings on revisions for the workshop productions at the New Dramatists, and the evenings were spent in rehearsals and conferences with directors. In between the mornings and the evenings, where my real interests were engaged, I continued to work not only on publicity and advertising for Knopf but on editorial projects—occasionally manuscripts I wanted to publish, but more often as a deputy with better-known writers for Alfred and Blanche—and on management affairs. By 1965, when my third play was presented at the New Dramatists and I was appointed a vice-president at Knopf, my two careers were headed rapidly for a collision. That June, Alfred suffered a severe heart attack, which curtailed his office activities and brought Random House executives more directly into Knopf management. My interest in my work diminished, along with my effectiveness in it. I had decided to resign when Blanche died in her sleep in June of 1966.

Without the stabilizing influence of that shrewd woman who had shared his life and business for over fifty years, Alfred was irascible, unpredictable, and suspicious. The announcement that my third play had been optioned for a Broadway production convinced him that I had been using Knopf for my own ends, not his. In a brief, uncomfortable discussion of my future, he told me I would have to choose eventually between being a playwright and being a publisher. Since I spent less time writing plays than other executives did playing golf, and since that time was stolen from my family and not from the office, I did not share his concern.

Once Alfred became convinced I would not give up writing plays or pledge myself to exclusive loyalty to Knopf, he withdrew his loyalty from me. Writers called me to say that Alfred had referred to me, at luncheons in his home, as Knopf's "resident playwright," implying that I was more interested in my writing than in theirs. Innuendos I had heard directed toward others were now directed toward me. I ignored them uneasily, telling myself that it was merely a temporary problem. Having watched him undermine editors with their authors before, especially those editors he wanted to get rid of but didn't have the excuse or courage to fire, I knew what to expect. My opinions were still solicited, but they were often turned against me. Not only were two careers in direct conflict, but a long and unacknowledged search for a father was dissolving itself, as it should, in my own parenthood. Both disappointed in the other, Alfred and I maintained a neutral relationship for some months, with an occasional unexpected reprise of the trust and affection we had once shared. There were infrequent moments when he became again the familiar paternal figure advising me in publishing relationships.

A popular middle-aged woman novelist had taken to telephoning me at home after a long day's writing and a long night's drinking. I am usually in bed by ten o'clock, and Dorothy, who had been openly snubbed by the lady the only time they'd ever met, quite understandably resented her insistent intrusion into our lives. Awakened at midnight from a sound sleep by an irritated wife, I suggested that the phone calls be discontinued after ten o'clock.

256

The next morning, Alfred called me into his office and announced that the author had demanded another editor, and he wanted to know why. He listened to my explanation with a mischievous smile. Back in the twenties, he said, they had hired young editors to be nothing but studs for menopausal lady novelists; I should have come to him earlier and he would have solved the problem. Then, shifting into his more familiar hostility, he said the author resented my talking about my work rather than hers. No amount of denial convinced him that was merely another weapon in her arsenal.

Generally, I enjoyed working with authors. Some, like Conrad Richter and Elizabeth Bowen, I had admired for many years, and they proved as graceful and admirable in person as their novels had led me to expect. Others, closer to my own age, like William Humphrey and John Updike, were refreshing men of original views and strong convictions. But, in time, I resented waking up in the middle of the night to ponder what was wrong with someone else's writing when it was clear that much was wrong with my own. Beyond that, I realized that Knopf needed a more vigorous, single-minded young executive, and certainly one more combative, if it was to maintain the standards and the reputation it had enjoyed for half a century. I had no regret about leaving a profession to which I was only partially committed; my concern was how I would support my family. It was unlikely that Random House would keep me on in any position once Alfred himself was no longer active, and I had to plan for the future.

R.C.A. had bought Random House; Knopf was now merely a small segment of an enormous industrial concern, not the family publishing house I had joined eight years earlier. Nor was I the deferential assistant Alfred and Blanche had relied upon. I no longer hid exasperation at decisions to publish manuscripts made by executives who didn't bother to read them. I had provided Alfred with the ultimate weapon of the bully by feeling sorry for him. Unwilling to hurt him, I had allowed myself to tell him what he wanted to hear rather than what I believed, becoming one of the toadies and lackeys I had detested when I first saw them surrounding him. Reacting strongly, if not sensibly, to my evaluation of myself, I began to tell him the truth even when he didn't solicit it, especially in those areas where his vanity sought gratification in editorial projects which his long-time associates agreed to in his presence but shrugged off as "Alfred's follies" when outraged salesmen at our conferences protested that they were hopeless.

I had decided to resign again but could not retrieve myself from an awkward position caused by Blanche leaving me a legacy in her will, as she had to most of those who had worked closely with her. The amount given to me was determined by Alfred, and it was generous and relieved us of debts that had pursued us since the children started school. I accepted the check with gratitude for their generosity and distress because it bound me to the firm as long as it wanted me. There was no way of refusing without insulting Alfred's self-esteem and Blanche's memory. I gave up my intention of resigning, and reconciled myself to the prospect of two careers, neither totally fulfilling.

Alfred resolved my dilemma at a banquet which posthumously honored Blanche. The chairman of the sponsoring group of book-industry women invited Alfred, through me, to bring his personal guests, including several well-known writers and their wives, into their cramped suite of rooms for cocktails before dinner. Within earshot of the women themselves beyond an open door, Alfred raged at my stupidity for exposing his friends to "frumps" and led them back downstairs to the hotel ballroom. Dorothy, aghast at seeing her husband treated in this fashion and perhaps even more surprised that I tolerated it, stayed behind with me. She glanced through the doorway at the unassuming women, some of them librarians like her, and as her father had been; then she stared down the corridor after the retreating tyrant who paid the salary that supported our children. Watching her, I realized that

258

once again I had invested a stranger with qualities I wanted him to possess. She had waited for years until I arrived at the acceptance of her estimate of Alfred Knopf as a man whose esteem was not worth the humiliations he exacted as its price.

In the spring, the New Dramatists presented a production of a play I had written several years before about American soldiers and German women at the end of the war. Since I was still working, the rehearsals were scheduled for the evening, under the guidance of a volatile European who had directed similar groups in Hollywood. Anne Meacham joined her classmate Marian Seldes in a cast that included two fine, unrecognized young actors, Ed Zimmermann and Addison Powell, and a once-famous film star, a boyhood infatuation of mine, whom I had persuaded to play the difficult role of an aging Bavarian countess. The cast would have been exceptional even for a Broadway production, but the first reading was a total disaster. The director obtusely antagonized the younger actors, all of whom were donating their time; three of them called me at my office the next morning and refused to work with him. I spent the day persuading the New Dramatists to replace him, and the film star refused to continue without him. We replaced her with Margaret Barker, a gifted actress who had been in the original Group Theatre, and who had directed me in stock twenty years before. I replaced the director myself, relying upon the actors, who knew far more than I did. A film commitment kept Marian in Hollywood for several of our ten-days' rehearsal period, and one minor part was cast three times as talented young actors left us to take jobs that paid salaries. The entire cast was onstage together for the first time at the dress rehearsal. They hardly knew their lines, but their performances vibrated with a raw force and credibility. Walking home elated from the final performance, I knew where I belonged and decided that, whatever the economic and personal consequences, I could no longer delude myself that I belonged anywhere else.

I delayed telling Dorothy, for I could still change my mind. The life I intended to re-enter was a morass of insecurity that breeds all sorts of neuroses and uncertainties; it was not a prospect to be lightly taken by a forty-five-year-old man with a family to support. I might possibly manage to retrieve my standing with Alfred; I might even overcome the now blatant hostility of those who freely echoed his antagonism. But I had found an unexpected delight in the freedom of working with actors who confront their differences with uninhibited candor. If Annie Meacham and I disagreed about her approach to a scene, we may have expressed ourselves with shrieks and tantrums on her side and groans and curses on mine, but when the rehearsal was over, we had a friendly drink together and met with complete trust in each other at the next one. At Knopf, however, tensions I could not understand were traced back to unstated differences which had smoldered for months between men who did not trust each other enough to be honest. At my final executive conference, the Gray Eminence, gloating in his survival of yet another favorite, suggested that I give serious thought to whether or not I was earning my rather high salary. Recognizing the message from the messenger, I thanked him, and silently thanked Alfred as well.

That night, walking home from a dinner party under the Greenwich Village trees where we had courted fifteen years earlier, I turned to Dorothy and told her I wanted to leave Knopf to become a free-lance writer but that I had no right to subject her and our children to the hardships it would probably bring to them. She looked at me for a long moment with the gravity I have come to rely upon as the only anchor in an insane world, and said, "I've been waiting for you to tell me that for years."

PART SIX

...and now...

A week after I left my job at Knopf, Stephen and Susan, then eleven and ten, suggested that since I would no longer be earning the salary we'd become accustomed to, I reduce their weekly allowance from a dollar to fifty cents. Just this year, when my income from teaching and free-lance writing finally matched what it had been three years ago, they hinted that perhaps they could receive a dollar a week again. We raised them to two dollars and a half.

My children, objects of often thwarted attention during my office years, now share the tensions and uncertainties of my life, as well as its gratifications. Even before leaving Knopf, I realized that the time I spent writing and rehearsing plays was stolen mostly from them, and I drew them with me into rehearsals so they would be familiar with what took me away from them. When Steve was ten, he attended the dress rehearsal of a play about my family, sitting engrossed alone in the back row until it was over, then strolled down to the stage to compliment Anne Meacham, Marian Seldes, and Nic Coster with a disarming suavity that reveals him more at home among actors than I ever was. He stayed behind to help me clean the auditorium, a chore all New Dramatists are obliged to do when they use the theatre. Banging down seats after collecting empty coffee containers, cigarette butts, and candy wrappers from the floor, he cross-examined me about the play. Did my mother actually use the words Anne Meacham said during the performance? Which of his four aunts was the one Marian Seldes played, and was Nicolas Coster really supposed to be me? Grateful that I had stumbled upon an appropriate occasion, I told him for the first time of his grandmother's illness and his grandfather's suicide, and explained to him the use of reality as a springboard for fiction. He listened gravely and walked silently with me back to our apartment. There his other grandmother, who had come up from Swarthmore to see the play the following evening, asked him how he had liked it. He replied, with the earnestness that occasionally makes him appear older than all the rest of us, "Well, Nana, that woman isn't exactly somebody you'd want for one of your noble ancestors."

My children have attended rehearsals of all my plays ever since, exposed at perhaps too early an age not only to violence and sexuality, murders and betrayals in my work, but to the uninhibited behavior and language that are endemic to theatre workers. But that is the risk I knowingly take so they understand what sends me to the typewriter in the mornings and out to rehearsals in the evenings. There have been moments when I've questioned the wisdom of my decision, as when I heard twelve-year-old Steve blithely explaining a slang term for a certain sex act to his mother during a rehearsal. But his explanation was much more accurate than mine would have been at his age, despite the obsessive discussions my brothers and I carried on behind the barn. Once, when they were somewhat younger, we overheard Steve in the next room furiously calling his sister "a dirty little kaput" and realized that the words they discover in my plays mean quite different things to them from what they do to me, or to anyone else.

My friend Addison Powell tells me that during the final rehearsal of my play about American soldiers in Germany, he heard,
as he straddled Annie Meacham for the brutal climactic scene,
a child's treble voice from the front row whisper, "Isn't he cute?"
Glancing up, he saw Susan's face, aglow with ten-year-old adoration. What my children see and know is far beyond what I saw
and knew at their ages, and even further beyond what their mother
knew. I cannot believe that exposing them to what gives me the
greatest professional satisfaction can damage them nearly as much
as shutting them out of it would. I refuse to believe that knowledge of human experience, honestly presented, is dangerous. When
Steve reads *Couples,* or *Portnoy's Complaint,* or *Myra Breckin-
ridge,* as he reads almost every novel that appears in our apartment, he is doing what I did when I was fourteen. Books have
changed because the world has changed, but it is the world he
must live in, and books can provide for him, as they did for me,
a route into lives beyond his own. He reads, too, every script I
write and, like his mother, is direct and uncompromising in his
criticisms. I sometimes have the feeling, dismaying for a playwright, that we are nurturing a future Stanley Kauffmann or
Clive Barnes within our nest.

Since I left Knopf, I have written three more plays, each of
which has been performed in workshop at the New Dramatists
and one on a college campus in the Midwest. During our summers
in Fire Island, my mornings are spent writing countless drafts
of a new play, the afternoons in the blueberry patches, gathering
ingredients for the pies Susan enjoys making and mulling over
ingredients that go into the plays I write, or on the tennis courts
with Dorothy to clear my mind of the disorder that is shaping
itself into characters, incidents, and dialogue. The winters are
spent revising scripts, earning a living by college teaching and
writing for television, and following up the various and usually
hopeless trails that might lead to a Broadway production. The
producer who optimistically optioned my third play released it

265

after eighteen months of frustrated efforts to locate a star prominent enough to attract investors and willing to be seen as a
shabby, deranged woman in her sixties. Broadway productions
would be gratifying, but they are no longer a paramount concern:
I have seen too many good plays arrive and depart within a week,
after blistering reviews, because playwright friends compromised
on casting and directorial matters in their hunger for production.
If my plays are any good, they'll be good ten years from now.
If they aren't any good, at least I have had the satisfaction of
writing them and of working with fine actors and directors free
from the pressures of Broadway. No matter who eventually plays
the woman I call Ada Moreau, no one will ever move me as
deeply as Anne Meacham did in a staged reading at the New
Dramatists. A slender, beautiful, foxlike creature, Anne Meacham
is no more like my mother in physical appearance than were the
movie stars of my childhood. But now when I think of the baf-
fling woman who carried me inside her body, I see superimposed
upon her stout figure the angular outlines of the actress who made
me acknowledge, finally and conclusively, the overwhelming love
I had always borne for my mother. That is my ultimate satisfaction in writing plays. In the meantime, agents set up appointments
with producers who express "interest" in my work, interest that
seldom extends beyond casual inquiries into what I really mean,
who the audience is supposed to be "pulling" for, and other
simple-minded questions producers usually ask and playwrights
generally cannot answer. The courteous, knowledgeable men of
twenty years ago who chatted with me about plays and actors
as I made the rounds have been replaced by businessmen, mostly
lawyers and real-estate tycoons, whose primary concern for in-
vestment makes meaningful discussion of a play unlikely. The
theatre is, at best, a special taste: more and more, it is becoming
the special taste of a special audience. Playwriting is something
else, and sometimes seems quite irrelevant to the theatre.

Several years ago, I was asked to teach drama in the English department of the School of General Studies at Hunter College. My students, who meet twice a week in the evening, range in age from twenty to sixty and in ethnic origin through the entire variety that makes up this country. Each semester, we meet in our first class, strangers on guard against each other, and we part four months later having revealed our own lives and natures in response to *Waiting for Godot, The Caretaker,* and *Long Day's Journey into Night.* Some of them have never seen a play on stage and have read only those assigned in high-school classes. Together, we examine why sons turn against mothers, husbands against wives, strangers against strangers, measuring experiences created by Samuel Beckett, Harold Pinter, and Eugene O'Neill against our own, theirs in Harlem tenements and East Side apartment houses, and mine in silos, dormitories, barracks, and domestic circles. Our candid, and sometimes explosive, explorations of what people do to each other and the words they use to do it is what the theatre is all about to me, not whether David Merrick options a play for Broadway or Clive Barnes praises or dismisses it. An unexpected comment from a hitherto indifferent student, or a rapt expression on a usually disinterested face, repays my long-standing debt to all those, from Agnes Clark to Virgilia Peterson, from Eldor Mainville to Charles Shaw, who taught me. My students—whose names and faces disappear just as they are becoming familiar, to be replaced by others—provide an essential link to people outside my immediate family.

Writing unproduced plays does not, of course, provide an income, and teaching one class an evening covers little more than the rent for our apartment. The first two years of our freedom were cushioned by shares of R.C.A. stock which I had bought under an option plan intended to spur me on to greater executive productivity. Now I earn my living by writing television dramas as disparate as one about abortion for the Catholic Archdiocese of New York, an adaptation of a futuristic novel for educational television, and countless scripts for a daily soap opera about

267

witches and voodoo. Checks come in slowly and go out quickly. The greatest advantage of our pleasant life is that what we most enjoy does not cost much. Outside of tuition for the children's schools, mortgage payments on a summer house, and rent for a large city apartment, our expenses can be adjusted to our income. My great good fortune, in this respect, is to share my life with a sensible woman whose values have never been distorted by a taste for furs, jewelry, wall-to-wall carpeting, and other expensive irrelevancies. If Dorothy hasn't bought a new coat in five years and if I wear suits given to me by the widow of a television producer who was my exact size, it's a price we happily pay to be where we want to be, to be who we want to be, at last.

Several years ago, Annabelle and her husband drove their five sons across the continent to visit her brothers and sisters in the East. Nearly twenty years had passed since most of us had seen her, so Marianne arranged a family reunion. Only Annabelle is a potent enough magnet to collect us all under one roof. The glue that holds the family together, she circulates round-robin letters of information collated from our infrequent individual letters, encloses snapshots of her boys, names and ages printed clearly on the backs, and remembers our birthdays, even when we forget them ourselves. After Frenchie was killed in combat, it was she who went through the tedious procedure of having his body brought back to be buried in California and sent us each a photograph of the white cross that marks his grave among the thousands just like it. It is she—from a distance of three thousand miles, and with a household of her own, as well as the responsible office position that partially supports it—who still plays the role of mother to the aging men and women who are her brothers and sisters.

Annabelle and her family were staying in our Manhattan apartment, since we were in our summer house. We came in from Fire Island by ferry, railroad, and taxicab, while others arrived by plane, car, subway, and bus, from Niagara Falls, Schenectady, Connecticut, and Brooklyn, meeting in Marianne's two-story house where our mother had spent the last few months of her life. With Frenchie long dead, Rudolph (way up north), and Ambrose (whereabouts unknown) absent, I was the senior Lemay boy present, caught in an eddy of memories, affection, and amusement that surprised me by its unexpected elemental force.

Douglas, leaning against a sideboard, laconically explained the black eye decorating the face once used for Marine recruiting posters by saying he had won a wager on a football game the day before but lost the fight that followed it. Vincent, now the settled father of three, regarded us placidly from behind horn-rimmed glasses and listened with tolerant skepticism to the stories we exchanged as we crouched on the floor, leaned against doorways, and sat on the stairway. Four daughters and five of the living sons repeated roles of hosts and guests played in our childhood by our parents and a multitude of uncles, aunts, and cousins. The television blared forth its unheeded inanities, food cooked on the gas range in Marianne's kitchen instead of the wood-burning stove of our farmhouse, and was cooled in a refrigerator instead of in an outside pantry. The rapid speech of the women, with strong north-country nasality, and the guttural tones of the male voices spoke English shadowed by a faint accent which softens consonant endings and darkens vowel sounds. Watchful eyes of children studied us from doorways and turned away blinking from our winks, as ours had from uncles and aunts. Family resemblances, the Lemay nose and the Beaupré mouth, a trace of Mohawk on a cheekbone, and a French heaviness on the bottom of an adolescent girl, connected the future to the past we had left behind us. We hugged the girls to us and rested our hands lightly on the shoulders of the boys. My daughter, her flat-tipped nose the only trace of the Indian heritage in a fragile, large-eyed face, scampered in and out of the rooms with a horde of cousins while her brother, darker than she in appearance and mood, sat absorbed in grown-up talk. My sisters, carrying heaping platters of food from the kitchen to the dining room, could have been my mother and her sisters, directing impatient glances at their men holding tumblers of whiskey and pretending not to hear the off-color stories that rode on waves of masculine guffaws. We could have been those dead and dying Beauprés and Lemays, gossiping thirty years before about relatives in Valleyfield and Fall River, or others locked away by snow or spring floods in desolate farmhouses, or by ailing children, from sharing this day of sudden laughter punctured by indefinable and half-acknowledged sadness.

Without visible envy, without defensive scorn, and without interrupting either our eating or our talking, we skipped along the surfaces of our lives. Now and then, our eyes rested upon each other with a question we could not ask: How is it with you? Are you all right? Are you happy, content? Oh, brother, are you at peace? We settled by asking what one always asks: What are you doing? I was, as expected, the freak, the outsider. After years of a salary none of them would ever match in a position most men would be proud to have, I had thrown it all aside to pursue still another dream. The suit I wore was older than those worn by brothers who had earned a fourth of my salary. The women regarded Dorothy with puzzled curiosity: she had given up, apparently without much concern, what they took most seriously, the security of a regular paycheck. The men accepted my evasive explanations as further indication of Harding's chronic dissatisfaction with his life, and dropped the subject. We carried our glasses from the table to the living room and sat side by side on the sofa, four brothers whose foolish grins and barnyard jokes belied the wrinkles, scars, and graying hair that life had extracted from us. One wife, a taciturn border malcontent whose marriage had been consumed in adamant opposition to her quick-fisted husband, rose from her seat on the stairway as we settled down, cradled an imaginary machine gun in her arms, and riddled us, with humorless eyes, from one end of the sofa to the other with

270

imaginary bullets. We roared as she joined the other wives in the kitchen, but her husband, staring after her with proud male possessiveness, said, "You think she's kidding, don't you?"

Marianne's living room was too small to contain us: we required the barns and pastures our uncles had sauntered through assessing the stock, the crops, and the weather. Free from those traditional rural concerns, we were thrown back upon assessing ourselves, as they never had and probably never could. Resurrecting boyhood boastfulness, we magnified adolescent potency (three of us, standing shivering in the hayloft, masturbating to see who came first), young conquests (Remember Emma Brown? She wore no underpants in school, and you could fuck her for a dime in the locker room between bells), and our adult freedoms (Hey, brother, how come they let you out of jail?). Embroidering or inventing incidents with competitive exaggeration, we avoided touchier topics. There had been three divorces among us since my own. Two of the girls had married Jews (no one on either side of the family had ever done that before!), one of the men had just married a vivacious black woman (no one in the family had ever known anyone who did that!), who watched us with cool amusement as she nursed her Scotch in the easy chair across from us. The past was safe. The present would soon enough become a past we could talk about at future reunions. And the future? Within the year, Marianne's oldest child would die of an undiagnosed brain tumor, Evangeline's husband of a heart attack on the golf course, and one brother flee with company money from marital discord into the anonymity of the current Alaskan oil rush. Life, which we had seen deal its blows to those who preceded us, would take us on, each in turn.

It may have been our unspoken awareness of that prospect which turned the talk into such outrageousness that mothers hurried children out of hearing and Evangeline urged her husband to herd us outside to pose before his motion-picture camera as we had posed for Aunt Maude's Brownie more than thirty years

271

before. In the twilight, far from field and silo, we made obscene gestures, tousled each other's hair, stuck out our tongues, and wiggled our fingers as the camera purred on. Somewhere, in a reel can in someone's attic, we are all recorded, in color, flickering shadows of the reality memory is already disguising.

For memory may be nothing more than another form of fantasy, in which we ceaselessly arrange and rearrange the incidents of our lives into a pattern we can accept. The honesty with which we present our motives to ourselves may be merely rationalizations for actions we no longer dare confront, and those we've loved, and hated, blur together into one haunting image. I sometimes dream of Alfred Knopf, alone and vulnerable, holding out yellowing photographs of Joseph Conrad for my inspection, or of my brother Ambrose, whose last message was a Christmas card several years ago from a dusty Southern town, waking me up in the bedroom above the kitchen by putting his manure-stained foot upon my naked chest and muttering, "Harding, it's your turn to get the cows." Waking, I reach to pull on my pants and stumble through the sharp edges of cropped cornstalks, but turn instead to Dorothy, sleeping peacefully by my side. I am safe once more, from the dreams and from the past. I dream, too, of my father confessing that I am the favorite of his nine sons; later, at breakfast, meeting my fourteen-year-old's speculative glance, I wonder. What will he remember? What will he invent to conceal what he does remember? What will I remember, ten or twenty years from now, of all this that seems so palpable today? Will it be the grin with which Dorothy turns my irritation aside on the doubles tennis court after we have each waited for the other to return a smashing drive down the center line? Will it be the radiance of a teen-age daughter, the grimace of a teen-age son, the sound of the screen door slamming behind them as they go out to smoke their forbidden cigarettes along the boardwalk, or to other diversions we dare not even consider? Perhaps memory can be trained to be faithful to reality. If it can be, surely it must begin early, before it retreats into imagination or escapes into other people's inventions to turn itself into self-protective fabrications of what could have been or should have been instead of what was or what might have been.

New York City
  and Saltaire, New York
June, 1967—August, 1970

71 72 73 10 9 8 7 6 5 4 3 2 1